Yeshiva Fundamentalism

Yeshiva Fundamentalism

*Piety, Gender, and Resistance in
the Ultra-Orthodox World*

Nurit Stadler

NEW YORK UNIVERSITY PRESS
NEW YORK AND LONDON

NEW YORK UNIVERSITY PRESS
New York and London
www.nyupress.org

Library of Congress Cataloging-in-Publication Data

Stadler, Nurit.
Yeshiva fundamentalism : piety, gender, and
resistance in the ultra-Orthodox world / Nurit Stadler.
p. cm.
Includes bibliographical references and index.
ISBN-13: 978-0-8147-4049-1 (cl : alk. paper)
ISBN-10: 0-8147-4049-9 (cl : alk. paper)
1. Ultra-Orthodox Jews—Israel. 2. Orthodox Judaism—Israel.
3. Jewish fundamentalism—Israel. 4. Jewish men—Religious life.
5. Yeshivas—Israel. 6. Jewish religious education of adults—Israel.
7. Spiritual life—Judaism. I. Title.
BM390.S727   2008
296.8'320954694—dc22   2008031657

New York University Press books are printed on acid-free paper, and
their binding materials are chosen for strength and durability. We
strive to use environmentally responsible suppliers and materials to
the greatest extent possible in publishing our books.

Manufactured in the United States of America
10 9 8 7 6 5 4 3 2 1

Contents

Las manos de mi madre
llegan al patio desde temprano
Todo se vuelve fiesta
cuando elle juega junto a otros pájaros.

Junto a los pájaros que aman la vida
y la construyen con el trabajo
arde la leña, harina y barro
lo cotidiano se vuelve mágico
se vuelve mágico

—Peteco Carabajal

The writing of this book was possible with
the care and love of my mother, Rachel, and
it is to her that I dedicate this book.

Acknowledgments

Many people helped me while I was writing this book, and I would like to thank them. First I thank my late teacher, Reuven Kahane, with whom I was privileged to work and who first shaped my thoughts and aspirations. His guidance, intellectualism, and encouragement enhanced my thinking and understanding of theory. I miss him very much.

The idea of writing a book about the changing yeshiva fundamentalism from the point of view of male piety came during a friendly lunch with Lynn Davidman at the Hebrew University campus in the summer of 2005. Both of us were talking about our books, and we together sketched out the framework of this book. I am grateful to Lynn for these moments and all her encouragement and help throughout these years. To Eyal Ben-Ari, I am indebted for guiding and collaborating with me on my research on various aspects of the Haredi culture. Eyal encouraged me to learn more about military aspects of yeshiva piety and joined me in my fieldwork with the Zaka Haredi teams. I thank him for his support and friendship.

My dear friend Oren Golan read the first draft of this book and commented on each of the chapters. With him I have experienced the joy of intellectual inspiration and conversation.

Through their friendship and intellectual insight, my colleagues and friends at the Hebrew University of Jerusalem sustained me while I was writing. I would like to thank Tamar Rapoport for her helpful suggestions about religion and gender and for her friendship. I thank Edna Lomsky-Feder for discussions about the challenges of ethnography in male fraternities; her experience contributed immensely to my work. I am grateful as well to Tamar El-Or, Gideon Aran, Yoram Bilu, Harvey Goldberg, and Yehuda Goodman for their helpful comments and suggestions.

I could not have completed this book without the help of my friends, colleagues, and teachers. I am grateful to Batia Siehbzehner, whose friendship and wise comments I greatly value. I thank David Lehmann for our conversations about aspects of comparative religion and the resurgence of religion around the world. My thanks are due too to Kimmy Caplan for our many discussions of contemporary issues in the Haredi world in Israel and to Samuel Heilman, whose work on the ultra-Orthodox communities in Israel and the United States has inspired my thinking and writing. I thank my friend and colleague Nimrod Luz, who always was able to explain contemporary and historical aspects of Muslim piety and fundamentalism, and Michal Biran for her nurturing friendship and coffee breaks when the reading room became too intense.

I also wish to thank Einat Mesterman, Sagi Ginossar, and Jonathan Ventura for their research assistance. I am grateful to Liron Bar who helped me with the bibliography, Peggy Brill for editing preliminary drafts of this book, and Doron Narkiss for his willingness to edit the manuscript. His insightful comments and suggestions influenced my work enormously.

Two places hosted me and made me feel welcome. First, the Department of Sociology and Anthropology at Hebrew University has supported my work through the years, and I greatly appreciate the constant help, warmth, and friendliness of Osnat Ben-Shachar, Revi Kamma, Ilana Amiad, Agnes Arbeli, and Hedva Danieli.

Second, the National Library at Jerusalem is a true sanctuary for reading, writing, and discussing ideas, and I wish to emphasize the importance of supporting this rare and important house of knowledge, especially because of the constant threat of financial crisis hanging over it. I thank, particularly, Elone Avinezer, Aliza Alon, Ruth Flint, and Zipora Ben Abu, who help and encourage me every day.

My fieldwork benefited from the generous support of various institutions during my research. Special thanks are due to the Israel Foundation Trustees, the Jewish Memorial Foundation, the Israel Science Foundation, the Shaine Center for Research in Social Sciences, the Harvey L. Silbert Centre for Israel Studies, and the Van Leer Institute for their financial assistance. I also would like thank the Faculty of Social Sciences of Hebrew University for a grant for editing the manuscript. I thank the Ginsberg, the Golda Meir, and the Lady Davis fellowships at Hebrew University for supporting my research.

I also would like to thank the Macahnaim Library for permission to use pictures from their books and Avi Greenberg from Greentec Marketing Ltd., Bnei Brak, for permission to use covers of their films.

Some of the ideas presented in chapter 4 appeared in a different form in my article "Is Profane Work an Obstacle to Salvation? The Case of Ultra-Orthodox (Haredi) Jews in Contemporary Israel," *Sociology of Religion*

63(4):455–74. Likewise, some of the ideas in chapter 5 appeared in "Playing with Sacred/Corporeal Identities: Yeshiva Students' Fantasies of the Military Participation," *Jewish Social Studies: History, Culture, Society* 13(2):155–78; and some of the ideas presented in chapter 7 appeared previously in different form in "Terror, Corpse Symbolism and Taboo Violation: The 'Haredi Disaster Victim Identification Team in Israel' (ZAKA)," *Journal of the Royal Anthropological Institute* 12(4):837–58.

I greatly appreciate the interest, support, and encouragement of Jennifer Hammer at New York University Press, and I also would like to thank the three anonymous reviewers whose suggestions for revisions were both insightful and inspiring.

To Vicky Izhaki, my dear friend, I owe a special debt for her inspiring and artful counsel. Vicky helped me with the photos, the book's cover, and many other aspects of the book. I wish to thank her for her infinite creativity and care for my daughters, and numerous hours of good company and mutual work.

Finally, I would like to express my enduring gratitude to my family: my mother Rachel and my father Asher for their patient and unflagging support; my two wonderful brothers, Giora and Shahar, whose shared memories of childhood and constant encouragement inspired me along my journey; and my husband, Jacob, for his good advice, flexibility, and love while taking care of everyday life as I was writing this book. Finally, my love and gratitude go to my daughters, Shira and Sivan, who have accompanied me and accepted my long absence. The writing of this book would not have been possible without their constant support and extraordinary capacity for pointing out the most amusing possibilities of looking at the world.

Preface

When the Zionist state was created, a new form of ultra-Orthodox (Haredi) fundamentalism developed as well, a postwar variation of fundamentalism invigorated by devotees struggling to defend a Jewish lifestyle destroyed in the Holocaust. In this rejuvenated religiosity, all men are confined to a life of studious devotion, in contrast to the traditional Jewish system in prewar eastern Europe, in which only a few were chosen for full-time study. By the late 1940s and early 1950s, however, Jewish scholars—in Hebrew, *bnei Torah*—were regarded as the last bulwark defending traditional, learned Judaism.

In Israel, the Talmudic seminar, or the eastern European yeshiva style, has become the center for male worship and fellowship. At the yeshiva, devoted men reinterpret sacred codes, revive Talmudic wisdom, and strive to set themselves apart and protect the community from the temptations and distractions of modernity and secularism. These yeshiva men are considered virtuosos of texts, a collective elite of the Haredi world who hold enormous sacred power. Because they consider the Haredi world the only body able to regenerate Judaism and a Jewish way of life according to the scriptures, they and their wives have been encouraged to produce large families and reestablish the studious ideal of piety in the Holy Land. Although this postwar Jewish fundamentalism has now become institutionalized, its basic religious orientations are currently being transformed by a new generation. Accordingly, in this book I examine these shifts in yeshiva piety, particularly its effects on the Israeli Haredim and generally the meanings of piety and resistance in fundamentalist culture.

Over the last three decades, scholars of fundamentalism have focused mainly on the first stages of these groups' creation and establishment in the modern state. In this book, however, I examine an entirely different stage and context. That is, my analysis is of the experiences and narratives of a new generation of fundamentalist yeshiva men as they reflect on their own history and reconsider the outcomes of the governing model of piety. Certain processes in this well-established fundamentalist society, both within and outside it, have sometimes caused the devotees to resist its model of piety. I demonstrate that the new generation of yeshiva men feel that this "ready-made," one-size-fits-all model of piety is no longer satisfying. In their view, fundamentalist piety has alienated them from state institutions (army, workplace, politics) and created uncertainty in their family life, gender roles, and everyday experiences. In their attempt to find solutions, these men have questioned major aspects of their life: their rabbis, the family as currently constituted, and their relation both to the state and its institutions and to civil society. Their conclusions are tentative and at times ambiguous, simultaneously accepting and rejecting the very same assumptions. Within their critique of piety, these men have formed an idealized image of their forefathers and, at the same time, have been forced to face the practical problems in their everyday life, financial situation, social position, marital and work options, morality, and future.

My own attraction to the contemporary Haredi yeshiva life in Israel evolved together with my interest in the sociology and anthropology of religion, especially the manifestations of worldwide fundamentalism. At first glance, the Haredi yeshiva world seems to provide a perfect opportunity to explore text-based religiosity and to study the modern aspects of asceticism, male virtuosity, extreme piety, modes of segregation, religious fraternities, and other aspects of the fundamentalist revival. The Haredi yeshiva culture is a community bounded by space; therefore it seems to present an ideal case study of the manifestations of extremist religiosity and the manner in which radical forms of devotion are played out just a short distance away from a dynamic, secular, modern state. Captivated by the lives of these *bnei Torah* or, more specifically, these men's studious lifestyle and enclave culture, I decided that the yeshiva world would be an appropriate case study. I also knew that the "inside story" of the yeshiva world had not been sufficiently studied by scholars of religion and Israeli studies.

I was encouraged by the generations of anthropologists who had entered closed religious communities, as well as their techniques for obtaining access, learning other languages, making friends, and becoming familiar with new ideas and concepts about other cultures. In addition, reading the extensive research on the worldwide revival of fundamentalism, such as "born-again" Christian groups in the United States, the pious Shi'ite Muslim movements in the Middle East, and Hindu fundamentalists in

India, inspired me to explore and compare them with the modern Jewish remaking of fundamentalist piety.

Entering the world of the yeshiva was obviously the first obstacle. I spent most of the summer of 1997 figuring out how to gain access to this world and finding ways to understand yeshiva life in Jerusalem. Because women are not allowed in this setting, in the beginning I was regarded with suspicion and faced with endless skeptical comments. I therefore had to convince the yeshiva students to meet and talk with me, despite the difficulties that I represented as a secular woman and researcher from the academic world. These challenges affected every step of my study. When I finally found a yeshiva student who was willing to meet me, I expressed my gratitude and tried to ask the pertinent questions with the correct attitude. Despite my eagerness to ask questions about piety and devotion, the most prominent obstacle in my first encounters was following the dress regulations and making sure to wear a calf-length dress or skirt and a blouse or top with long sleeves and a high neck. Adhering to the strict regulations concerning modesty was the prerequisite for my initial access to the students' worlds, but these first encounters only added various methodological and conceptual complications. After conducting a few interviews with the students, I realized that in order to proceed with my fieldwork, I had to design new tools to investigate their models of piety and masculinity which also considered the scriptural nature of the yeshiva male-based world. Because I had to conduct my interviews outside the confines of the yeshiva, I decided to simulate yeshiva learning by working with the students as my teachers of sacred texts. Consequently, in the first chapter I spend considerable time exploring these issues of access that affected my research on the segregated male yeshiva fraternity.

My interviews and simulations with yeshiva students led to several dilemmas and limitations with regard to interpretation. In order to widen my focus, while conducting interviews I also collected a wide range of popular materials, which I was able to incorporate in my work as valuable sources of knowledge. As a secular woman, and thus restricted from entering the yeshiva, I could not observe the everyday aspects of yeshiva learning and devotion, but I could examine and interpret what was made visible, published, distributed, and performed outside the yeshiva. I also could use the many books, manuals, and films which represent a creative and popular Haredi religiosity, with its meanings, interpretations, symbols, and ideals of piety constantly being debated and negotiated. These, then, are my materials: the analysis of the views expressed outside the yeshiva by the students with whom I met, and the themes and symbols conveyed through books, pamphlets, posters, and CDs of sermons and films, most of which were available in Haredi shops.

During my nearly ten years of fieldwork (1997 to 2006), I came to know yeshiva students whose talents and personality greatly impressed me. Naively believing the research on fundamentalist socialization and institutions published since the 1980s, I expected to meet conformist subjects, enlisted into the missions of the fundamentalist regime, soldiers of God ready to fight modernity and its dreaded consequences. In contrast, I met students who expressed disapproval of and dissatisfaction with their worlds, families, and contemporary rabbinical authorities. Early on, I met yeshiva students who were not just followers being manipulated and circumscribed in their religious socialization by the powerful fundamentalist elites and leaders of their culture. Rather, I spoke with rebellious students who were even reformers in certain aspects of their lives. I met text virtuosos on the path to status and power in the Haredi world who were challenging their own position and culture.

Through my conversations with more than sixty Haredi students, I began to question some of the accepted wisdom regarding the so-called quiescent fundamentalism of the yeshiva and the model of stagnant piety as expressed in the literature on fundamentalism. This led to a new set of questions about yeshiva piety in Israel and the ways in which yeshiva students identify and represent themselves. Gradually, my presence and the many taboos I represented in my own existence and lifestyle—which had acted as a barrier to the whole project and jeopardized my first steps— were beginning to work in my favor. My very impartiality, noninvolvement, or downright alien-ness with regard to the issues that concerned them, allowed them to voice, I believe, criticisms of the yeshiva and yeshiva life and norms, and observations of some of the changes in this world. As I became more adept, I received surprising expressions of curiosity, self-observation, inner scrutiny, and self-examination, which form the raw data for much of this book.

Following my personal encounters with these students, reading the guidance manuals and watching films, learning about their worldview and the dramatic shift occurring today became clearer, challenging the masculinity and piety as currently viewed. Through their reflective criticisms, these students were reevaluating their life in my presence. As much as the leaders of the yeshiva world would like to keep the community isolated from the pernicious influences of the larger society around it—such as a loss of faith, reduction in religiosity, changing gender roles and family patterns, and global capitalism—these forces have nevertheless affected the yeshiva world and its students. Despite the founders' and contemporary rabbis' efforts, modernity has made inroads into this enclave. Various modern and Israeli discourses, images, practices, and bodies of knowledge have necessarily found their way into the community's context and practices, as this book demonstrates. In a period troubled by matters of security, welfare issues, identity politics, and a growing militarism, yeshiva students see no virtue in studious poverty, in conditions of overcrowding with no professional training and with self-enclosure leading to alienation from the Israeli public sphere. So the Haredi enclave is striving to create new strategies of inclusion and identity while at the same time defending their faith and unique lifestyle.

Based on these interviews and popular texts, I discuss the incorporation of several key dimensions of the modern world and the state: a this-worldly definition of masculinity and piety along with a transformation of the Haredi family, of gender roles and fatherhood and their attitudes toward livelihood and sacrifice. This changing view comes with a demand for participation in civil society, in the labor market, and even in the military, and the establishment of organizations that aid, at the scene, the victims of mass bombing incidents and other disasters.

The students' reflections on piety provide a perspective on their passions and fantasies and on their ideas about the Israeli state and modernity, on the one hand, and on their attitudes toward religiosity, worship, prayer, and study, on the other. Through an analysis of these themes, I argue that fundamentalism changes not only because of adaptations to modernity but also because of criticism from within by new generations of devotees. While facing new challenges, the yeshiva world is reevaluating its models and institutions toward a this-worldly orientation that would enable devotees to engage with the world and to be more adaptive to these changing circumstances without immediately relinquishing their traditional social values.

In this book I analyze five aspects of the evolution of piety in Israel's Haredi fundamentalist enclave. Paralleling my slow adaptation to and acceptance by the community, I recount my attempt to open a dialogue about these men's approach to the "evil inclination" and sexuality, which are strongly embedded taboos in the model of yeshiva fundamentalism. Most manuals describe the inner struggle of pious men as a powerful concept, one that was not questioned as often by my interviewees and popular writers. The second aspect of piety is these men's renunciation of profane work and the withdrawal from the modern Israeli labor market.

Very different from sexuality, these men's attitudes toward work generated strong criticism. Their withdrawal from work was interpreted as a manipulation by the yeshiva rabbis to achieve full control over the students' freedom and minds. Students are challenging their leaders to change to a this-worldly orientation toward work that would make earning a living an intergral part of their life.

The third aspect of piety is the men's approach to military conscription. The interviewees argued against otherworldly piety and redefined it with the use of militaristic images and hegemonic models of the Israeli combat soldier, heroism, and sacrifice. Yeshiva students imagine an active, heroic, and militaristic form of piety, although currently they do not translate work and military orientations into everyday practices.

The two other aspects of yeshiva piety, prescribed gender roles and participation in civil society, are strongly contested by the students and have been translated into new religious meanings and practices. Students criticize the gender division and their separation from women's domains and household matters. They want to be involved in family life and to undertake domestic tasks by redefining fatherhood, challenges that are being translated into the variously active roles of fathers and spouses.

Finally, as a case study, I analyze my fieldwork experience with the ZAKA volunteers, the male Haredi aid organization, to examine their changing attitudes toward civil society. ZAKA expresses piety through a new approach to death and to helping the victims of mass incidents, especially by collecting body parts for burial and helping identify the dead. Participation in ZAKA represents the new this-worldly Haredi piety, the alternative to the model shaped in the first stages of fundamentalism. Death work, aid, sacrifice, heroism, and masculinity all are part of this process of transformation. The change in models of pietistic interpretation highlights the new possibilities of fundamentalism's changing nature today, options that may be realized by other fundamentalist groups in the future.

1

Introduction

Redefining Male Piety and Fundamentalism

As a result of and in response to the challenges of modernity, male piety is now being reconsidered and reconstructed in the fundamentalist world. Piety has always been at the heart of religion and is expressed in a variety of ways: through abstinence and mourning, with a selective self-disciplined faithfulness, or via sexual renunciation or zealous attachment, all of which are ways of preparing the body to receive the spirit of God (Brown 1988, 68). Piety also is at the center of modern religiosity, especially as performed by fundamentalist groups. The encounter between religion and modernity, however, raises questions about the unique nature of piety in the context of modern religious experience. How is it shaped, institutionalized, or transformed?

Students of fundamentalism usually describe models of piety as monolithic, especially the strict fundamentalist forms of men's piety, which are usually regarded as holding power and thus as being static. Piety is often portrayed in the scholarly literature as a collection of religious practices used to protect and maintain the group's boundaries (Almond, Appleby, and Sivan 2003; Eisenstadt 2000; Marty and Appleby 1991). Throughout this book, I argue that piety is not a fixed model, that instead it is always shifting and constantly being revised, reinterpreted, and contested by the members of the fundamentalist group. To my surprise, while analyzing piety, I found that those who are seen as the strictest and most prestigious models of piety are often the ones who hold the most powerful positions in the community, who are most likely to resist accepted forms of piety and to try to change its nature. How is it, I wondered, that members of a fundamentalist elite would want to undermine their own position of superiority? While refracting various images of the religious persona, the characteristics of this piety—its configuration, power, and defiant nature—also reveal the possibilities of changing the structure of religious society and its politics.

In the fundamentalist world, piety is composed mainly of devotion and self-restraint. The presence of these qualities in a person, either a man or a woman, leads the devotee to try to reclaim those spaces that have been or are in danger of being secularized and modernized. Underlying this pietistic activity is the assumption that the world has entered a final period of moral, religious, and ethical decline and that the secular world, always a source of danger, is now a greater threat than ever. In the fundamentalist view, piety, with its mastering body regime, is the only force capable of changing or restraining the secular and heretical nature of the world and thus perhaps of ensuring its future, if not present, redemption.

Fundamentalist leaders also use piety as an ideological motive to convince members to become active, albeit with almost no visible rewards. Indeed, piety is a political tool, used by fundamentalist authorities to control the enclave and its boundaries, as well as members' relations with the state, politics, and civil society (Almond, Appleby, and Sivan 2003, 17; Sprinzak 1993). In order to persuade people to join and work for the group, the moral ideology must be all-embracing, implemented in all spheres of its members' lives by creating a politics that persuades them that they are part of the "chosen." This ideology defines devotees as elected by God, chosen to fulfill his missions on earth, for which all others are too frail, pitiful, and wretched. The "outside" is thereby polluted and demonized, whereas the "inside" is constantly purified by the sacred work of pious men and women (Harding 2000). The concept of piety in contemporary fundamentalism blends the traditional features of devotion, asceticism, and awe (see Valantasis 1995) with the latest applications of communication, technology, science, and consumerism and with postmodern notions of the representation of the self.

Sociologists studying fundamentalism contend that fundamentalist groups consist of educated, text-based, intellectual elite men, who are accepted in their communities as virtuosos of the canon (Antoun 2001, 3; Riesebrodt 1993, 9). These men transmit ideas to the new generations in special institutions, and their duty is to use piety as a defense against the outer world. In sum, piety is a set of techniques used to constitute a model of the docile devotee, usually a man, to regulate members' bodies, to form restrictions, and to enforce rules. Power and status are protected by these valorized devotees who are constantly performing, defending the sanctity of the group. Trained and impressed with the stamp of proper desire, selfhood, masculinity, morality, and knowledge, the pious fundamentalist is conditioned to aspire to transcendental qualities, which safeguard him from the corrupt world and, by extension, safeguard the entire community.

Most scholars see piety as a model of moral perfection, an authoritative requirement to be accepted without criticism or challenge (Antoun 2001; Emerson and Hartman 2006; Lawrence 1989; Riesebrodt 1993). In this book, however, I suggest an alternative view. I argue that piety is not only learned, used, protected, and reinforced by fundamentalists but that it is also critiqued and reshaped by individuals and, over time, by generations. Moreover, those fundamentalist figures who embody the highest level of piety in the group and whose dominant position would seem to lead them to protect and reproduce the sources of sacred power sources are precisely the self-reflective agents who are constantly refining and critiquing their own religious paradigms. At certain moments, elite devotees challenge the very nature and validity of what is considered sacred in their culture. This critique involves a change in not only what is experienced as sacred but also in the very meaning of the sacred order (Demerath 1999, 1).

Piety and devotion are not merely parts of a system protecting and defending its own boundaries; they also are a paradigm of active resistance, revision, and the incorporation of otherness. Thus, devotees worship and accept the sacred and, at the same time, rearticulate its very meanings, structures, and boundaries. Fundamentalism is not, as many see it, necessarily static just because it is conservative; instead, it presents an innovative challenge to orthodoxy on its own grounds, and it is the somewhat unpredictable growing point of religiosity. Therefore, we should not be too surprised that in its challenges to the accepted foundations of piety, fundamentalism encourages devotees to consider new possibilities of the sacred. In doing so, fundamentalism deals with the roots of the idea of the sacred, sometimes risking transgression and at other times yielding new religious orientations.

Revealing the dynamic nature of piety in fundamentalist experience and uncovering its new meanings—especially its implications for masculinity and power—is at the heart of this book. These ideas both question the hegemonic view of male fundamentalist piety as static and explore the creation of alternatives to the model of pious masculinity. Indeed, revealing the contemporary change in piety allows us to rethink how fundamentalism has shifted the core of religious performance and institutions over time and shows how the idea of the sacred is being contested by a new generation of devotees in their constant negotiation with modernity, the state, civil society, and other institutions and apparatuses, to create new forms of piety.

The fundamentalist group on which I focus in this book is the Jewish, ultra-Orthodox, Haredi community in Israel or, more specifically, the male yeshiva culture. This is an enclave culture that is interacting with other worlds while remaining self-contained and in which many of the transactions in and the transformation of fundamentalism and piety take place. At the Haredi study hall, students are taught to become virtuous through the expert study of the Talmud and its commentaries. Indeed, Torah studies in the yeshiva are considered a value on which the continuity and survival of the Jewish people depend in both a spiritual and a physical sense (Friedman 1993, 184). In Haredi culture the yeshiva—that is, a seminary for higher Talmudic learning—is an institution exclusively for men. Men who excel in yeshiva studies become rabbis, adjudicators, and scholars; members of the elite; and authority figures in their worlds (Heilman 1983, 1).

The yeshiva men I interviewed for this book use the word *Haredi* to distinguish themselves from other Orthodox Jews. The Hebrew term *Haredi* (or the plural, *Haredim*), meaning "those who fear or tremble," appears in Isaiah 66:5: "Hear the word of the Lord, you who tremble at His word" (cited in Heilman and Friedman 1991a, 198). To specify their religious devotion, these students also use the Hebrew term *ben Torah*—literally "son of the Torah" or the "disciple of the wise" (*Talmid hackham*), the true pious man (see Selengut 1994, 236)—to stress that they are fulfilling the truest male piety.

When I first became interested in the Haredi yeshiva world, I realized that although it posed enormous difficulties for research, it contained near-laboratory conditions for uncovering the workings of male piety in fundamentalism. In order to explore this world, I needed to examine the members' various experiences and stories and then to analyze the meaning of their experiences from different perspectives, observing the manner in which they oppose and reshape piety.

As this book demonstrates, even though the official leaders of the yeshiva world have attempted to establish a religiosity that reinforces particular models of piety and purity within a certain apprehension of the sacred, modernity has made inroads into the yeshiva world, affecting these time-honored models and shifting the understanding of the sacred. We look at how different modern features have altered these modes of yeshiva religiosity. By analyzing the specific characteristic of yeshiva fundamentalism in Israel, I show that the traditional type of fundamentalism, based on male asceticism and the devotional study of texts, is currently being contested.

I further contend that the new generation of yeshiva students, despite being expected to defend the enclave, is rebelling against the main principles set by the rabbis to govern their interaction with the secular world around them. This is part of the wider development of an "oppositional culture" of young Haredi men who chafe at the limitations that the older constructions of yeshiva masculinity in Israel have imposed on them. I show how they are actively seeking a religious model through which to incorporate, rather than oppose, some of the models offered by secular Israeli society. I demonstrate that these men, although assured of their power and status, are resisting the traditional model of piety, especially the other-worldly orientations of their forefathers, and are redefining the basic meanings of the sacred. To replace this model, they are suggesting a this-worldly orientation, more politically and physically active, taken from military images of the Israeli combat soldier, Jewish/Zionist heroism, voluntarism, and active forms of citizenry, especially those connected with terrorism and care for the dead and the wounded. In their search for a new religiosity, yeshiva students are trying to incorporate several dimensions of secular, national models: they are redefining masculinity, "Israeliness," and family relations; participating in civil society through the labor market and the military, setting up voluntary social aid organizations; and offering services in their unique areas of expertise for the public beyond their own community. These new features, derived from ongoing pressures such as constant war, terrorist attacks, factional politics, and economic burdens, are being incorporated in a manner acceptable to the community, thereby necessitating a new formulation of fundamentalism and power.

While the details may differ from one fundamentalist group to another, the presence today of these kinds of dynamic forces is not unique to Israeli yeshiva students but can be found in fundamentalist groups around the world. Fundamentalism thus has become a comparative theoretical tool used by scholars to explain a variety of religious experiences, including Hindu nationalism, Shi'ite Iranian revolutionaries, evangelical Christians in the United States, radical Egyptian Sunnis, Sikh militants in India, and Sri Lankan Buddhist fighter monks, all of which can be examined using the same analytical framework (Almond, Appleby, and Sivan 2003; Juergensmeyer 2000; Obeyesekere 1995). As Marty and Appleby (1991) argue, a comparative analysis of these trends allows an in-depth look into particular traits, similarities, and differences among distinct radical religious platforms and among expressions or religious resurgences that appear to share similar models of reaction to the values of modernity. Their exploration here, I hope, will also serve as methodological tool for further research of fundamentalist communities in general.

Varieties of Fundamentalist Piety

Over the last two decades, anthropologists and sociologists of religion have focused on the ways in which fundamentalist religions have absorbed modern ideas and practices (Ammerman 1987, 2005; Davidman 1991; Deeb 2006; Mahmood 2005). Scholars have analyzed the resurgence of fundamentalism worldwide since the late 1970s and early 1980s, studying processes of conversion, devotion, disaffection, and the social organization of fundamentalist communities (Almond, Appleby, and Sivan 2003; Ammerman 1987; Antoun 1989, 2001; Beeman 2001; Bruce 2000; Hervieu-Léger 2000; Kepel 2002; Riesebrodt 1993). Within a few years, however, it became clear that although fundamentalism appeared to be monolithic, nonliberal, and entirely traditional, it actually is, and always was, in dialogue with and affected by the larger culture in which it exists. Fundamentalism's antagonistic stance toward secular and Western liberal traditions makes them its defining other, which must be incorporated in order to be opposed. In turn, this positioning has influenced major changes in the beliefs and practices of these conservative religious groups.

The word *fundamentalism* dates back to an early-twentieth-century American religious movement, which took its name from *The Fundamentals: A Testimony of the Truth*, a twelve-volume work published between 1901 and 1915 by a group of Protestant laymen. This movement was part of the tradition of evangelical revivalism that inspired the Great Awakening of the early nineteenth century. The term *fundamentalism* originally was applied only to the beliefs and practices of Christian sects, but it expanded to include similar ideas and behavior in other religions and is currently used to describe several modern religious expressions (Eisenstadt 2000, 83; Lehmann 1998; Stolow 2004, 110). The context and features of modernity, especially secular state education, the mass media, and technology, seem, both individually and collectively, to contain distinctive inclinations toward religious fundamentalism. Accordingly, the fundamentalist phenomenon can be explained as a product of the contradictory pressures of modernity and a surprising series of reactions: secularization led to religious revivalism; the consolidation of feminist ideologies caused a backlash against modesty and family-based ideologies; the rise of secular education brought with it the cultivation of the religious ethos; and technology and free access to knowledge seem to have led to religious confinement and censorship.

The term *fundamentalism* in the modern Jewish context may offer a better understanding of the exclusiveness (historically as well as culturally) and differences of present-day Jewish movements. The scholarly literature on Jewish fundamentalism recognizes three groups: The ultranational Gush Emunim (bloc of the faithful), the Lubavitch-Hasidic or Habad movement, and the Haredi community (Aran 1991, 1993; Friedman 1994; Heilman 1994, 1995; Ravitzky 1994; Soloveitchik 1994a; Stadler 2005). These groups are distinguished from conservative and reformist trends in Judaism, the Haredi Mizrahi (Sephardi), and the charismatic or New Age Haredim (Breslaw and others), as well as from Haredi communities in other historical periods. Scholars (Cromer 1993, 164; Friedman 1987, 1995a; Heilman and Friedman 1991b) dealing with Haredi fundamentalism have defined the community in Israel as having four dimensions: resistance to modernity, scripturalism, the massive institution building of fundamentalist institutions in Israel, and separatism.

The first dimension of fundamentalism is what Shmuel Eisenstadt calls the "modernity" of these groups (1995, 259, 2000). Even though fundamentalist movements oppose modernity (Marty and Appleby 1991, ix), they are the inevitable product of it (Ammerman 1987). Modernity, especially the modern liberal state, is commonly seen as the symbol of the outside and of evil forces. Although Israel is officially a Jewish state, its governmental system is constructed as Zionist and secular, which is a cause for rejection and resistance by ultra-Orthodox believers. Nonetheless, the existence of Israel's Haredi community in its current form depends on the nation to protect it and provide for it materially, and it demands these rights as a minority in a liberal state.

Past and current leaders of the Haredi community, such as Abraham Isaiah Karlitz and Elazar Menachem Shach (Caplan 2007, 77, 69), provided believers with a set of religious, pietistic strategies by which to protect their religious identities and culture in these modern surroundings. This fundamentalism rejects or disregards modernity by using religious reasoning to explicate history and tradition as well as contemporary reality. Although Haredi historical discourse reflects historical and mythical events in the life of the secular state as well as the Jewish nation, it uses a different causality.

First, fundamentalists perceive their faith as a link in a glorious unbroken tradition beginning with the earliest prophets and practitioners of the faith. Haredim, especially Ashkenazim, feel this most poignantly because of the Holocaust. They consider themselves a remnant of the glory of European Orthodox Jewry and its only continuation in the present, custodians of a tradition that, because it was once nearly lost, must be kept alive at all costs. Modern culture, the antithesis and nemesis of that world and of the Western lifestyle in general, is strongly condemned. Like Muslim and Christian fundamentalists, Haredim do not permit abortion and homosexuality and actively oppose them.

As other fundamentalist groups have done, Haredim have constructed their unique identity by means of a selective retrieval of doctrines, religious symbols, and beliefs. The sacred texts—the Torah, the Qur'an, or the Bible—all are accepted by their adherents as being of divine origin (Almond, Appleby, and Sivan 2003, 96). This acceptance is known as *scripturalism*, which is the second dimension of fundamentalism (Antoun 2001). These symbols and meanings are selected from a sacred imaginary past and are used by devotees to respond to what they perceive as challenging, troubling times. Fundamentalists purposely select specific elements from their traditional sacred texts to incorporate in their future plans, visions, and fantasies. According to Talal Asad (2003, 11), in fundamentalist imagery the scriptures are used to establish and authorize a particular interpretation or view and to empower a particular authority.

By selecting certain elements of tradition, fundamentalists try to remake the world according to their own goals and desires. For example, currently in the yeshiva world, the commandment in Deuteronomy 6:7 to study Torah "when you sit at home and when you walk abroad" has been given absolute centrality. That is, this commandment orders all male members to join the yeshiva as part of belonging to the community and its legacy.

In the Lithuanian Israeli yeshivas, this obligation is underscored by symbols drawn from their imaginary or invented cultural and traditional past, used especially by the rational school of the *gaon* (genius) of Vilna, Rabbi Elijah Ben Solomon, and his disciple Rabbi Hayyim of Volozhin. This use of tradition to legitimize participation contrasts with the historical account of the European tradition. Among eastern European Jewish communities in Lithuania, only a handful of prodigies, members of a select elite, dedicate their life to studious activities, whereas today most adult male Israeli Haredim must devote most of their lives to the yeshiva. As a result, Haredi members regard anyone who accepts the legitimacy of modern culture as being essentially anti-Jewish and therefore a potentially contaminating influence. Haredim rationalize their scriptural choices by seeing themselves as the elite whose piety will save all Jews. But this studious way of life is not for everyone, hence the desire for change.

A third dimension in the scholarly literature defines fundamentalism as extensive institution building. The nature of scripturalism has reinforced the importance of founding new educational and religious institutions such as religious seminars, yeshivot, madrasas, churches, theological schools, and Bible schools. To construct a specific, modern, model of piety, new socialization methods are used. The yeshiva hall, exactly like the madrasa, is the key element of the fundamentalist operation, in that both serve to maintain a cadre of experts who can invigorate a moral rearrangement (Heilman 1995, 78).

Because the fundamentalist imagination views the ancient past as a time of true piety, the devotees' fathers and forefathers are perceived as not having been sufficiently religious. Therefore, the mimetic aspect of socialization in these communities—or the strong tendency to imitate the behavior of other members of the family—has been reduced. The family is thus not considered as the sole significant institution for socialization and education. As in the example of the Habad movement, special nursery schools and children's after-school activities are based on the implementation of the Habad style of life. Members of these groups must participate in these institutions, whose purpose is intensifying their religious aspects and constructing a fundamentalist consciousness. They thus tend to become total institutions, meaning that they encompass and are responsible for all fields of their members' everyday lives (Friedman 1994).

The fourth dimension is separatism. Students of religion define fundamentalist groups as "enclave cultures" (Almond, Appleby, and Sivan 2003, 34; Sivan 1995), or distinct entities with defined cultural and moral boundaries that are strongly protected by the divide between the virtuous saved and morally superior from the depraved (Sivan 1995). Fundamentalists are kept apart from the defiled, thus thwarting the demonic forces that try to subvert the enclave (Almond, Appleby, and Sivan 2003, 34, 36). In this sense, the outside is seen as polluted, contagious, and dangerous, even though, as Sivan pointed out, "It seems as though it partakes of the same tradition as the inside, while being in essence its very negation" (Sivan 1995, 19).

These four features of fundamentalist piety dominate the study of the yeshiva world and its forms of male piety. Scholars have focused on the foundation and institutional growth of the society of learners and their methods of studying. Their resulting works highlight the texts and structures of the early stages of yeshiva fundamentalism in Israel (Friedman 1991; Heilman 1992, 1995; Sivan 1995), describing Haredi culture as traditional, God-fearing, and otherworldly. These studies describe yeshiva piety in detail and define it as the center of the fundamentalist Haredi enterprise. But these studies have not paid much attention to the changes in Haredi fundamentalism in general and in yeshiva piety in particular. Therefore I suggest taking a more dynamic approach to yeshiva piety, one that concentrates on challenges to the sacred. My analysis demonstrates that the model of studious piety is being transformed and that the sheer volume of activity makes obvious an issue that previously was invisible: that yeshiva students are constructing, and have been for some time, a new conception of what it means to be a righteous person, one who is more of this world, sensitive to issues of the Haredi family, gender equality, politics, and civil society.

Piety, Gender, and Resistance

A large body of literature has examined the intertwining of fundamentalism with gender relations, especially in the creation of a new model of gender, piety, and authority (Bendroth 1993; Brasher 1998; Deeb 2006; Griffith 1997; Mahmood 2005; Muesse 1996; Nason-Clark and Neitz 2001; Stacey 1990). By thus situating women's piety and resistance, this literature has contributed to the study of fundamentalism and change. Scholars have concentrated on this through two central issues, the effect of the inherent domination of men in these groups and the different religious experiences of the sexes. Scholars argue that gender is a pivotal factor in transforming the nature of the fundamentalist movements from within (Brasher 1998, 18). Most studies look at the paradox of women's participation (whether they joined or were born into the group) in these religious groups: an oppressive patriarchal culture, on the one hand, and women's ability to exercise power within the repressive religious group, on the other.

Judith Stacey (1990), for example, points to the high level of Christian fundamentalist working-class women's participation in gender-restrictive religion. Fundamental congregations are attractive to these women, she maintains, because they can find support there for the difficulties in their lives, especially economic uncertainties, while constructing a family that suits their needs.

In *Godly Women* (1998), Brenda Brasher examines Bible-believing women and contends that fundamentalist women are powerful agents in their religious group, even though it is generally conceded to be organized around their disempowerment. She explains how devoted women who stay involved with fundamentalist congregations construct new positions and exercise power within their religious group. The key to this empowerment is the women's ministry program of each congregation, which is led by women for women. Besides adding capable women to the churches' ministerial staffs, these women-only activities create a special symbolic world that empowers them, encourages them to develop female religious enclaves, and provides a network of support in everyday and public activities (Brasher 1998, 3, 5). This construction of female piety is thus part of the resistance to and the formation of new authority.

In *God's Daughters*, Marie Griffith argues that the specific realities of being "submissive wives" in an evangelical organization are negotiated, constructed, challenged, and transformed by women (Griffith 1997, 139; see also Gallagher 2003). Thus Pentecostal women have negotiated between politics and theology to construct powerful new models of religious involvement. Using biblical terms, Griffith shows how women integrate their husbands' and fathers' authority and discipline into what they interpret as freedom and self-empowerment.

The consolidation of fundamentalist piety and women's active participation in the revival of the Jewish fundamentalist world has been studied as well. Lynn Davidman (1991) analyzed two groups of Jewish women who turned to Orthodox Judaism in adulthood. She explains why not particularly observant Jewish women have chosen an Orthodox way of life and seek legitimacy through the authority of that tradition. Here again we see, as in the evangelical context, that while they are shaping their piety, these women also are devising strategies, ranging from compromise to resistance, for dealing with the world.

Tamar El-Or (1993a, 2002, 2006) stressed the centrality of literacy to women's religiosity in their construction of piety and the spreading practice of intensive learning. In her studies she demonstrates women's creativity and involvement in the project of fundamentalism and its reshaping. El-Or contends that women's literacy is bringing about a profound transformation in Orthodox Judaism in particular. Women study the Torah together, observe the Jewish commandments, and deemphasize the gender of the believer so as to enable female devotees' participation in public debates. In this shift, the tension between piety and the modern secular world has been exacerbated by religious women's pursuit of Torah knowledge, and this increased tension has led to a change in the social situation.

Tamar Rapoport (1999) studied the link between women's piety and the construction of subjectivity in Zionist religious fundamentalist education. Based on her fieldwork in an all-girls' religious boarding school, she argues that these girls translate and reinterpret their daily experiences of modesty in these fundamentalist institutions and their anticipated experiences as wives and mothers (Rapoport, Penso, and Garb 1994, 1995; also Rapoport, Penso, and Halbertal 1996).

Saba Mahmood (2005) also explored piety, literacy, and modesty, demonstrating these changes in the revival of Muslim women's participation since the 1980s in mosques in Egypt. She shows how women have reconstructed piety and a modest lifestyle by reading and teaching a variety of canonical sources which interpret for them their daily conduct, thereby reshaping the nature of female piety. Similarly, in her fieldwork with a pious Shi'ite community in Beirut, Lara Deeb (2006) claims that women's piety has changed because of the uncertainty of how to be modern in Lebanese culture. Deeb investigated the symbolic aspect of religion and explains how public piety is cast as the current women's jihad, which has implications for women's lives, clothes, rituals, lifestyles, and politics in Lebanon.

This ethnographic body of research has shown the experience of piety as being an active, innovative, and powerful enterprise in the lives of women fundamentalists. The combination of these insights into piety, gender, and resistance tells us that fundamentalist identity, despite being constructed within a conservative religious framework, is nuanced, not monolithic. And unlike outsiders' all-too-common misperception, the members of this framework, whatever their gender, are not necessarily victims of oppression or domination any more than are the members of many other communities.

Despite the wealth of recent studies illuminating religious women's experience, neither male piety nor the construction of models of religiosity for Jewish fundamentalist men has received as much attention. Male piety and religiosity have many different archetypes, drawing on different eras and traditions. In the Christian tradition, men's religious heroism has always been a central issue and has been interpreted in a variety of ways. For example, the model of the monk, the ascetic, or the martyr is represented by what Michael Kimmel describes as the "reedy man with long bony fingers" image of Jesus (Kimmel 1996, 176).

Alternative models of piety also were constructed by male fraternal orders and institutions. From the medieval tradition of the church militant, struggling both physically and spiritually in this world against sin, to the nineteenth-century model of muscular Christianity in Britain and the United States, a fraternity of men strove for piety and male character building through sports, against a perceived cultural feminization (Kimmel 1996; Putney 2001, 3). That is, sports were used as a tool to masculinize evangelical Christianity, disseminate religion, and convert nonbelievers (Bartkowski 2004, 31; Kimmel 1996). Anthony Rotundo (1993, 224) maintains that this male piety was oriented to the body, emphasizing the body image of Jesus as vigorous and strong. In these different models, religious men acquired their power and status from different models of religiosity and masculinity. Daniel Boyarin (1997, 23) points to the various models of piety and manhood in Judaism, with the Talmudic culture as the ideal traditional form of Jewish maleness, embodied in the yeshiva student. But Boyarin also claims that Westernization is what brought a new model of piety, creating a "muscular Jew" in the image of the "muscular Christian," dominated by discourse of "the body" rather than solely as an organism for transmitting knowledge.

In contrast to women's studies, only few studies in the field of fundamentalism have looked at piety from the viewpoint of men's desires to change and reconstruct their own piety. I would argue that this oversight is connected to the assumption that fundamentalist men, in general and not only in the Jewish context, serve as the protectors of the faith, defenders of the enclave who are expected to preserve the power of scripturalism that is in their hands. The thinking is that because they are the elite, they are not likely to struggle for change. But in this book, I demonstrate that this assumption is wrong. Those men who are assumed to protect the fundamentalist enclave, its sacred structure, can and do challenge models of piety and power and are currently reconstructing their religiosity. My aim is thus to provide a detailed account of this changing piety in the heart of fundamentalism. I contend that by resisting piety, fundamentalist men are reconstructing a model that not only is based on religious power but also blends together several other bases of social power and religious revival.

John Bartkowski's analysis of a male religious revivalist group in *Promise Keepers* (2004; Messner 1997; see also Williams 2001), examines the construction of new forms of Christian masculine piety. These men seek to replace the old notions of "godly masculinity" based on an "instrumentalist" definition of manhood, characterized by aggression, strength, rationality, and goal-oriented behavior. The new model of male Christian piety, "expressive masculinity," focuses on its members' involvement in family life and the expression of emotions and gender egalitarianism, as opposed to male domination.

My book explores the involvement of Jewish fundamentalist men in formulating new meanings of piety in their fundamentalist world by creating new models of godliness and maleness. I analyze shifts in fundamentalist piety through the prism of the Israeli Haredi yeshiva culture, which is composed mainly of young men both representing the culture yet looking to expand the definition of piety in order to cope with the reality of their world. My findings define a way of resisting traditional masculinity and piety in the fundamentalist world. Thus, fundamentalist men are not only the defenders of their faith and the performers of models invented by their forefathers; they also are the challengers of their own culture. Despite their position as part of the elite, they are struggling to exercise new power and change the meanings of piety.

Being a Woman Researcher of Male Fundamentalism

As I stated in the preface, my conclusions presented in this book are based on more than sixty in-depth interviews with Haredi men, most of them students at Lithuanian yeshivas. I decided to focus on the Lithuanian segment of the Haredi community because the ideology of male-based yeshiva culture in the Haredi culture is strong and because this is the most dedicated group to the all-yeshiva, male-based ideology in the Israeli Haredi culture (including the various Hassidic or other groups in the Israeli Haredi community today). I analyzed sermons, speeches, popular writings, videos, manuals, pamphlets, children's books, films, photos, and artifacts that I collected during almost a decade of extended fieldwork in the Haredi world. For each of the chapters, I used different materials and methods to explore the various themes.

Gaining Access to Their Worlds:
The Key Informant and the Forbidden

Reflection on the hardships and challenges of "entering the field" is a sub-
genre that has recently become very popular in anthropology. A notable
part of this genre was written by scholars studying religious movements
and communities, including the ultra-Orthodox Haredim. Even though
the fieldwork on ultra-Orthodox communities is extensive (Belcove-Shalin
1988; Davidman 1991; El-Or 1994; Kaul-Seidman 2002), few scholars have
done fieldwork studying the world of the yeshiva and its experiences. In a
landmark work, William Helmreich (2000) presented the life of the postwar yeshiva world in the United States. Raised as an Orthodox Jew, Helmreich was, as he says,

> familiar with the Talmud and spoke Hebrew and Yiddish fluently, which
> were invaluable in establishing contact and maintain[ing] rapport with
> those in the yeshiva. The most significant practical outcome was that I
> was able, as a student in a class, to find an acceptable role and blend in
> more easily. (2000, 332)

Helmreich used his familiarity with the yeshiva world to enter these closed
institutions and to interview, characterize, and define this religiosity.

Samuel Heilman, who has a similar background, gives in *The People
of the Book* (1983) a detailed account of his entrance into the Talmudic
study circle in ultra-Orthodox communities in Jerusalem and throughout the United States. Using the participant-observer approach, Heilman
tries to comprehend the meaning of *lernen* (study) by providing a thick
description of the experiences of those who engage in yeshiva practices.
As a male researcher familiar with the Torah world, he used the "native
as stranger" approach to join various groups involved in Talmudic studies
(Heilman 1983, 9).

Reading Helmreich and Heilman left me feeling frustrated. Unlike
these men, I could not possibly enter a yeshiva and join the students in
their study groups or ask direct questions about their lives. I had no Talmudic or other Jewish background. And as a secular woman, my efforts
might even be held up as an example of the moral ills of modernity, my
every step into this world being considered a violation of the enclave's
morality and sacred order.

When presenting my work, I always am asked about the exclusion of women from the Haredi world: "How, as an Israeli woman, could you possibly meet and interview these men?" Indeed, as a secular woman researcher, I had to overcome many obstacles. In this world, the presence of a woman is viewed as a distraction from the men's dedication to study. Thus the foundation of anthropological methods—the intimate encounter between the researcher and the informant—posed a threat to the community's basic definitions of masculinity and femininity and its sacred order.

As a comparison, I used Lisa Kaul-Seidman's account of gaining access to the anti-Zionist ultra-Orthodox Neturei Karta community in Israel. Because she was a woman, Catholic, and of Indian origin, she decided to present herself unvarnished as a researcher and to make direct contact with members of the community. During her interviews, she had to follow certain rules when speaking to men: meeting them only in the presence of another woman and only in the formal setting of a structured conversational meeting. She was, however, able to interview women, unaccompanied, in informal conversation (Kaul-Seidman 2002, 37).[1]

The attitude toward women in the yeshiva has other dimensions as well. According to Michael Satlow, "All of the rabbinic comments that condemn female Torah studies do so on the grounds that because a woman does not have the requisite amount of self-discipline, she will use her Torah knowledge for ill" (1996, 33). Women are considered to have little self-restraint and thus are seen as having limited access to the primary means of a relationship with God (Satlow 1996, 35). Moreover, an educated woman is portrayed as dangerous to the manly yeshiva fraternity and its order. I thus had to adopt a cautious and sensitive approach, not only to gain an "honorary male" position in order to meet and interview students, but also to craft a method that would enable me to attain insights into the lives and experiences of Haredi yeshiva men today. I therefore decided to use my exclusion to my advantage and model the interviews as much as possible on the familiar pattern of a study encounter.

Following other ethnographers (see Krannich and Humphrey 1986, 477), I first located a key informant who could help me enter this male-based world and meet with the men.[2] My plan was to find a yeshiva student who would be willing to help me resolve the difficulties of meeting and talking to other students. I looked for someone who could accompany me and help minimize the tension in meeting with these men. I assumed that if they saw me talking with someone who was like them, they would agree to cooperate with me. I was fortunate to find a young yeshiva student who agreed to be my key informant and whom I call Rashi, after the famous commentator on the Bible and the Talmud. I was hoping he would be my commentator on piety at the yeshiva world.

Rashi was a young yeshiva student whom I met through friends. He was eighteen years old at the time and was studying at a well-known Lithuanian yeshiva. He was willing to meet me and conversed freely about himself and his daily experiences at the yeshiva, including timetables, lesson schedules, curricula, books, and teachers. At the beginning I did not use a tape recorder, but after a month of many meetings, I asked his permission to tape most of our conversations.

Rashi described himself as an excellent student but also an outsider. In later conversations, he often defined himself using this contradiction. For example, he claimed to be very skeptical about the way that yeshiva studies were conducted in Israel and often voiced his desire to leave the yeshiva and try a different lifestyle. At the same time, he frequently expressed his full devotion to Haredi values and to the yeshiva world. This contradiction was repeated many times throughout my research and in interviews with other students.

I also realized that the inclination to define oneself as an "outsider" or "unique" or as desiring to experience other lifestyles than that of the Haredi was very common among this age group in general. When I asked Rashi about this contradiction, he explained that he was at a stage of examining his Haredi identity and devotion. Perhaps he was uncertain of his own future in the community, and my presence also may have been an excuse for him to explore his fluctuating identity. He expressed these uncertainties about his future in the Haredi community especially with regard to his livelihood and marriage. For example, he often mentioned his aspiration to become a religious judge (*dayan*), yet in other conversations he mentioned the possibility of leaving the community and becoming a computer expert. Rashi was not alone in his struggle with such contradictions; indeed, they exist in the heart of Haredi yeshiva life, expressed by many of the interviewees to whom Rashi introduced me. Rashi was well connected in the community, and many of the students he knew were considered the most successful in their yeshiva. All of them were older then he was, between eighteen and twenty-eight years old, yet Rashi's doubts about various aspects of the yeshiva life reflected, as I show throughout this study, those of many of these students as well.

Winning Rashi's trust was the first step. His familiarity with Talmudic studies enabled him to teach me some of the yeshiva texts and to learn more about male yeshiva practices and experiences. I was so fascinated by his knowledge and descriptions that I tried to meet with him as often as possible. Rashi encouraged me to interview other students too, so I could also hear their opinions on many issues, and mentioned some of his friends. I tentatively asked him about the problem these yeshiva students might have about meeting and talking with a woman. He emphasized that I needed to learn many things and thought about "the most appropriate method" to approach the students. He decided that I must concentrate on the *kavana*, meaning the purpose of my work, and not on its limits. I was surprised because by relating to my purpose, he was not pointing to my faith or lack of faith. That is, he was not interested in my religious orientation. Generally, I was not a target of proselytizing at any stage of the research. My experience differs from that of other studies, in which members of the group saw the researchers as potential converts (Ammerman 1987; Davidman 1991, 54; Neitz 1987; Peshkin 1986, 19). I believe that Rashi's willingness to introduce me to others was not for reasons of possible conversion; rather, it indicated his trust and confidence that I would be honest and respectful of my potential informants. Rashi also was attracted by my curiosity to learn about yeshiva life in general and his life in particular.

In my first meetings with Rashi, I explained my ethnographic interests, and he described his life and experiences at the yeshiva hall. We discussed problems that we could face in interviews with other yeshiva students and possible solutions. His knowledge of the yeshiva and the many levels of students' lives became apparent during these first meetings. From this point on, we spent most of our meetings preparing and discussing ways of meeting and interviewing other students. For example, Rashi and I talked about my appearance. Haredi members emphasize their differences by wearing a distinctive style of dress. Haredi men usually wear formal black overcoats over white open-necked shirts, and wide-brimmed black hats. Women's clothes vary in different Haredi groups and contexts, but they all dress modestly, with only their faces and hands visible, their heads covered by a wig, a scarf or veil, or a hat. These dress regulations deliberately keep Haredi women away from modern fashion trends; women buy their clothes exclusively in Haredi shops or make their own. With this in mind, I had to decide on my own attire. If I dressed like a Haredi woman, wearing clothes bought in Haredi shops, I might end up trying to look like something I was not, and this could damage my credibility. But I understood that maintaining certain laws of modesty was crucial. I did not want to offend my interviewees or risk forgoing the encounter (see Friedl 1996). After long discussions with Rashi, we decided that I would take the middle road, maintaining Haredi modesty regulations by wearing an calf-length dress or skirt, long sleeves, and high neck, but they would be my own clothes. In this way I believed I would show respect for the Haredi dress regulations but not present a false appearance that could be misinterpreted.

With Rashi, I learned much about the debate about excluding women from the yeshiva realm, especially by reading with him some of the current Haredi writings on women. Many of these books cite the distraction caused by women as the main explanation for their exclusion from the yeshiva (see Boyarin 1997, 153).

We decided that for the purpose of my study, recreating the environment of yeshiva learning would make possible my encounter with men. For our interviews, we decided to work with the following themes: work, livelihood, studiousness, gender, and marriage. We selected texts pertinent to these themes and had long debates about each one in order to produce questions based on them. These debates enabled us to decide on the accepted norms for each issue and how specific texts would be selected to support them. For example, we learned about the various texts emphasizing the importance of Torah studies and their relations (or tensions) to other aspects of life, especially work, marriage, raising children, and other subjects. Rashi instructed me how to select these texts, and we added them to a list that served from this point as the initial stage of every encounter or formal interview, as well as a basis for questions during interviews with other students. As I will explain later, because we worked outside the yeshiva walls, it was important to recreate the familiar settings and logic of the yeshiva.

We also decided to draw up a list of possible interviewees from different Haredi yeshivas in Jerusalem and Bnei Brak. Before meeting with them, we thoroughly discussed their background. Usually Rashi recommended what he called "serious" students who were considered prodigies (*iluyim*) in their yeshivas. He claimed that they would be the best sources of information about yeshiva life because they were the most dedicated students.

In the first stages of the research, Rashi made the initial contact. He asked the potential interviewee whether he would be willing to take part in a research interview with two participants, a female from the university and a student from a well-known Lithuanian yeshiva. When the answer was yes, he explained in detail the themes that we would like to discuss and pointed out the particular texts that were to be used. During this conversation Rashi also asked the yeshiva student about other texts on the chosen topic. After these first contacts I found my own way of looking for interviewees. After each interview I asked the student to suggest other persons and wrote down their names, phone numbers, and the name of the yeshiva they attended.

In order to prepare for the meetings, Rashi and I often studied the texts suggested by the students, and in the last phone conversation before the meeting, we decided on a time and place for the interview, its length, and its structure. On most occasions the interviewees invited me to their parents' homes and asked if we could pick them up from their yeshiva after the last evening lesson. Accordingly, most of the interviews took place in the students' homes, usually at their parents' houses. In many cases the students waited for Rashi and when they left the yeshiva, we drove them to their homes for the interview. Otherwise we went to their parents' homes right after the last lesson. The interviews were usually scheduled very late at night, after 11 P.M., and lasted until early in the morning.

Most of the interviews consisted of three people: Rashi, me, and one yeshiva student, although sometimes we would interview two or more yeshiva students at a time. The interviewees always came prepared for these meetings, bringing with them (from the yeshiva library or their personal collection) those texts they thought were most central to the issue to be discussed. When the student entered the car, we began to converse, easing into the encounter in a friendly manner. Meeting in a student's home usually, however, caused embarrassment. Perhaps going to their homes emphasized my strangeness. But the uneasiness created by my presence was partly alleviated by the presence of Rashi, with his warm demeanor. In addition, many of the books and texts we brought to the meetings increased the student's curiosity and encouraged conversation. The question of why they accepted me into their study circle still puzzles me. I prefer believing that their desire to learn and debate was stronger than the tensions raised by my presence.

Some of these tensions derived from my belonging to the larger, secular Israeli community in which Haredim are criticized for such issues as their lack of participation in the military and the labor market. My using the ideology of learning, which was their central goal and activity in life, and my structuring all interviews as lessons, allowed them to feel comfortable and believe that they were still engaged in their consuming work of Torah study. While describing his encounters with Tuhami, Vincent Crapanzano defines his interviews as a dynamic dialogical event:

> As Tuhami's interlocutor, I became an active participant in his life history. . . . Not only did my presence, and my questions, prepare him for the text he was to produce, but they produced what I read as a change of consciousness in me, too. We were both jostled from our assumptions about the nature of the everyday world and ourselves and groped for common reference points within this limbo of interchange. (1980, 11)

I, too, felt that my interviews functioned as a mutually active creation of knowledge that was shaped by my modeling their native yeshiva images and their learning activities. I blended some of the traditional features of the Haredi learning experience and knowledge transmission with some of the standard anthropological methods. According to my field notes (April 1998),

> Whenever I took the [prepared] Talmudic text and presented a copy to the interviewee, he was stunned. He first looked at me to examine my face and body but then looked again at the pile of texts and read them. At this moment an expression of seriousness altered his look, and he responded with an interpretation or a question . . . this reminded me of Bashevis Singer's *Yentl the Yeshiva Boy* [1962]. . . . When I got home, I looked up the story: "After exposing her femininity to Avigdor the two went back to their Talmudic conversation. It seemed strange at first to Avigdor to be disputing holy writ with a woman yet it was the Torah that reunited them."

The benefits of this position are apparent: a secular woman does not pose a threat to men's authority over the interpretation of the sacred scripture; there was no way that I could construct alternative bases for authoritative religious expressions. Through these encounters I learned how men reproduce knowledge in the community and how yeshiva students distinguished between sacred and profane activities, such as study and work. During these interviews, students interpreted the most significant texts to explain different aspects of Haredi lives, piety, and religious experiences (see Yamane 2000, 184). Typically, Rashi and I presented an argument about a particular theme, followed by the interpretations of several rabbinical figures and the debates among them. These interactions with my informants, focusing on sacred texts, highlighted the enormous variety of possible interpretations of the canon. In each chapter I exemplify this approach by showing how the students interpreted different canonical texts.

Despite their recitation of standard yeshiva ideology, however, occasionally I was able to hear alternative voices and expressions. Although I was exposed to the official script and the rabbis' accepted interpretations, I also detected some of the criticisms of the yeshiva institution and its way of life. When I discussed these contradictions with Rashi, he suggested that we should sometimes bait students with some "missing texts." By missing texts, he was referring to central scriptures in the canon that had not been cited by our interviewees and represented meanings different from those discussed in the interview. This debate provoked stormy arguments between Rashi and the other yeshiva students. Rashi explained that these events resembled the dynamic of the study group (*hevruta*)[3] used at the yeshiva (Breuer 2003).[4]

This dialogue facilitated a close observation of the learning process, revealing informal codes of constructing knowledge and ideas that went beyond the official interpretation of the canon (Kahane 1988, 1997, 213, 214, 216). The dialogue in the study group created for the students an atmosphere that allowed them to discuss their worlds and experiences and even to reflect on them and on how these yeshiva experiences influenced their everyday reality. Many students pointed to what they referred to as the rabbis' "unreasonable messages" about studious excellence and chastity, which they felt were absurd and irrational and caused hardship in their lives, especially regarding their obligation to get married and to provide for their families. In this way, they were able to express their yearning for changes in the yeshiva lifestyle in particular and in the Haredi lifestyle in general. Through the simulation, we exposed the various tensions between the yeshiva students and the Haredi authorities and their frustrations with yeshiva life and duties (see Asad 1986, 14).

The students also talked about their discontent with the Haredi community's economic conditions, their exemption from military service, and the cultural marginality of the yeshiva student in Israel. Because they were experts on the texts, they expressed their ambivalence through the use of canonical sayings; ironically, these quotations supported their disappointment and anger. By expressing their ambivalence, they were calling for significant transformations in the yeshiva world that might lead to a turning point in the Haredi community.

It is curious that these men of the yeshiva, required to follow its codes, agreed to cooperate with me, particularly considering their position as members of an enclave culture that would seem to have much to lose and little to gain by these interviews and encounters. I believe there were several reasons for their agreement. First, most of the students believed that the yeshiva both had achieved and was still achieving its great theological mission: to restore Judaism to its former glory and to support the Jewish people in its God-given missions. Second, the students were curious about secular life and the nonreligious world outside the yeshiva. Third, they needed acceptance and legitimacy from someone outside their world. In Israel, yeshiva students endure a great deal of criticism from the public on many issues, especially their automatic deferment from military service. For these students, explaining the world of the yeshiva to a secular person, one who comes from the university and is eager to listen to their views on Talmudic studies, seemed worthwhile.

The stereotypes of their world are familiar to these students. My conducting these research interviews as if they were a yeshiva lesson and giving the students the opportunity to discuss texts with me allowed them not only to express their worldview but also to criticize their religiosity. The students' lack of participation in citizenship obligations, especially the army and labor force, are major causes of conflicts with the secular majority. In contrast, talking about their experiences gave them an opportunity to point out the positive aspects of their world, such as sacredness and the joy of study, and to elaborate on ideas and norms that were obvious to them but were not understood by secular people like myself. Finally, these interviews were opportunities for them to criticize their own culture, their rabbis, and the current leaders of their world.

Visiting Haredi Shops: Books, Films, and Other Artifacts

During the winter of 1997, I was in the last stages of pregnancy with my first daughter, Shira. At that time I also was trying to contact yeshiva students and conduct in-depth interviews. The most vivid memory I have of this period is my obsessive need to prepare the most appropriate questions for these encounters. I read texts and books recommended by Haredi men whom I met informally in Haredi bookstores in the Geula area of Jerusalem. I assumed that I could find information and insights while wandering

Figure 1.1. A Haredi bookstore in Mea She'arim, a Haredi Jerusalem neighborhood, winter 2006.

through the Haredi streets and stores, so I decided to do some serious book shopping. Haredi neighborhoods are filled with friendly bookshops that are loaded with manuals, handbooks, sacred books, pamphlets, and also films and cassettes for the Haredi public (see figure 1.1).

At least at first glance, these bookshops looked like mysterious containers of Jewish sacred wisdom available only to Orthodox eyes. I thus entered these shops with some apprehension, not sure how Haredi people would react to a secular woman asking questions. In the first shop I found myself leafing through the books next to Haredi men from different sects. Only in retrospect did I realize that in these first encounters, my visible pregnancy was my safe passage to these shops. I would ask for books on pregnancy, birth, and raising children and was immediately offered help and advice; my pregnancy was an opening to conversation with men as well as women. What I saw initially as background research for my main topic turned out to be an overwhelmingly rich source of materials for the research and analysis that constitute this book. Along with canonical books such as the *Shulchan aruch* ("set table," the code of Jewish law, written by Rabbi Yosef Karo) and *Mishneh Torah, Yad ha-hazaka* (the code of Jewish law written by Rabbi Moshe ben Maimon), one can find in Haredi bookshops a variety of instructional books for yeshiva students, grooms, brides, parents, and children, as well as children's books and pamphlets. The booksellers, most from the various Hasidic sects, always were friendly and ready to offer advice and opinions on books and other topics. Visiting these shops regularly enabled me to engage, however marginally, with the community's vast written world, with publications for yeshiva students in particular and other aspects of Haredi published culture, and to do so in a manner that supplemented my interviews.

Since the 1990s, Haredi bookshops also have stocked videocassettes, films, CDs, and DVDs. The demand for these materials shows an awareness and consumption of nontraditional media covering many topics. Some of these topics had previously been discussed in popular Haredi books (thoughts about the military, the Jewish state, economic problems, marriage), but some of them were new (action films, drama, adventurism). I decided to collect this material regularly and use it along with my interviews and observations. As a result, this book is based on a mixture of several different data sources, texts, tape and video cassettes, and photographs and films.

Bartkowski (2004, 45) explains how he analyzed a sample of best-selling men's advice manuals written by the elite Promise Keepers on subjects such as the essence of godly manhood, the importance of Christian men's fellowship with one another, the pursuit of godly marriage, and strategies for effective fathering. Haredi society, like other fundamentalist communities, publishes popular texts and advice manuals. During the last decade, books written by rabbis for yeshiva students became very popular. And especially since the 1980s, rabbis have produced a wide range of books, manuals, and journals dealing with the regulation of everyday life: gender, family, Jewish festivals, rituals, food, leisure, and more. These books and pamphlets target different Haredi audiences and are published and sold in special shops located in the community.

Many of the materials I collected in Haredi shops pertain to ethics. One of the most interesting shifts in Jewish fundamentalism is the emphasis on morality. That is, the study of the Torah is not only a way to worship God but is also a tool for intellectual pride (cf. de-Lange 2000). Yeshiva students seek in the scholarly life the virtues of holiness and piety. Thus, in contemporary yeshiva settings, in order to address the work of character building and the idea of moral education, the role of the spiritual supervisor (*mashgiach*) is regarded (Halbertal and Hartman-Halbertal 1998, 465) as necessary for moral education. Accordingly, in the yeshiva curriculum, in addition to the study of the Talmud, literature dealing with virtues and moral questions is read as well.

For my research I selected two hundred popular instructional handbooks used as tutorials for yeshiva students. These include manuals instructing yeshiva students on issues of everyday life. In order to collect these texts I regularly visited the Haredi shops, especially in Meah She'arim in Jerusalem and in Bnei Brak. Some texts were recommended by the yeshiva students I interviewed and others, by rabbis. I divided the themes that recurred in most of these publications into the following categories: study, family matters, work, gender, and sexuality. I read these texts to gain insights into the world of yeshiva piety as seen by various writers. This focus then enabled me to analyze the particular rhetoric used by these authors to build a stable worldview of Haredi piety, both reflecting and articulating its nature and relevance to current times. All the students I interviewed were familiar with these texts, although they did not read them uncritically. Those who referred to them expressed their own views about the ideal types of behavior and religiosity promulgated by these manuals. By reading these publications regularly, I was exposed to the rabbis' pronouncements on many issues of everyday life, and I used these books to provoke responses to the publications themselves and to the subjects they discussed, especially the family, gender, work, education, and the military. By listening to their reasoning, arguments, and ideologies raised in response to these books, I tried to understand how these publications might be interpreted by members of the group.

Bookshops in Haredi neighborhoods distribute only electronic media—audio, video, and DVD—produced by Haredi companies. This growing industry uses computers and other such technological devices, for the Haredi world was quick to grasp the implications of this new technology, even though most of it is not allowed into the home or the yeshiva. As a result, the Haredi film industry is flourishing, despite the opposition of many rabbis. The religious authorities post polemical billboard warnings (*pashkevils*) and publish newspaper articles opposing the use of computers and DVDs (see figure 1.2). For example, *Yated neeman*, a popular Haredi newspaper, published the following warning:

Figure 1.2. Haredi men watching the posting of the most recent *pashkevil* in Mea She'arim, 2006.

Recently we have detected a new kind of executor, one that our fathers did not anticipate. Their evil inclinations appear surreptitiously, through computers, the killing poison, that threatens to exterminate the sacredness of the Jewish home. . . . Every film is pollution and therefore prohibited . . . [and] those who resisted buying a computer have saved their family from temptation and sin. (*Yated neeman* 1998, cited in Ba Gad-Elimelech, forthcoming)

These publications notwithstanding, many Haredi homes now own computers, and the Haredi film industry continues to grow. Many Haredi writers explain that they were likely to lose this battle, and as they did in the popular books industry, they judiciously decided to cooperate with

Figure 1.3. Billboards covered in *pashkevil*s in Mea She'arim, Jerusalem, winter 2006.

the distributors by becoming trustworthy critics, describing the plot on the cover and approving the contents. Sometimes they even are present at the film's production. The presence of the rabbis gives legitimacy to the film and also strengthens their control over the products. Nonetheless, the very nature of these media also allows them to display new ideas, never fully discussed in the Haredi public, such as marriage problems, education, violence in the family, and the position of women in the community (see figure 1.3).

For this book I collected films and audiocassettes dealing with daily issues related to yeshiva students, such as military service, the life of studious devotion, one's livelihood, and marriage. Indeed, today the distribution of audio- and videocassettes is one of the principal ways of spreading the ideas of rabbinical authorities in the community (see Caplan 2007, 51–58), especially sermons and lectures on morality and belief.[5] But these very media also offer views of the worlds outside the text and canonical interpretations, allowing for new images and aspirations to infiltrate the official religious orientation of the community and its founders. To illustrate these popular narratives and meanings, I have organized interviews, manuals for students, and films and cassettes portraying a number of central themes, including sexuality, the family, work, the military, and volunteer work. Through my analysis of these particular themes, I am able to explain the official view of each one and show how these themes are represented through popular manual books for *bnei Torah* written by young yeshiva rabbis, through the students' discourse, and through films and videocassettes. These popular narratives and artifacts shed light on the complex meaning of current Haredi piety.

The Outline of the Book

I support my argument regarding the transformation of piety by examining in this book five major themes in yeshiva life: sexuality, work, the military, the family, and volunteerism. As my fieldwork revealed, the current generation of yeshiva students is challenging the ideas of their rabbis and suggesting different ways of defining the group's fundamentalist nature. Their voices, however, are not monolithic, as the students' attitudes, interpretations, and practices all differ. As my study shows, the students offered a range of responses to the questions that turned out to be central to them. On some subjects, students were merely critical but did not seek or find change, whereas while talking about other subjects, they not only resisted traditional interpretations but also were actively making structural and behavioral changes in their lives. Students thus are demanding, I claim, different levels of changes in the different spheres in which they find their own piety.

The order of this book's chapters is in ascending priority for change in Haredi life. Students accept most of the ascetic norms of the yeshiva and do not seek to change sexual behavior or disagree with the notion of evil inclination. They are more critical of renouncing work and livelihood but have not yet been able to suggest new sources for their livelihood. They are much more troubled by the image of manhood represented by the ascetic scholar. They wish to join the military and adopt Israeli models of masculinity, are especially drawn to the image of the heroic combat soldier, and wish to update the codes of manly piety accordingly, though usually without being able to achieve this directly. The nontraditional approach is perhaps implemented most fully in the new model of spousal and parental relations that has been gradually materializing in the Haredi community. Another expression of change in this fundamentalist community is the rise of voluntary organizations that, staffed almost exclusively by Haredim, is serving the entire Israeli public with great success.

The integration of new pietistic thought and practice within and beyond the traditional spheres of family life and voluntarism is an example of the way that the aspirations of the younger generations can lead to changes in the yeshiva world. In turn, these changes are bound to prompt changes in the other areas discussed here, such as openness to the labor market and participation in some form of national service.

I develop my argument in the seven additional chapters. Chapter 2 gives a short background of the yeshiva movement in Israel by situating the world of the yeshiva in a broader historical and cultural context. I begin by exploring the yeshiva's religiosity and the students' experiences. I show how the heroic Jewish model of piety created by Haredi leaders in Israel after World War II led to a renaissance in the modern Jewish state. I contend that this heroic piety, fulfilled in the past only by a select elite in the community, has become a resurgent movement in Israel, influencing other religious groups (such as the national Zionist Jews, spiritual groups, and so-called New Age movements), the state, and civil society. The following five chapters form the core of my thesis: the change in the model of piety in yeshiva fundamentalism today.

In chapter 3 I analyze the shaping of yeshiva piety through the mechanism of sexual restrictions and bodily prohibitions. I show that the ideal of Torah studies uses a set of techniques of the body, that is, Pierre Bourdieu's ideas (1977, 76–78; cf. Comaroff 1985; Foucault 1997) about the habitus of sitting, speaking, moving, and reacting to fellow men. Piety is stressed by means of a courageous fight, overcoming hardship and realizing a heroic studious asceticism. In the study hall, men acquire their status by learning how to overcome bodily desires, to control lust, and to dedicate their body and soul to the goals of the yeshiva. Men are trained to transcend to high spiritual levels and to renounce, as much as possible, worldly affairs. The rabbis teach them that many evils lurk in modern society and the secular city. Potentially sinful hazards are everywhere here, leading to the abundance of restrictions and prohibitions. The fulfillment of male devotion and perfection is associated with the idea of rising above earthly limitations, although this may eventually lead individuals to violate the rules in the name of spiritual freedom, which in turn is limited by the threat of ostracism. Most of the prohibitions on students are related to their bodily needs, of which the most dangerous are hunger, sleep, and sexual desire. These represent weakness, which is distancing the student from his true goals. In discussing the theme of sexuality and piety, I focus on one central aspect, that of the evil inclination (*yetzer hara*). I analyze how the concept of the evil inclination is interpreted in current Haredi texts and narratives.

I show that although some shifts in the definition of the model of the fundamentalist body and sexuality are apparent, the basic model as it was defined by the first rabbis in Israel is generally accepted by members of the yeshiva world. Although bodily restraint requires much effort and is difficult to achieve, it is the only way that yeshiva students can maintain their dominant status in the community. This is the reason why students are reluctant to criticize, change, or even discuss transforming these models of sexuality, because they represent their power and status. In comparison to other resources that are less important to their power and masculinity, sexual renunciation and the control of the body are still the primary category of power and manhood in the yeshiva world.

Chapter 4 considers the challenges to the traditional model of piety as a result of the attitudes of the younger yeshiva students toward work and livelihood today. Haredi piety is based on a model of manhood that is separate from the economic realm that usually defines status and power in the modern world. In the fundamentalist yeshiva world, hierarchy and power are constructed through consecration to yeshiva activity that must be kept "pure," that is, detached from the economic and entrepreneurial realms. Excellence and achievement are the most important features, not work, profession, or material goods. Economic responsibilities are defined as corporeal, bodily, and physical tasks, unsuitable for men. Those who engage in work and earn a living are considered inferior to Talmudic scholars, whose riches—virtue and piety—enrich others as well. Men's success is measured by their ability, and availability, to dedicate themselves to studying the Talmud. The less that one works, the more time that one has for study, and by application and memorizing, one can become adept at interpreting the scriptures for one's own sake and capable of applying this accumulated knowledge to practical questions of contemporary Jewish life.

In this scheme, women are responsible for earthly needs. By nature, women are worldly, practical, and functional, and they are expected to support their husbands and families financially. In Israel, because the yeshiva world sees itself as responsible for "authentic Judaism," the secular state has been viewed for many decades as responsible for supporting yeshiva students in particular and for maintaining the Haredi family structure in general. In this chapter I show that students are critical of this model and thus are challenging the Haredi work ethic. They oppose their withdrawal from the labor market, as this results in their own unproductive behavior, poverty, backwardness, and lack of professional knowledge and training. By questioning the prevailing model of fundamentalism, devotees are calling for a new kind of piety that takes into consideration the ideals of work and livelihood in the modern state.

Chapter 5 looks at the Haredi students' response to their exemption from compulsory military service. One of the basic characteristics of Haredi culture is its rejection of, and refusal to participate in, the mystique of earthly power, which includes all manifestations of military life. The warrior or soldier was never a key symbol of masculinity, or, rather, it was replaced by its Jewish mirror image: that of the devout, pious ascetic. In particular, the army was seen as an affront to piety: instead of allowing the divine plan for the Jews' return to their ancient homeland to work itself out in due course, the army took it upon itself, as the executive branch of the generally impious liberal Israeli state and its institutions.

Whereas the military is a major locus for the construction of Israeli male identity, Haredi men reinforce body discipline, control, and mortification through Talmudic training. Sacrifice and fraternity are perceived to exist in their purest forms only in the sacred yeshiva setting. I argue that in yeshiva culture, the rejection of the ideal of the Israeli Defense Forces (IDF) soldier, influenced by military symbolism and militarism as they are constituted in secular society around them, has produced frustration and new impulses. Haredi yeshiva students have described to me their fantasies of enlisting and acting heroically in a military regimen, just as they try to do in a religious setting. Here, one does not replace the other but represents, in militarized discursive and symbolic practices, the previously combative but nonmilitarized zone of pious achievement. Contrary to their own stated ideology and that of their rabbis, these young students express a desire to participate in the military and bear arms, thus demonstrating a conceptual transformation of Haredi piety and masculinity. In doing so, they also are contradicting their own rhetoric of exclusivity by adopting the inclusive hegemonic models of masculinity that dominate Zionist culture and the secular Jewish state.

Chapter 6 explores how yeshiva students are challenging the traditional norms of spousal relations. I show how young Haredi men are currently reinterpreting family and gendered behavior, despite the traditional yeshiva expectations that they maintain a high level of asceticism and studious dedication. Through my analysis of yeshiva instruction books, I demonstrate that the writers of newer popular texts are instructing young yeshiva scholars to integrate their studies into their family tasks and functions. These books direct yeshiva ascetics to provide aid and emotional support to their wives and children. Accordingly, these young men are now being advised to spend more time with their families and to become teachers and therapists to help deal with their wives' frustrations, and they are encouraged to be aware of and relate to their wives' emotional needs. This approach represents a big change in family relations that is redefining new ideals of manhood and Haredi piety. The new books and cassettes offer the yeshiva scholar a repertoire of popular psychological texts on human nature, medical and biological knowledge of women, and "female instincts." Many instruction books include chapters on the psychological profile of women, their ambitions and desires. Instead of emphasizing the "yeshiva brotherhood" and the distance from any form of femininity, the new discourse promotes a model of unity and companionship between the sexes. This process of domestication also includes a redefinition of fatherhood and encouragement toward a more emotionally involved relationship with the children, the family, and the community.

Chapter 7 examines the ZAKA, an acronym for "identification of victims of disaster," a countrywide search-and-rescue organization composed mainly of Haredi men who help with the treatment of bodies after unnatural death such as from terrorism, traffic accidents, and murder, in accordance with Jewish rites. ZAKA was established by Haredi men for the express purpose of ensuring that victims of bomb attacks received proper religious treatment, including locating and reassembling dismembered body parts, cleaning blood from disaster sites, taking responsibility for the victims' bodies, and transferring them to the Israeli Institute of Forensic Science.

The analysis of this Haredi organization offers a new possibility of fulfilling male piety in the community today. ZAKA is a new Haredi way of challenging the traditional culture and finding a new religiosity, which is the focus of this book. It is one possible way of channeling yeshiva students into new everyday practices. Indeed, various volunteer organizations, of which ZAKA is only the most visible, have become legitimate outlets for Haredi male members to leave the enclave for short periods of time and to offer their specific knowledge to the greater Israeli society, even at the risk of endangering protected boundaries. Through their training and participation in ZAKA and other organizations, Haredi volunteers are challenging their own identity and reconstructing the traditional male practices and piety. By assuming a public position as specialists and death workers in Israel, these Haredi volunteers provide alternative religious models that contradict the ascetic vision of the Haredi man and find new ways to enact their critiques of the established models of ultra-Orthodox religiosity.

Chapter 8, the conclusion, examines the study of yeshiva fundamentalism in the broader sociological context and its contribution to the understanding of piety and fundamentalism in general. I discuss the contribution of my book to the study of the fundamentalist elite, their family life, and their place and meanings in the current changing fundamentalist world. I argue that the politics of the fundamentalist elite and the ideals of the family are the most significant problems facing these groups today. Fundamentalist groups are changing because of challenges to these basic aspects of life. I end this chapter with a discussion of two puzzles deriving from the examination of fundamentalism and piety: the recreation of power in elite groups, and the performance of severe body regimes in postmodern societies. They suggest responses to these questions, using this book's approach to piety and modernity.

2

Yeshiva Fundamentalism in Israel's Haredi Community

> The study of the Torah is greater than the daily sacrifices of the Temple.
>
> —Babylonian Talmud, Megilah 3b

The Haredi Community in Israel

The Haredi community in Israel today comprises between 6 and 10 percent of the country's population (Berman 2000; Dahan 1998). There are two main Haredi centers: the Mea She'arim neighborhood in Jerusalem, and Bnei Brak in central Israel. Because the capacity of such neighborhoods is limited and the cost of living is relatively high for Haredi families, Haredi quarters were built in development towns like Ashdod, Nathanya, and Beit Shemesh (Shilhav 1998, 6). The dispersal of the Haredi population then led to the construction of more towns and suburbs especially designed for Haredim, such as Modiin Ilit, Beitar Ilit, and Elad. These towns contain all the services necessary for community life: yeshivas, synagogues, kosher food groceries, ritual bath services (*mikve*), bookstores, and Sabbath arrangements. In these towns, Haredim are involved at all levels of management, planning, and maintaining the city (Shilhav 1998, 7).

Menachem Friedman (1991) characterized Haredim as belonging to the east European Jewish tradition and strictly observing Halakha, the corpus of legal codification. They are required to study the Torah, to take an anti-Zionist stand, and to proclaim a collective trauma resulting from the choice of numerous Jews—the majority of Jewish society, in fact—to leave the traditional life in favor of other options. Although unified by their adherence to the strictest version of Jewish law, Haredi members are not monolithic but are divided into sects, communities, and movements that struggle over power, authority, and resources. In Israel, the historical split (during the eighteenth century in eastern Europe) between the Hassidim and those who opposed them (the Mitnagdim) has been blurred, and in the modern state, different new boundaries between the groups have been erected. Whereas Friedman (1991) divided the Ashkenazi Haredim in Israel into four groups—Lithuanians, Polish Hassidim, Hungarians, and Jerusalemites—Caplan (2007) asserts that today the Haredi community is mostly divided into the Ashkenazi Haredim, of European or American descent, and the Sephardic Haredim, of Asian or North African descent. This division is marked by separate political parties and educational systems which protect the ethnic-cultural division (see Lehmann and Siebzehner 2006).

My analysis of the yeshiva world is based on the Ashkenazi Lithuanian sector of this group. The history of the Sephardic Haredi yeshivas is related to what Lehmann and Siebzehner (2006, 79) call "the machinery of 'Tshuva,'" or the return to Judaism, which has been widely discussed in the literature (see e.g., Caplan 2001, 369). In contrast, the Lithuanian sector has several distinguishing characteristics, of which politics is central.

Since the establishment of the Israeli state, the Haredi Ashkenazi sector has been represented by the Agudat Israel (Union of Israel) Party, established in 1912, and the Degel Hatorah (Flag of Torah) faction, today known as Yahadut Hatora Hameuhedet (United Torah Judaism). This Haredi party is under the auspices of the rabbinical elite and has consistently sought to ensure that yeshiva students would be able to continue studying after they reached the age of eighteen, that they would be exempted from military service, and that the government would increase funding for the Haredi educational system and other institutions as well as increasing welfare stipends for large families.

In the 1998 elections the Agudat Israel Party added three to the number of its seats in the Knesset (the Israeli parliament), out of a total of 120, reflecting a dramatic rise in the Haredi parties' political power. This growth was due to their increasingly nationalistic orientation and the muting of their opposition to Zionism and the Zionist state (see also Liebman 1993, 72). Together with other fundamentalist parties, especially the National Religious Party, the Agudat Israel Party's influence on Israeli culture and public policy has expanded since the 1967 War and especially after 1977 with the election of a right-wing government that overturned almost thirty years of Labor rule and again with the fundamentalist parties' support of the Oslo accords in 1992 (Horowitz 2002, 11). The Haredi public usually leans to the right politically and takes a hawkish position toward the Arab–Israeli conflict. This position is part of a general reaction in Israel to recent events and to the escalation of tension between Jews and Arabs in the region, beginning with the Palestinian intifada of the 1990s, the second intifada in 2000, and the second war with Lebanon in 2006. The constant conflict also has led to the Haredis' demonization of local Arabs as enemies of the Jews and agents who throughout history have worked toward the destruction of the Jewish people.

The growth of the Haredi parties' political power and involvement also is related to the economic conditions of the community and its constant need for more resources. Haredi families are different from the general public. That is, ultra-Orthodox men and women marry young, have more children (7.7 per family versus 2.6 for the Israeli population as a whole), and seldom divorce. In addition, Eli Berman reports that the proportion of Haredi men aged twenty-five to fifty-four who do not participate in the labor market because they attend yeshiva full time rose from 41 percent in 1980 to 60 percent in 1996 (2000, 913–14). These levels are unprecedented among Jews in other Orthodox sects and far exceed yeshiva attendance abroad, where young men seldom remain after the age of twenty-five.

Most members of the Haredi community maintain a modest lifestyle, live in crowded housing, and rely on state support (Berman 2000; Dahan 1998; Shilhav 1991). Although the level of education is high, poverty and unemployment are on the rise. Moreover, the state support of Haredi families has recently been drastically reduced, leading to less time for full-time study of the Torah. Since the 1990s, a number of these trends have been converging. Because the concept of the welfare state has changed, the state no longer can support those in need to the same extent, which is critical in regard to children. As a consequence, the ideology of asceticism has become a burden to Haredi families. Although some families collected income from property in Europe or received Holocaust pensions from Germany, over time these sources of income have been lost or used up. This loss of income plus the high birthrate, the decrease in child support, and the public's continuing image of the Haredis' high cost of living have worsened their economic situation and deepened the tensions inside the community (see figure 2.1). In this atmosphere, Israel's yeshiva system has been transformed.

Figure 2.1. Yeshiva students at the Hebron yeshiva, Jerusalem, 2007.

A Brief History of Yeshiva Fundamentalism

Yeshiva is the Hebrew word for "sitting," which is associated with the places, namely, academies of learning, where men sat as they studied Jewish sacred texts, as opposed to standing in prayer. In premodern times, yeshivas were usually administered by the local community and existed wherever there was a sufficiently large Jewish community (Selengut 1994, 239). Designed for a male elite, the yeshiva served as local institutions for transmitting knowledge and gaining access to sacred wisdom (see Breuer 2003, 7, 29). Although it is beyond the scope of this book to provide a full recounting of the history of the yeshiva movement in general and its manifestation in Israel in particular (see Breuer 2003; Friedman 1991), I will try to outline its background.

In eastern Europe during the nineteenth century, an extensive system of all-encompassing yeshivas was established along with the community-based, traditional system of Yeshivot (Zalkin 2006, 131, 132, 137). The establishment of the Valozhyn yeshiva in 1802 in Lithuania in accordance with the inspiration of Rabbi Hayim Valozhyn, a student of the Vilna *gaon*, transformed the traditional model of Torah studies. According to Selengut (1994, 240), the Valozhyn yeshiva emphasized the formalization, centralization, and rationalization of Talmud study. Moreover, in contrast to the local premodern yeshivas, Valozhyn was centrally located in an area containing hundreds of potential students. The Jewish leadership, rabbis, rabbinical judges, and legal decision makers of Jewish law (*poskim*) all were trained in these schools (see Selengut 1994, 240; Stampfer 2005, 14; Zalkin 2006, 144). Valozhyn thus became the ideal model of constant Talmudic learning as an act of male piety and male Jewish spirituality (Selengut 1994, 240). Indeed, scholars of Jewish history argue that the Valozhyn yeshiva became the prototype of all other Lithuanian yeshivas in eastern Europe, such as Ponevezh, Mir, Telz, and Slovodka (these yeshivas usually were named after the town in which its rabbi was born or flourished).

By the end of the nineteenth and the beginning of the twentieth century, yeshiva Torah studies were being influenced by the Musar movement and its moral ideology. This was mainly a religious movement, influenced by medieval Jewish literature and the ethical teachings of Rabbi Israel Salanter (1810–83). Although these teachings aroused some opposition in the yeshiva world at that time, they greatly influenced the curricula of the Lithuanian yeshivas. The Musar movement emphasized personal piety and social improvement as necessary complements to intellectual studies of the Torah and Talmudic wisdom. Consequently, what had been primarily an enterprise among individuals studying this literature turned into a social movement in Lithuania and elsewhere in eastern Europe. The movement predictably extended into the schools and changed the teachings and methods in the various yeshiva institutions (see Breuer 2003, 48; Stampfer 2005, 273, 281, 287).

Among these eastern European Jewish communities, only a few members of a select elite dedicated their life to studious activities; others devoted only few years to learning, work, and family obligations. In these Jewish communities, the home was the basic unit for imparting knowledge and values. Social behavior was transmitted mainly through imitation of the behavioral models of the family and the community. For example, at the *cheder* (literally "room"), a one-classroom school, a *melamed*, a religious teacher, taught reading to children as young as three or four and Torah and religious studies until the age of ten. These provided the basic schooling and behavioral skills necessary for men to participate in the normative Jewish way of life. The next stage for some, but by no means all, boys was the yeshiva hall, which provided advanced Talmudic studies and, as such, was intended for those who would require expertise in everyday Jewish laws (Soloveitchik 1994b, 216). Since yeshiva studies were a relatively rare commodity, the yeshivas could selectively accept candidates, which led to recognition, education, and upward mobility for many bright but poor students (Selengut 1994, 240). World War II, however, ended most of these teachings and their institutions.[1]

The Holocaust brought to Israel and the United States rabbis and leaders of numerous European yeshivas, mainly from Lithuania, where they founded institutions modeled after their European predecessors (Helmreich 2000). After the war the eastern European (Ashkenazi) ultra-Orthodox Jewish community was determined to rebuild its way of life and reestablished a network of religious organizations to fill the vacuum created in Europe and across the world (Friedman 1991, 37). This period of renewed postwar yeshiva culture is defined in current literature as the first appearance of yeshiva fundamentalism (Selengut 1994, 241). Again, in these yeshivas, rabbis considered full-time study for all men as the only way to repopulate the vanished world in the land of Israel, as well as a way to return to piety, whose loss was seen as partly responsible for the calamity of the Jews in Europe and as a reaction to the clear impiety of the modern–secular Israeli state. During this time, these leaders created a new type of yeshiva system and founded new, ultra-Orthodox institutions.

Numerous men have contributed to the yeshiva movement in Israel, but their histories, biographies, and influences are beyond the scope of this book. But I must mention some of the earliest of these leaders and their works, such as Rabbi Finkel Eliezer Judah, who reestablished the Mir Yeshiva in 1944, one of the most prestigious yeshivas in eastern Europe and today an important current Talmudic center in Israel. Rabbi Yehiel Michel Schlesinger and Rabbi Baruch Kundstadt, both from Germany, founded the Kol Torah Yeshiva, first in the center of Jerusalem on King George Street in 1939 and then in Bait Vagan, also in Jerusalem. One of the most influential figures in the creation of the Ashkenazi Society of Learners was Rabbi A. I. Karlitz, known as the Hazon Ish (1878–1953), after the title of his famous book (Friedman 1993, 187; Kaplan 1992). The Hazon Ish immigrated to Israel in 1933 and settled in the Haredi city of Bnei Brak. He soon became a recognized authority of all matters of Jewish law, life, and institutions, even though he was not the head of any yeshiva. Rabbi Joseph Shlomo Kahaneman (1886–1969), head of Ponevezh Yeshiva in Lithuania since 1919, escaped the Holocaust and immigrated in 1939. He settled in Bnei Brak and in 1943 reestablished the Ponevezh Yeshiva as one of the most prestigious in Israel. Kahaneman helped found several Haredi educational institutions for teenagers and families connected with the Ponevezh Yeshiva in Benei Berak, as well as educational institutions located throughout Palestine and, later, Israel. Eliezer M. Shach (1898–2001) was the head of this yeshiva and later the leader of the Haredi–Lithuanian community in Israel until his death. Also at this time, yeshivas from other Orthodox sects were established as well. Among them, Merkaz Harav, a Zionist yeshiva established in 1924 by Rabbi Avraham Izhak Hacohen Kook, became a center for religious Zionist learning.

The history and structure of the Jewish Sephardic system in Israel took a different direction under the authority of Rabbi Ovadia Yosef (for a comparison, see Lehmann and Siebzehner 2006; Zohar 2004). Although he and many others were responsible for reestablishing the yeshiva world in Israel, their biographies and their enormous institutional endeavors have unfortunately been almost entirely neglected in the academic literature (for details, see Caplan 2007). A systematic study of these men and their work would have been a huge contribution to the arguments of this book.

When Israel was established as a modern secular state in 1948, the ultra-Orthodox were a small and impoverished minority, with almost no means of physical or cultural renewal. Moreover, the secular Zionist ideology that arose in this period tried to eradicate all traces of the Diaspora and its associated image of the passive Jew. The dominant secular Zionist ideology viewed religion in general and its leaders in particular as residues from the past that were likely to disappear in time under the influence of a modern culture and secular institutions. In a society that was in the process of establishing a modern state, the ultra-Orthodox way of life was denied as atavistic behavior, adapted out of necessity in diasporic conditions, its practitioner's ghosts of the past now rendered immaterial. The Hebrew man of the Zionist ideology was the very opposite of the image of the Orthodox man. Religious Jews were considered an anachronistic remnant that would inevitably vanish with the establishment of a secular Jewish state and Western secular ideologies. Indeed, Zionist ideology encouraged the opposition to the Haredi lifestyle, consolidating its image of the "new" Jews. These Sabra (prickly pear cactus), as they became known, were native-born Israeli Jews who spent their life working and earning a living through their own labor in a mutually supportive community. In contrast, the Haredi Jews were seen as unproductive and unfit, in both character and training, for the physical and mental challenges that the settlement of the land required. This viewpoint can be traced to traditional notions of Haredim masculinity, which were thus expected to disappear when the modern Jewish culture had been established (Almog 2000, 128).

Zionist resistance to Orthodox Jewish life and its social and cultural models was directed in particular to the devotion to Torah study, which regarded dedication to studious activity as leading to the degeneration of Jewish culture (Almog 2000). The Zionist ideology emphasized productivity, utilitarian work, and, most of all, the notion of individual free will. The ideological struggle against both religion in general and critical attitudes resisting the ultra-Orthodox lifestyle in particular was also part of a growing global attitude condemning religion while stressing the secularization of people's lives (Stark 1999, 249). While the Israeli state was being consolidated, these notions contributed to basing the culture and state institutions on a liberal-democratic model.

Nevertheless, scholars of the Haredi community agree that despite the obstacles placed by the state and its secular, Labor Party–oriented ideology and despite the weaknesses of the Haredi community and its leadership, it was precisely during this period that the infrastructure for this community's success was constructed (Friedman 1991, 1993, 179). Menachem Friedman contends that "the secular and permissive city and the Zionist secular State of Israel constituted a fertile soil for Haredi rehabilitation, where the ideal of Torah study flourished with unparalleled intensity and scope" (1993, 179). This growth can be seen in the data collected and published by the Tal Committee, which was mandated to seek a legal basis for the issues related to recruiting yeshiva students into the military (see Ilan 1999, 2000).

The Yeshiva System in Israel

It is true that there were yeshivas in Palestine, particularly in Jerusalem, starting in the nineteenth century, the best known being Etz Haim, Haiy Olam, and Torat Haim. Although these yeshivas continued to exist after the establishment of the Israeli state, they were marginal to the revival of yeshivas in Israel (Friedman 1991). Rather, Friedman links their revival in Israel to the new Jewish settlement in the area which, he claims, was more influenced by the Poland-Lithuanian model than by the local Jerusalem model. The east European yeshivas were considered more selective and competitive than the Jerusalem yeshivas and represented a renaissance of Jewish wisdom and spiritualism. Accordingly, it was only after the destruction of World War II that a yeshiva revival can be said to have begun (Friedman 1991). Haredi leaders were convinced that the secular Zionist state would deny religious Jews the opportunity to educate their children and so created a yeshiva system under its auspices. As Friedman argues (1993, 185), the establishment of the state of Israel as a Western welfare state formed ideal economic and social conditions for rebuilding and expanding Haredi education. Paradoxically, the modern state has encouraged the rise of yeshiva fundamentalism, as illustrated by its education laws and its policies concerning birth control.

The law passed in 1949 making education compulsory encouraged the Haredis' Agudat Israel (Union of Israel) political party to submit a bill for its particular educational needs, to be underwritten by the state. This meant that the secular state would supply the necessary budget, services, and infrastructure to support the Haredi community and especially its educational system (Schiffer 1998, 7). What the state would not provide to the ultra-Orthodox sects under the 1949 Compulsory Education Law would be contributed by Western Jews, especially from the United States. According to Friedman (1991, 73), these funds ballooned after World War II. During the 1950s, the infrastructure of the Haredi yeshiva system was put in place, along with a cultural, educational, and emotional support system that could be seen as leading to the Haredis' present success.

Even though yeshiva students are not permitted to become involved in civic affairs, and the yeshivas in Israel do not teach secular subjects, most Haredi educational systems are supported by the state, which also provides stipends for yeshiva students. In addition, the Haredi educational system receives funds for transportation and extended study hours, and Haredi institutions also collect money from nonprofit organizations (Schiffer 1998, 14). Consequently, yeshiva education in Israel is constantly growing. During the 1980s, the number of students under the category of *Torato omnuto* (Torah as vocation) exceeded 30,000, rising in the 1990s to more than 70,000 students affiliated with specific yeshivas, or *kollels* (yeshivas for married men) (see Schiffer 1998 and the Tal Committee at http://www.knesset.gov.il/docs/heb/tal.htm), indicating a revival and a renewal of yeshiva education and the Haredi lifestyle in Israel (see Caplan 2007).

The support of the yeshiva culture is related also to the development of Israel's welfare policy. The Israeli social welfare system encouraged a high birthrate and fully supported large families (Horowitz 2002, 18) There thus was little motivation for Haredi men to leave the yeshiva before the age of forty, as they had no working skills and were unemployable in the

Israeli labor market. This is why in Israel today, Haredim live in relatively poor conditions (Berman 2000; Dahan 1998; Shilhav 1991), and large Haredi families are totally dependent on communal support systems. This situation is unique to Israel. In the United States and in some European countries, Haredi men join the modern labor market and fulfill their local civic obligations and, in countries like the United States and Britain, are considered part of the middle class. In contrast, in economic terms, the majority of Israeli Haredim are defined as belonging to the lower or lower-middle class (Caplan 2003a, 79).

In the liberal Israeli welfare state, especially during 1950s and the 1960s when the ideology of the all-inclusiveness of the yeshiva intensified, full-time study for all men in the community was the Haredi norm. After the 1967 War and during the 1970s and 1980s, more yeshivas were constructed and the new religious ideologies were tested. This revival is exemplified by the large number of religious institutions, which began to be constructed in the 1980s and 1990s. Those neighborhoods and towns undergoing a religious resurgence are conspicuous by the appearance of not only new residences but also many new religious buildings. The very architecture of these institutions reflects the degree of the neighborhood's religiosity, its religious and cultural affiliation, and the dominant sect for its education.

The architecture of yeshivas, in fact, has much in common with that of other fundamentalist groups, such as Christian and Muslim, in that by choice or necessity, they adhere to the simple yet functional architecture of madrasas and evangelical or Pentecostal Bible schools, usually using plain and inexpensive materials. The emphasis is on the ability of these institutions to spread as expeditiously as possible and to engage pious members willing to devote themselves to faith and God.

What kind of religious institution did the modern state want? The principal goal of the founders of the Haredi community was to produce devoted Torah scholars. Thus, secular studies such as math, English, history, and technology were banned, as they were thought to pollute the students' minds and distract them from their obligations to God and Judaism. In the fundamentalist framework, and for the same reasons, after marriage men were encouraged to continue studying at a special academy for married men, the *kollel*. This institution helps married men continue learning and is another affirmation of the community's values and the validity of dedication to religious studies (Friedman 1991).

Haredi-style yeshivas differ from those of other religious sects in Israel, such as the nationalist yeshivas reinforced by religious Zionist movements that encourage radical political activism (Don-Yehiya 1994, 284). Instead, the new Haredi system stresses exclusivity, scripturalism, and withdrawal, and studying at a prestigious yeshiva is a prerequisite for status, marriage, and success at all levels of life (Stadler 2002).

To reinforce their piety, males must devote their life to the yeshiva and its goals. The way of life once practiced by only few in the ultra-Orthodox community is now the choice of many (see Caplan 2007, 205; Selengut 1994, 247; Zalkin 2006, 155). This religiosity is based on texts and requires a wide network of institutions to transmit and enforce new ideas and rituals. According to Haym Soloveitchik (1994a, 200), in this emerging culture, texts assumed a new role. In contrast to other Jewish groups in history that were regulated by religious law, the new Haredi culture in Israel was governed by rules and the stringency of textual interpretation, or what scholars of fundamentalism call *scripturalism* (Antoun 2001; Goldberg 1987).

This reliance on scripture and on rabbinical interpretations to justify every detail of behavior is a nontraditional reading of traditional texts, which is selective by nature because it focuses on certain parts of the scripture while ignoring others, which usually contain variations, gaps, and contradictions. The parts selected, often marginal and seemingly unrepresentative, become a comprehensive explanation of reality and a guide to behavior. Yohanan, a former spiritual supervisor at a famous Lithuanian yeshiva, described the ideal student as requiring an extraordinary state of mind:

> If you look carefully at our students, you will see that their heads and minds are fully engaged in the study of the Torah. Even when they are not at the yeshiva, their minds are immersed in the Talmudic world, and they are deep in an intellectual state. This is a remarkable mental condition for the students, which can be achieved only after hard work and endless study. Any distraction can disrupt this process, so continuity is a necessary part of this exceptional state.

During my interviews, many students described the glamour and rewards of achieving pious masculinity. They bragged about their status in the community and how important it was for them to belong to a famous yeshiva, with its benefits for their families and their status in the eyes of young women of the community. According to this view, such piety is related to marriage and success. Some students even complained that young

Haredi women were so intent on finding the perfect husband that they overlooked the man's personality and qualifications, concentrating only on the yeshiva to which he belonged or his success in his studies. "All girls want is a smart yeshiva boy," the students declared during the interviews. Many told me that young women were not even interested in economic matters and that in personal meetings they asked only about their yeshiva, studies, friends, teachers, and rabbis.

Yeshiva piousness is protected by a strict separation of the sexes. Women are excluded from the yeshiva world and are educated in their own institutions, particularly in the Beit Ya'akov (House of Jacob, Exodus 19:3) schools. Based on its roots in Poland after World War I, the Hazon Ish established the ideological foundation of Beit Ya'akov in Israel (see Friedman 1995b, 284), as institutions where girls would be educated to raise families and obtain jobs in order to allow their future husbands to devote their time exclusively to the yeshiva (Friedman 1995b, 284).

Their separate educational tracks socialize Haredi boys and girls differently. Three-year-old boys are introduced to the religious studies that will remain their main vocation for years to come, whereas girls are guided toward mundane tasks (Bilu 2000, 34). Yoram Bilu showed how the separation of genders and males' identification with Torah practices are achieved through separate rituals, such as the Jewish ritual of circumcision (*brit milah*), the rite of *bar mitzvah* ("for those to whom the commandants apply," i.e., thirteen-year-old boys), and the first haircut (*halakha*, at age three, a ceremonial marker of entering the world of Torah, study, and commandments) (Bilu 2000, 47). When boys reach three, they enter the *cheder* (the room), a religious preschool, which constitutes the first step of a Haredi boy into the world of study, piety, and masculinity.

After the *cheder*, Haredi boys move to a Talmud Torah, a yeshiva elementary school, until they turn thirteen, the age for their bar mitzvah. Between thirteen to sixteen, they attend the small yeshiva (*yeshiva ketana*), in preparation for the senior yeshiva (*yeshiva gdola*). The big yeshiva holds a few hundred students whose ages range from sixteen to forty (and sometimes older; see Halbertal and Hartman-Halbertal 1998, 458), divided according to their study abilities and their achievement in scriptural studies, Talmud, Jewish law, and rabbinic commentaries. At the yeshiva, studies are regulated by the rhythms of lessons, self-study (*limud atzmi*), and peer-group study (*hevruta*).

One of my interviewees described the meaning of the yeshiva to his life:

If we think about worldly achievements, then this is the less important part of my life . . . religiously I am commanded to sit all day and study the Torah. Primarily, I study the Torah for its own sake because it is a Jewish commandment that is central to the entire yeshiva world. Personally, I see the study of the Talmud and its wisdom as a light that leads me along the way, showing me the right path in life.

Yaakov Friedman described the yeshiva as follows in his popular book *The Soul of the Yeshiva* (*Nefesh ha-yeshiva*):

A thick barrier divides the yeshiva world from the world outside. A barrier of pleasure, a barrier of pain, of feelings and yearnings. A barrier of the "internal world" a stranger will never understand. A barrier that divides the curved back, and the sparkling eyes of anyone who was blessed to place foot inside this world. (1997, 17)

Every manual for Haredi students that I examined opens with a description of the ideal of *torato omnuto*, or how to live a life of the Torah as a vocation. Here the rabbis explain to their young disciples that lifelong exposure to the sacred texts requires their withdrawal from all worldly practices and devotion to intellectual and spiritual activities. In this view, continual Torah study should be a man's goal and the center of daily male activity. Interrupting this sacred duty, for any purpose, is forbidden and considered sinful. For this reason, participation in general economic or civic activities and duties of the state, especially work, the labor market, and the military or national service are banned (see Friedman 1991).

Yeshiva Learning

The centrality of the yeshiva lesson as a learning technique is rooted in the Jewish tradition and is the primary form of men's acquisition of knowledge from childhood onward. Today, the lesson is a basic unit of the Haredi community's transmission of text-based knowledge (cf. Qur'anic schools, see Antoun 1989; Gellner 1981). Most of the students I interviewed claimed that the Hevruta was the most effective and preferable mode of study, as it was constructed to improve study techniques, memorizing, competence, and debating skills (T. Friedman 1996, 458; Heilman 1983, 203). In this dyadic learning format, two yeshiva students learn by means of a shared study experience. Students told me that the dialogue between two students makes learning more active, vivid, and interesting. In contrast to self-study, when they learn together their interpretations must be more accurate. In addition, the accumulation of dozens, and sometimes hundreds, of small discussions creates a loud and steady background noise, accompanied by hand gestures, rhythmic body movements, different ways of leaning on the stand (*stender*), and a variety of animated facial expressions (Halbertal and Hartman-Halbertal 1998, 458). Students also acquire a set of body techniques: they learn how to talk to one another; how to walk, sit, and stand; and when, where, and how to eat.

In various official Haredi texts, the representation of yeshiva religiosity reinforces a model of maleness, that of the pious student, an otherworldly soldier constantly engaged in the work of God. Paradoxically, the pious ideal that appears in traditional texts as an impossible aspiration was made a reality in the Zionist state for the first time in Jewish history. For example, while explaining the ideal of yeshiva piety and maleness, many of the yeshiva students I interviewed mentioned the scholarly tradition of Rabbi Eliyahu, known as the *gaon* of Vilna (1720–97), the genius from Vilna. Students stated that in their studies, they aspired to the pious model of the *gaon*. By stressing his life and piousness, the students also were emphasizing the ideal of the ascetic scholar who dedicated his life and family to the Torah. These students told me heroic stories about how the *gaon* shunned sleep, food, and social relations while studying and how he devoted all his time to the Talmud. Many expressed their wish to achieve this kind of piety, which they defined as the most heroic act possible.

Scholars of the ultra-Orthodox community in Israel agree that the development of this model, albeit at the expense of some of its original sophistication, made these institutions in Israel more attractive to youth searching for authenticity and absoluteness in the secular–liberal state (Friedman 1991, 1993; Selengut 1994, 251; Soloveitchik 1994a, 1994b). The necessity and ability to fulfill the ideal of Jewish manhood and piety in Israel, especially after the Holocaust, was an explanation I also heard many times during the interviews. Students claimed that Judaism, almost eradicated during the war, could be renewed only through intensive Torah studies and the growth of yeshivas. In this view, yeshiva masculinity is connected to Jewish revitalization after destruction and defeat and is used as a key factor in a divine scheme. When I asked what motivated them to stay at the yeshiva for so many years, the students told me that they had the task of reviving the yeshiva's past, an exclusive sacred mission that could be fulfilled only by their full-time devotion to the yeshiva.

Yeshiva scripturalism and the new status of yeshiva studies also awarded a special status and authority to the yeshiva's leaders, teachers, and especially the heads of the yeshivas. In many of the interviews, the students stressed not only the ideas of the rabbis who were considered to be the founders of the community in Israel but also the importance of the current Haredi authorities. For example, when discussing the motivation for their studies, the students always mentioned a rabbi, a spiritual supervisor, or the academic head of a yeshiva, who in their view fulfilled the Haredi ideals in Israel. That is, they based their own incentive to study and to stay in the yeshiva world on these ideal figures, their moral standards and persistence. During the interviews, the students recounted how different rabbis had encouraged them to engage in yeshiva life and how rabbis in their yeshivas had helped them through difficult times by means of personal meetings and extensive involvement and spiritual support. The students asserted that these rabbis were their most important models, who fulfilled many positive functions, such as generating students' creativity, inspiration, and drive.

Scholars agree that despite its currently active and creative character, the yeshiva model of masculinity was originally designed in Israel as one of quietism (Selengut 1994, 246; Soloveitchik 1994a, 222). In the first stages of the model's establishment, Haredi actions were mostly defensive against the intrusions of the state and society and not activist political demonstrations or ideologies. The pious ethos created by the leaders was of scholarship, of being engaged in yeshiva Talmudic studies and unconcerned with worldly matters. This position was in sharp contrast to secular and national symbols of masculinity, especially that of the warrior, which reinforced heroism and a capacity for violence and activism (Morgan 1994, 165). During this period, both the yeshiva student and Haredi life as such were constructed as passive, waiting for divine intervention, which does not require action in this world. Yeshiva men therefore were told to reject Zionist and other activist models of behavior as well as militaristic activities, either defensive or offensive; any involvement in politics; and any aggressive models of behavior. Nonetheless, the connection to the Zionist ethos is still available through both social systems' willingness for sacrifice.

The Shifts Paradigm

Anthropologists and sociologists have recently turned their attention to the study of Haredi communities (Aran 2003; El-Or 1994; Goodman 1997;

Hakak 2003; Stadler 2002). They agree that since the 1990s, the Haredi community in Israel has been changing radically. The community's dedication to the Torah, exclusion of women, male yeshiva asceticism, separatism, and withdrawal—all features that defined the quiescent nature of yeshiva fundamentalism at its inception—have been challenged by members of the community. Now Haredi leaders, rabbis, politicians, and members all are reacting to many changes in Israel that are crucial to the continuity of the yeshiva world in Israel.

Transformations in Haredi fundamentalism can be explained using different paradigms. For example, changes in the Haredi lifestyle and religiosity in Israel are taking place in a dynamic social context. Since the 1990s, when Israeli society began coming under the daily threat of suicide bombers, political instability, war, and the redefinition of sovereignty and state borders, different social groups (immigrants, religious Zionists, ethnic minorities) started to redefine their relations with both the state and civil society. Scholars of the Haredi community argue that this shift was related to the Haredis' changing relations with the Israeli public as a whole. By gradually accepting elements of Israeli identity, Haredim have been able to minimize the tensions between the state and civil society. Others claim that the economic crisis is the most relevant to the yeshiva world (see Lupo 2003, 12). Although the ideal of religious poverty remains strong, its current deterioration is affecting even the most devoted members, as seen in the numerous discussions about professional training for Haredi men, that is, about their obtaining a secular education. These debates are continuing and have generated much controversy, and the underlying economic pressure has raised questions for Haredi leaders.

The Haredi community also is participating in this process of inclusion and change. Indeed, the realization of the need for change has transformed many aspects of Haredi life, and as a result, Haredim have changed their views on politics, religion, economics, medicine, aid, modern technology, the state, culture, gender, and the family. Consequently, even as a small, isolated community, the Haredis have gained a political strength that exceeds their electoral weight. The recent new relationships among Haredim, the secular segments of Israeli society, and the state seem to have influenced the dramatic revision within the community (see Caplan 2003b; Sivan and Caplan 2003). One example of this is the shift in the Haredi orientation toward the state and citizenship. Many Haredim are becoming more nationalistic and have demonstrated an increasing interest in joining the military and participating in the labor market. Haredim now use modern technology, especially computers, cellular phones, the Internet, and DVDs, which give them access to worlds of knowledge previously forbidden. Haredi participation in aid institutions such as ZAKA, Hatzolah, Magen David Adom, and Yad Sara also are important manifestations of these transformations.

In addition, in recent years the religious options in Israel have multiplied and diversified. Ultra-Orthodoxy is no longer the sole prototype available to actualize authentic Jewish life. New alternative and attractive ways to fulfill a Jewish lifestyle in the Israeli setting can be found in some contemporary Hasidic groups, such as Habad and Breslav, the Conservative and Reform movements, New Age Jewish groups, and the various Sephardic groups. An analysis of the meaning of these changes reveals how the new religious orientations have affected the relationship of fundamentalist groups with the liberal state and civil society.

Accordingly, to explain the shift in the Haredi yeshiva culture, we must develop a new set of theories, for I believe that this transformation in the masculine model of piety, in the criticism, and in the ideas emerging today and reshaping the religious experience in Haredi yeshiva culture helps explain the shift in its fundamentalist nature. This is what I shall discuss next.

3

On the Edge of Transgression

*The Study of the Talmud and
the "Evil Inclination"*

Sin crouches at the door.

—Genesis 4:7

Any form of transgressive discourse, of anti-language, implies
an alternative reality.

—Halliday 1976, 572

After a long interview with Moshe about yeshiva life, I asked
him about its many prohibitions. Moshe asked me whether I was familiar
with the writings on the evil inclination and explained his view of these
restrictions:

> We know that the evil inclination is there all the time. . . . We know that
> when you are with people, it is much harder to overcome your desires, that
> God is huge and stronger than us, that we can pray and worship God but
> that when we meet people, this is when we have to deal with our nature and
> truly fight the evil inclination. We must do this every day and every time.
> With the Torah we can accomplish this mission, this daily trial that is striv-
> ing for our final defeat. . . . I try every day to fight it. The evil inclination is
> here all the time, but sometimes when I survive it, I feel good, spiritually
> satisfied, and I feel that I deserve to rest in Olam Haba because I have fought
> it, and even though I have failed many times, I did my best every day.

We can examine the shaping of Haredi piety and yeshiva masculinity in Israel by looking at the meanings of sexual restrictions and bodily

prohibitions. Along with studious activities at the yeshiva, students are educated to restrain their bodily desires. Prayer, repeated rituals, memorization, and debates are some of the techniques used to reinforce self-control and create a pattern of behavior associated with the yeshiva piety. The ideal of Torah studies entails a set of body techniques, what Pierre Bourdieu calls the habitus of sitting, talking, speaking, moving, and reacting to other members of the group (1977). This ideal model, a product of the early modern Ashkenazi–Jewish yeshivas, is what defines piety in the community today as it is constructed and tested every day in the yeshiva (see Biale 1992a, 1992b; Boyarin 1997, 154; Satlow 1996, 21).

When talking about the practice of Torah study, the students I interviewed used various metaphors of love, stressing the pleasure of wisdom, otherworldly satisfaction, and regeneration and, at the same time, emphasizing bodily hardship and toil. The enchantment of Torah studies and piety accentuated in current Haredi writings and narratives is accompanied by a strong emphasis on the body's struggle with the secular temptations of modernity. Ideals such as self-mastery, physical restraint, and the constant war between the self with endless internal and external distractions are major themes in the popular discourse of yeshiva students and manuals.

According to the new generations of Haredi rabbis and students, piety is a continuing and courageous battle between the higher self and the body and its desires. In the study hall in the modern city, yeshiva students learn how to overcome desires and temptations, to control lust, and to dedicate their body and soul to their Talmudic tasks. All men are trained to ascend to high spiritual levels and to distance themselves as much as possible from secular and state affairs. The new yeshiva books interpret piety as heroic, for it is even harder to achieve under the current social conditions of the modern Israeli state. Transgressions are abundant, scattered everywhere in the modern, secular city. The Haredi response has been to add to the prohibitions already governing the yeshiva students. To become a pious, virtuous man, the student first must be able to fight his bodily desires, to master and purify his body and become a hero. To do this, rabbis and writers emphasize constraint, abstinence, and the strict regulations regarding marriage and refer to the morality literature (*sifrut musar*) for students.

My interviewees accepted without question this piety and its worthiness as a guide for their actions. They did not contest it or complain that it was unnecessary or too rigorous. Instead, the students expressed their fear of transgression and stressed the need to overcome their bodily desires and seek purification. By reinforcing this discourse of overcoming their sexual desires, the students were able to achieve a courageous piety and maintain the group's religious dominance and social power at all levels of community life, both inside and outside the yeshiva itself, thereby minimizing any criticism of or challenges to these aspects of sexuality and the body.

In contrast to the other topics discussed in this book—namely, work, the military, the family and gender relations, and volunteerism—my interviewees had almost nothing negative to say about the notion of limiting sexuality (see also Davidman and Greil 2007; Goodman 1997). Although constraints on sexuality are demanding and difficult to observe, the students recognized these obligations as their most important mission, which offered the greatest rewards, transcendental as well as social. As we have seen, the ideal of the disciplined body and the model of male sexuality in the community are considered the religious foundation for consolidating the normative Haredi family, their social position as key commentators and pious virtuosos in the Haredi community as well as ambassadors to the secular society.

Nonetheless, my analysis of the rhetoric used to reinforce the yeshiva's piety did reveal some discrepancies. To explain the struggle with bodily desires, rabbis and other writers incorporate modern and Israeli features into the traditional religious moral texts, like the eleventh-century *The Duties of the Heart* (*Hovot halevavot*) by Rabbi Bahya ibn Paquda and *Path of the Just* (*Mesilat yesharim*) by Rabbi Moshe Chaim Luzzatto.[1] Such features might be metaphors of Israeli wars, images of Israeli soldier-heroes, and various modern medical and scientific terms in which the yeshiva student is compared with an infected body struggling with a fatal disease, and a psychological discourse on the student's own personal experiences and his life at the yeshiva, including problems of solitude, sexuality, relationships, and the yeshiva's authority.

To protect the fundamentalist enclave from the threat of modernity, fundamentalist leaders of all sects use prohibitions concerning sexuality and the body. Almond, Appleby, and Sivan (2003) borrowed Mary Douglas's argument (1966) concerning the maintenance of symbolic boundaries and the importance of unity in religious experiences. They argue that the advice given by fundamentalist leaders, particularly to men, is intended to improve the means of protecting the body and to raise barriers to contain and distance the temptations and ills of modernity. As a spiritual exercise representing social control and an awareness of their propensity to deviate, men should limit both their own sexuality and their contact with women.

Indeed, Jewish, Christian, and Muslim fundamentalism all have instructions for using the methods and laws of the sacred canons to purify their devotees' activities by reinforcing ethics and practices of sexual constraint (see Griffith 1997; Mahmood 2005). One measure of the centrality of this issue is the number of books and audiocassettes for these groups that deal with controlling lust, and especially what is called the "problem of male desire." These fundamentalist leaders refer to women's sexuality as evil, and many of their writings and public sermons explain why and how encounters between men and women should be minimized or avoided altogether, using an abundance of biblical or Qur'anic texts to attack modernity.

Discipline of the Body and Yeshiva Piety

In the winter of 1999 I received a telephone call from Jonathan, a yeshiva student who was considered a prodigy by Rashi and his friends and someone I had wanted to interview for a long time. He asked me to pick him up at 11 o'clock at night, on a corner not far from the yeshiva. Jonathan is a typical yeshiva student, wearing the regulation black suit, white shirt, and a black Lithuanian hat. When he saw me, he immediately got into the back seat of the car and retreated to the farthest corner. He looked shy, self-conscious, almost cringing. Despite his evasive body language and his reluctance to make eye contact, we immediately started a conversation. In contrast to his body language, his voice was firm and clear. He instructed me to leave this street because he did not want anyone to see him with me and "get the wrong impression." I told him that I appreciated his time and effort to come to talk to me. He answered by stressing the importance to talk with someone like me, that he wanted the world to know about the good Haredim and their positive contributions to both the continuity of the Jewish people and the country of Israel. He told me that despite the problems with meeting someone like me and the problem of *bitul Torah* (i.e., doing anything, usually pleasurable, other than studying), he was committed and willing to talk because he knew I would listen and write about the qualities of the community and the important work of the yeshiva world. Taken aback, I asked him to explain what he meant by "a person like me." He smiled and kept silent. I insisted, "Do you mean meeting with me can be interpreted as sinful behavior?" He said, "Yes, you know, our rabbis, they are very traditional, and of course they are right, but I am willing to take this risk if you listen." Jonathan cited two areas of potentially transgressive behavior in our meeting. One was "the wrong impression" that people might have of his meeting a woman alone, at night, and secretly. The other was the incompatibility of the yeshiva habitus with his present surroundings. Either one or both of these could have been demonstrated by his body language.

The gap between the accepted norms of the yeshiva and the manner in which students actually behaved appeared as a major obstacle in my interviews. The years of yeshiva socialization in an all-male group were apparent in the interviewees' demeanor and behavior during these encounters. Their embarrassment, distance, and limited eye contact were common to all our meetings. During the interviews, students seldom ate, even when food was served, and once they had sat down, they controlled their movements and tried not to stand, just as they would do in a yeshiva, until the end of the meeting.

In contrast to these physical limitations and constraints, the interviewees usually spoke freely about their problems in meeting with me, often explaining their willingness by stressing the importance of my role as a mediator between Haredi life and Israel's secular, academic world. They legitimated their encounters with a secular woman researcher from the university by emphasizing the importance of refuting the stereotypical views of Haredi life, especially yeshiva life. Such an attitude calls for some caution on the researcher's part, and in some cases I was forced to approach a topic obliquely. It became clear, for example, that under the circumstances, I could not discuss the evil inclination directly. The tensions of meeting with a woman were such that I did not feel it would have been helpful to bring up sexual issues. But when I asked my interviewees about manners, behavior, and family life, they usually recommended manuals written by contemporary rabbis on the various topics of their everyday lives. How yeshiva asceticism is justified in modern-day Israel and how it is interpreted by members of the fundamentalist Haredi culture were my main interests. I therefore collected and regularly read these pamphlets, particularly those recommended by more than one student.

These manuals are extremely popular in the yeshiva community as a whole, and large sections of them explain how yeshiva students must restrain their bodies in everyday life, as well as how to deal with the problem of the evil inclination in the yeshiva experience. Reading these manuals was a first step into this world. They told me how piety is interpreted in terms of sexuality and the body and clarified the students' behavior during our meetings and interviews. As a result, most of my interpretations of the evil inclination in this chapter are based on the popular texts and manuals that my students recommended, most of which I read after I had finished the interviews.

The current Haredi writings identify those aspects of body discipline in which the evil inclination dominates. Indeed, the evil inclination is a common theme and appears in various Jewish sources. Boyarin (1995, 460) even argues that it often becomes almost a synonym for sexual desire itself (cf. Tishby 1989, 803). This term has now gained new attention and meanings, especially in regard to the battle with bodily temptations in the context of modernity and the secular city. As Eilberg-Schwartz (1992, 20, 1994) observed, Jewish scholars have long debated the problem of the body. In the Haredi view, the tension between the body and the sacred text is a major concern (see Goodman 1997) and an important stage in shaping and reviving yeshiva fundamentalism in Israel. To be able to study the sacred texts, yeshiva men must keep their bodies clean and pure, so Haredi male rituals related to the purification of the body are inculcated from childhood (see Bilu 2000, 37).

In order to attain purity, one first must understand the enemy, the evil inclination. Many fundamentalist writings reify the enemy and provide ways to fight it (see Almond, Appleby, and Sivan 2003). The current manuals for students describe the evil inclination as jeopardizing male bodies as well as the existence of the community and Judaism in general. In Mary Douglas's terms (1966), the internal battle of the masculine body is a symbol of the external danger of extermination and the conflict in which the fundamentalist enclave itself is engaged, a minority fighting for its existence in the antagonistic modern world.

Haredi texts, especially the manuals, portray the evil inclination as an independently existing entity, a dominant, deceptive persona with demonic-erotic attributes. In this view, this evil incubus is present in male bodies from the day of birth, clouding their everyday experiences. The yeshiva student is thus considered to be a frail, unrestrained vessel, always in danger of violating taboos concerning dietary laws, sexual limitations, or other norms. These frail bodies must struggle with seductions not only or primarily in the secluded space of the Haredi community but also in their contact with the modern state and in the interstices where secular modernity might infiltrate Haredi space.[2] This is why these books teach

Figure 3.1. A street poster in Mea She'arim demanding that Haredi girls dress modestly and specifying a dress code (objectionable items "includ[e] tight blouses like cotton and lycra, tight or short skirts, open neck [blouses], diaphanous stockings").

students to stay within the confines of the yeshiva and to remain continuously involved with Talmudic studies, lessons, and ritual practices. The lessons, which form the yeshiva's core activity, are themselves the practice of moderating the body and the self. The long daily lessons in large study halls transmit not only Talmudic knowledge but also techniques to oversee, regulate, and overcome men's passion by stressing the right behavior in the enclave (Goodman 1997, 47).

The world outside the yeshiva's walls is considered dangerous. The secular streets contain dozens of temptations, shops, theaters, and scantily dressed women, but far worse is the distraction, while studying, of the memories of these scenes (see figure 3.1). Time spent outside the yeshiva or beyond the shelter of Torah is thereby considered a literally life-endangering activity. Most large Haredi communities are, however, located in or near a modern, secular city full of foreign, non-Jewish ideas and false wisdom, which is often referred to as a den of snakes and scorpions. This degenerate secular urban space is the seat of abomination, profanity, and insanity and is often described as the product of brutal rape or disease. In contrast, the fragile masculine body, socialized to study and fulfill the sacred work of God, is depicted as collapsing under the attack of the dark forces of desires and sin (see Aran 2003).

The inclination for evil is related to a loss of male spiritual power and the risk of being oppressed and dominated by other forces, especially women. It is analogous to and represents the fear of being dominated by modernity and the politics of the state. The only way to avoid this weakness is by reemphasizing the presence of the sacred and following its practices. Piety can be achieved only by minimizing one's physical needs and overcoming corporeal temptations. Men who can control their physical needs and remain at the yeshiva can proclaim their dominance over all other forces: women, secular men, traditional rabbis, previous generations, and alternative models of piety in Judaism.

To reinforce male heroic piety, many Haredi manuals concentrate on particular anatomical features, such as the heart, eyes, and mouth. Each organ serves as both a receptor and a filter for different kinds of modern seductions and secular contaminations. The organs must be taught to distinguish between what may and may not be ingested and must be strengthened according to the kind of damage they may sustain, and so kabbalistic medicine is based on the relative strength of various areas and organs of the body. Because the pollutions of modernity infect the inner organs and demonize the self and the body, both physically and spiritually, the student must struggle heroically to repel these invaders through techniques of the body and prayer, in order to protect both his own body and, by analogy, the organs of the community. The student is viewed as a body in contact with sickness or disease, plagued by germs, or containing a pathological cancer. Some examples illustrate this view of the yeshiva body and its limitations.

The evil inclination is thought to be particularly likely to enter through the eyes, mouth, or the heart. In fact, the idea of the heart as the dwelling place of the evil inclination is common in Jewish sources (see Tishby 1989, 789–90). Contemporary Haredi writers relate the heart to fears of modernity and emotional insanity as a result of a person's encounter with the secular city. Fear is related as well to wider issues of secular knowledge, participation in state affairs, and the domination of women because of their secular study and work experience (see Caplan 2007, 223).

Once the heart of the student has been infected with external influences, the body is out of control; and if the yeshiva student, a paragon of virtue, becomes infected, it is but a short step to the infection of the entire community. In both cases, the heart is the central organ pumping evil into the entire body and culture. This image highlights both the students' vulnerability and corporeal impulses, and the challenge and responsibility imposed on them, a struggle intrinsic to current Haredi masculinity and fundamentalism (see Aran, Stadler, and Ben-Ari 2008).

Some Haredi writings define the heart in opposition to the brain. Many students pointed out to me that at the yeshiva the body ideally should be controlled only by the mind. But when the evil inclination takes over, it is the tempted heart that dominates the body, and emotions cloud the mind. Emotions are both uncontrollable and unforeseeable and are identified with insanity and irrational features such as femininity, secularity, impurity, and spontaneity (see Douglas 1993). This dichotomy arrays forces from both inside and outside the community against the always imperiled notions of the sacred and male piety.

Yeshiva students are portrayed as what Boyarin terms (1993, 399–421) carnal bodies exploding with desires and externally exposed to a constant barrage of temptations. Students are weak, with a tendency toward irrationality. They lack willpower and are easily inclined toward sin and transgression (see Stallybrass and White 1986; Taussig 1998), which are naturally exacerbated by the modern city and the liberal state.

The books I studied depicted students' bodies as vicious battlegrounds on which the evil inclination and modern forces fight. In these texts, the evil inclination is invoked to refer to all that endangers the student's progress to piety. In *The Kindness of Your Youth* (*Hesed ne'urecha*, Jeremiah 2:2), a book addressed to young yeshiva students, the author, Moshe Friend, described the constant state of battle:

> Your body has two inclinations. The first can make you angry and upset, and this can distract you from your studies and prayer; only in war will you be able to dismiss and remove it. The second [inclination] can harm your thoughts. It will always be after you, and even if you fight it, it might return to harm you. . . . My only advice here is to lock yourself in the study hall and learn the sweet words of the Torah with enthusiasm and joy, and your soul will be invigorated. (1995, 24–25)

Like many other books for yeshiva students, here the author describes the evil inclination as a powerful independent agent liable to attack at any time. But since the source of evil lies within the student, he has the power to fight back. At these moments, only a determined, even heroic, internal struggle can enable the forces of virtue to prevail. Resolution can be achieved only through discipline and isolation. The Torah is always cited as the only tool for ordering, mastering, and realizing true piety for men. Moreover, the Torah and its ways are the only tools to fight the technology and science of modernity.

In various manuals for students, the term *sweet words* reinforces the tradition of Torah studies as sweet food, like honey, nourishing and tasty. More than a metaphor, as Yoram Bilu explained (2000), in some Jewish communities when the boy enters the *cheder* for the first time at the age of three, he participates in a ritual of licking honey from letters of the Hebrew alphabet. Digesting the words of the Torah as food marks its entrance into his body (Bilu 2000, 47–48). Likewise, popular yeshiva books often describe the Torah as a food that purifies the body and can be used as a remedy for internal transgression and external threats. This relationship of sacredness and food can be compared with the eating of Christ's body in the Christian ritual of the Eucharist (Bynum 1987, 3). As the yeshiva students mature, the idea of eating the sacred words, digesting the holy, or making sacredness a concrete practice is replaced with a moralistic order to use the sacred text as a barrier, a wall between the students' bodies and the secular world.

In the manuals for yeshiva students, the eyes are central images of the battle with the evil inclination, and they are regarded as windows of the soul.[3] Accordingly, the focus of many chapters and even whole books is on the problem of the eyes, as Haredi men in secular spaces are in danger of being contaminated through their eyes (see figure 3.2).

Many of my interviewees explained that if the eyes are misused, for instance, by looking at polluted things, they will become dark windows of sin. The guidance concerning the eyes instructs that they should be restricted or even blocked, as even a narrow breach may allow the evil inclination to take over the body and destroy it. But apparently the eyes are expressive as well. Thus the problem of the eyes in men is similar to that of speech, the evil tongue, in women.[4] In an instruction book for yeshiva students, *The Ways of the Just: A Moral Handbook for the Yeshiva Student* (*Orchot yesharim le'ben yeshivah*), Wegshel explained the problem of the eyes:

> In our world there is no better way of guarding the heart's desire than keeping the eyes shut. Although the eyes see, the heart lusts, so if a man can avoid seeing [what is not decent], he will be saved from lust. . . . There

Figure 3.2. "Please Do Not Pass through Our Neighborhood in Immodest Clothes." Mea She'arim, winter 2006.

is a great danger in looking at something corrupt, since [in this way] the evil inclination can penetrate the heart's desire. (2000, 36)

The eyes are the windows of the soul and thus the opening for modern and secular forces to enter the body. Since men's eyes are weak and easily induced to gaze, especially at women's bodies, this must be avoided. Many writers believe that the eyes must be guarded, covered, and continually occupied and that only the sacred texts can do this effectively. Reading these texts and using them as screens protect the student from possible interruptions. Constantly reading the Torah is like wearing blinders to protect the eyes from outside temptations. According to these books, in order to deal with bodily weaknesses, students are advised to learn the sacred texts by heart and to repeat them over and over again (see also the interviews in Shalif 1995). These practices not only are assumed to improve students' memory but also are recognized as powerful techniques to heal and defend the fragile male body from modern threats.

Piety, Militarism, and Medical Definitions

In his work on the rabbinical construction of masculinity, Satlow argues that "whereas the 'warrior' in the Hebrew bible is the man of war, to the rabbis he is the one who exercises self-restraint" (1996, 27). In current Haredi texts, the male struggle with the evil inclination is expressed in images of war, soldierhood, and illness and other medical definitions (Morgan 1994). The principal manifestation of the struggle can be found in Israeli military rhetoric. Accordingly, these texts use expressions of military preparedness and strength to construct the yeshiva's heroism. This discourse reveals an important blend of religious ideals, Jewish sources that deal with the evil inclination, and modern metaphors of war and Israeli soldierhood. These images also reflect the shift in the community's expressions of different religious aspects, such as the yearning for the corporeal and for participation in Israeli society.

Haredi books and manuals describe students as needing to be quick, strong, skilled, properly equipped, and armed, attributes that parallel those for socialization in the military, such as the unquestioning readiness to obey, to fight, and to die for the country. In his *Guidebook for Yeshiva Students* (*Sefer hadracha le'ben yeshiva*), a popular manual for students, Aharon Melovitzky described this kind of heroic piety:

> He [the Lord] ostensibly is willing to forgive you for your mistakes and your defeats. The meaning of this is a supreme strengthening and a sense of calmness in the soul of the combatant fighting in the most stressful war. Despite his courage, he fails again and again. Some yeshiva boys give up in despair and decide to leave and desert the battlefield [the yeshiva]. This is a hasty decision that stems from not knowing the canonical rule, "to lose the battle but win the war"; it is not your task to win right away. To you is given the task of the fight itself, to show your willingness to win. The last victory is won with God's help. (1994, 107)

Melovitzky also uses (1994) war imagery to describe the daily struggle of the yeshiva student. As in other texts, the yeshiva student is called to fight a religious war in a modern secular city and to struggle with the evil inclination. To fight this war, the student is armed just as any other soldier would be. Melovitzky (1994), Wegshel (2000, 38–40), and other writers describe the warrior with heroic military qualities: "He starts a holy fire against his enemies"; "he is armed with a sword"; "he fights the most vicious battle against his own lusts" (against the possibility of becoming an animal); "he fights against the enemies of the nation" (against becoming a person without a nation or people). The struggle goes two ways: students act against their own impulses both to give Jewish morality and spirit to the secular modern realms and to thwart the enemies of the Israel, foes that threaten Judaism and the Jewish state. In this war, the yeshiva student is called on "to stand upright against his enemies," "to stand strong and firm on guard," and to learn how to use actual war tactics. For example, in *The Kindness of Your Youth* (Jeremiah 2:2), Friend asserts:

> In these moments when your desires are boiling hot, immense protection is needed. In these instances, we should not let the evil inclination do what it pleases. When it begins, you are seduced little by little, and your passion grows. Therefore, you should recite the words of the Torah, and they shall be sharpened like arrows in the hand of a war hero. . . . But you also must protect yourself from the external enemies entering the room, permitting them to speak with you only when they are outside. . . . Therefore all your battles will be fought outside, and there you shall thwart him and then you will conquer him. (1995, 160–61)

This quotation emphasizes a critical moment in yeshiva life, when a student's desires take over, and it describes them empathetically, as an experience of every yeshiva man. This is a critical moment in a young man's life when he is the most vulnerable and in the greatest need of protection and goodness. Those who triumph over the internal evil inclination, over lust and desire, must and will overcome any external interferences as well, which may come even from within the household. In both cases, and as a general rule of piety, study should be used as a weapon so that the "battles will be fought outside." A man who can do this will protect himself, his family, and the teachings of the yeshiva.

Because the student must concentrate on his inner battle, he is warned not to transform his inner struggle into violent behavior. This masculinity, which emphasizes inner struggle as heroism and not as physical violence, lies at the heart of Haredi ideology today. It can be demonstrated in the hidden connection between the outer consequences of the inner struggle and the seeming passivity of the Haredi warrior.

In *The Joy of the Torah* (*Rinat hatorah*), the author shares his views about boarding a bus in Jerusalem during a spate of suicide bombings:

> There I saw a yeshiva student sitting and learning a page of Gemara for its own sake, and I realized that only through this, his study, he has interrupted and prevented a suicide bomber from exploding and massacring people, even far away from him, and we realize that through his studies he has saved many souls in Israel and that only those who rise to heaven can understand this act and comprehend how the Torah provides life to its possessor. (Vaanunu 1998, 1)

Here the writer surmises that by reading the Talmud, that is, by doing the work of God, the student has prevented a suicide bombing and all other catastrophes. Seeing the young man reading makes the writer "realize" that learning is a way to engage with the way of war. He too has learned and passes on this learning on as further validation of the practical worthiness of Haredi studiousness. In the book *Enlighten Our Eyes* (*Veha'er eineinu*),[5] Goldsmith writes:

> Your way is the way of all wars; there is no war without injury. As in any other war, in which every soldier is at risk of dying, we do not know whether he will return dead or alive, but we do know that statistically some soldiers will die because we know that there is no war without risks, without death. . . . This is exactly the same with the war against evil inclination. It is clear that sometimes the evil inclination will win because there is no war without causalities, and although this is something that we must examine and respond to, it is not an indication of our weakness or victory. Real victory can be declared only at the end of the war, and he who actually determines the war is the winner. But as long as the war continues, sometimes one party will win and sometimes the other. (2004, 80)

Here again students are encouraged to fight a war like all other wars and to risk dying as soldiers in the Israeli Defense Forces do. The idea of giving in to the evil inclination is compared with the death of a soldier, a central theme in yeshiva books. Students are taught to struggle and win the war; death, like the death of a soldier, is considered heroic.

In Israel, the motif of the fallen soldier is a model of heroism and patriotism that is mainly restricted to Israeli men. Bereaved families have a special status in Israel, as they have made the ultimate sacrifice for the collective, giving their sons as part of the heroic national myth (Doron and Lebel 2003, 199). Haredi writers use the same motif to underscore the danger of death and heroism as well as the risk, sacrifice, and perseverance demanded of the yeshiva student and his contribution to the Jewish collective. In this way, they build their own trials of masculinity (cf. Ben-Ari 1998) and dramatize the students' fight, stressing heroic masculine features and warning against the consequences of failure.

The battle of the yeshiva student thus relates and refers to iconic dimensions in the discourse of Israeli manhood, such as military preparedness and war. Then, to reinforce the notion of potential damage and destruction that the evil inclination leaves in its wake, the struggle is compared with a serious physical condition, along with the use medical terms.

To be possessed by evil inclination is a serious mental illness that can be treated only by sacred means. In *Body and Society* (1988, 421) Peter Brown shows how sexual desires in early Christianity were repudiated using the medical terms of that period. He argues that framing sexual temptation and its treatment in this way also described a fearsome and debilitating trial, especially including the fear of the lingering power of male sexual fantasy that eroded the joy of the saints (1988, 422).

The Haredi writings that I analyzed use current medical terminology to define masculine piety. For example, in his interviews with Haredi men, Goodman describes their giving in to sexual desires, especially through masturbation, in terms of mental illness and the need for immediate institutionalization (1997, 47). Haredi books also use medical and scientific terms to explain how to fight the evil inclination and to employ medical strategies to cure the body and achieve male piety.

Many books demonstrate the sickness of the body through the vulnerability of the eyes. An infected eye is understood as resulting from a yeshiva man's sinful gaze. In *Enlighten Our Eyes*, Goldsmith cites doctors and experts to emphasize the basis for Haredi morality and philosophy (2004, 29). He uses scientific research and information to show that sinful thoughts can affect the memory and damage the eyes. The only way for the eyes to be worthy of transcendental rewards is to keep them closed and thus protect them from infections. Moreover, infected eyes are related to a student's most dangerous state: insanity.

A person who has left the Torah and become enslaved to the evil inclination is regarded as insane. A person who cannot resist the evil inclination has no future and no joy in life. He is destroyed, possessed by worlds of his imagination and fantasies, created by the evil inclination. The evil inclination forces the possessed student to violate his norms and rituals, and to behave in a self-destructive manner. He no longer can use his intelligence, which is what makes him a rational creature, but instead follows his lower instincts. This state is defined in many Haredi writings as a state of mental illness, underscoring the irrational nature of modernity. The Torah and yeshiva techniques and morality therefore are also techniques to protect and heal students, the only remedy for their insanity. A student who loses his mind can be treated only with the power of the texts.

Yeshiva Piety and Emotional Crisis

Along with the images of war and illness, images that are used to shock and dramatize the seduction and destruction of the evil inclination, I was surprised to find in the manuals a psychological discourse dealing with emotional crisis. This discourse explains the harmful results of the victory of the evil inclination over the student, which leads to suffering, depression, and despair. According to these texts, even though yeshiva students are likely to undergo an emotional crisis while studying, they are advised not to blame themselves. Rather, crisis is an inherent weaknesses and a medical emergency that requires extensive therapy.

In this sense and in this context, "crisis" appears to be a new phenomenon. One explanation is the yeshivas' fear of students—particularly the more sensitive and brilliant students—who may develop a sense of failure and unworthiness and consequently leave. Writers use common psychological terms such as *crisis, mental stress,* and *instability* to acknowledge the students' situation, as well as to name the problem and offer assistance (Y. Friedman 1997). In this way the students are encouraged to share their fears and learn that they are not alone. Here psychological strength is linked to the call to return to the yeshiva and continue God's work. This therapeutic terminology is used to reinforce the religious calling. A crisis therefore becomes a transitory, even necessary, cathartic experience that, with the correct treatment, can be cured. Many students told me how their crisis at the yeshiva affected their decisions and how they overcame it and returned to the yeshiva, even stronger.

Crisis is defined as the opposite of piety and masculinity and is a weakness that did not exist in previous generations of disciplined yeshiva scholars. Crisis is therefore identified as afflicting the new and exceptionally weak generation of students. Some writers explain that because students are now exposed more often to modernity and secularization, they are more likely to experience emotional crisis. In response, their books suggest new methods of coping with modern challenges.

An example is the book *The Soul of the Yeshiva* (*Nefesh ha-yeshiva*). The author, Yaakov Friedman, demystifies what he sees as the invention of a condition known as a student's emotional crisis:

> *Crisis*, this is a new word invented by this generation and newly introduced to the yeshiva vocabulary. *Crisis.* . . . This repulsive word did not exist when yeshiva students had "spiritual muscles" [*shririm nafshiim*]. Today these moments called crisis are the backbone of the student's soul. (1997, 241)

In this passage Friedman stresses that piety was always difficult to achieve but that at one time, students were spiritually more resilient. "Why do yeshiva students prefer the word *crisis*?" he asks.

> Because *crisis* is considered the most severe and desperate word in the Hebrew language because it means "spiritual escape," the "collapse of the personality onto the nearest spiritual stretcher" (*alunka nafshit*), and the wait for external forces to come and influence him. (1997, 241)

Emotional crisis also is defined as a result of the burden of long hours of study of complicated theological issues. Although Friedman (1997) holds to the old model, he tries to approach the new generation of students by expressing sympathy for their problems. He uses common psychological terminology for emotions, which is evident in the interviews as well. Even though he still describes the student's soul as weak and vulnerable, in order to return to God, his soul must be treated with new methods. My interviewees contended that the self should be treated with physical and emotional means and that the solitude of the yeshiva only softens the students' souls and weakens their spirits, making them more likely to experience emotional collapse.

Together with the psychological effort to help students in crisis, many books state that eating particular foods and observing proper eating behavior can improve students' concentration and physical well-being. In *The Soul of the Yeshiva*, continuing his demystifying move, Yaakov Friedman explains in clear scientific terms the importance of specific nutritional elements to improve concentration and motivation:

> After the morning prayer, men need food that contains protein, like eggs, meat, and fish, to prevent fatigue during the day. Many yeshiva students regularly suffer from physical fatigue and think this is a result of depression. But in fact they are tired because of a lack of protein. It is a pity to suffer so much from a problem that is so easy to treat. At breakfast and lunch, they should avoid eating carbohydrates, such as bread and baked and sugary foods, which have no nutritious value and are the main cause of tiredness. (1997, 244)

Here protein is used to explain the weakening of student's body. Caroline Bynum (1987) showed that in many ascetic cultures, food habits are linked to the construction of piety. Likewise, at the yeshiva, modern scientific approaches to food are used to enhance piety. In *The Soul of the Yeshiva* (1997), for example, Yaakov Friedman insists that the proper use of food can strengthen learning abilities and enhance concentration. That is, eating the right food can affect the student's Torah studies. Here again the focus is on internal issues of the body. Moreover, fatigue is just another manifestation of the evil inclination that causes the crisis and distracts students' minds from their purpose at the yeshiva. Therefore, it too needs to be addressed at a basic bodily level, such as through the students' diet.

Tiredness is often confused with depression, says Friedman, an expression used by students to explain their problems at the yeshiva. He, however, avoids this interpretation and instead uses scientific language to explain how nutritious foods can help cope with fatigue and improve learning abilities. Food can help keep the body functioning in order to fulfill sacred activities, especially concentration (Bynum 1987). In sum, a student's psychological crisis is seen as a misidentification of the underlying cause and understanding of the performance of the physical body and its durability.

Besides the relation of food to concentration and the ability to achieve piety, rabbis and students also acknowledge the importance of taking care of the physical body. The writers of students' manuals therefore encourage students to keep their bodies fit and to exercise regularly; this improves the brain's operation and produces better study results. Food and exercise are used to strengthen the body. Yaakov Friedman tells the following story:

> One of the greatest rabbis in a famous yeshiva told me that one of his brightest students came to him one morning brokenhearted. He confessed that he had a strong urge to get up, escape . . . and leave everything behind him . . . and ultimately leave the yeshiva. . . . The rabbi listened and instructed his student to run every morning for an hour in the open air. . . . This experiment turned out to be a wonderful thing. The student's spirits returned to him, he got stronger again, a deprivation was filled, and he was ready to dedicate his senses to the work of God. (1997, 245)

Yaakov Friedman here reveals the rabbis' worst fears, the possible desertion of their best students from the yeshiva, the triumph of the evil inclination. The purpose of his story is to show that what is called a crisis can beset even the most successful students and that they too can benefit from simple and seemingly spiritually unproductive exercise. Exercise not only raises the spirits and strengthens the body, but it also fills some felt deficiency, which, when satisfied, enables "the senses" to return to the study of the sacred. Friedman connects physical training to success at the yeshiva, and failure, to the lack of exercise:

> We all know how many students have fallen in their journey, just because no one told them that they need to work and fortify their bodies, to exercise constantly. . . . How many students have wrongly assumed that they did not belong to our world, only because their kidneys, lungs, and muscles did not receive their natural due . . . ? Physical exercise will not harm students—walking, training, and so on—some reflection on the health of the body. . . . We are called on to reinforce our souls with the spirit of the Torah; however, we also must protect our flesh, milk, and blood! (1997, 246).

This dualistic approach, endorsed by the rabbis, reflects new thinking in the fundamentalist struggle for piety. At the yeshivas, students have traditionally engaged in practices to prepare them for long hours of study, but physical exercise and physical work have always been discouraged.

This idea of fighting the evil inclination with activities that have a direct physical benefit thus marks a shift in the approach to piety that is evident in many aspects of Haredi life today. Among these changes is the presence of Haredi men at gyms, especially in Jerusalem. Gyms, which used to be out of bounds for Haredim, are now being remodeled under pressure from their Haredi clientele and according to their requirements. Alternative ideals of how to achieve piety have affected the manner in which Haredi men relate to and think about their bodies, and going to the gym is another way of using mechanisms that are not by nature necessarily textual or Haredi.

Conclusion

Men's physical, emotional, and spiritual struggle with the evil inclination is at the center of fundamentalist yeshiva piety. Today, however, in the yeshiva books and narratives, this religious struggle has been depicted using new images. War, with its vocabulary of weaponry, defense, attack, triumph, defeat, and heroism, must be waged on the evil inclination. This is war in the military sense, a fight against disease in a medical sense and along the psychological dimensions of crisis, all of which emphasize heroic piety and masculinity. Avoiding the transgressions and sins that modernity and the secular city make available forces yeshiva students to redouble their efforts to achieve piety.

Boyarin (1997, 3) discusses the metaphors used in early history to glorify Torah studies and argues that such metaphors as nursing, feeding, and giving birth and the comparison of Torah studies to the creation of life have been used to feminize the act of Torah studies and to glorify the ideal of pious masculinity. The process of studying has been connected to love, longing, and passion. Haredi writings cite the traditional texts that feminize Torah studies as an implicit counterbalance to the evil inclination, but at the same—and the first—time they use images of male soldiering and war, thus relating the struggle of the pious to the context of the Israeli state and its heroic masculinity. Furthermore, the body of the devoted student is defined as being (in) a battlefield, where he must act heroically to save not only his own body and soul but also those of the entire community, however defined. Studying the Torah thus is not only a practice of rebirth and regeneration but also an acceptance of a constant condition of war and soldierhood.

The sexual aspects of piety are accepted, and new, active, masculine images of the heroic ascetic warrior are reinforced. Moreover, piety is also related to the fear that the so-called crisis of the self, whether or not "real," will lead to the abandonment of the yeshiva life. This crisis is explained in psychological terms as an emotional rite of passage that, given the right treatment, will pass. Yeshiva life can be harsh, causing less emotionally robust or physically unaware members some fatigue and self-doubt, but these should on no account be confused with depression or insanity. Again, with the right treatment (using psychological tools), this can be cured. Therefore, the student must be taught to eat the right food at the right time and to exercise. Then he will be able to return to his sole duty to God: his Torah studies. During their interviews, the students reaffirmed this course of physiological, emotional, and spiritual treatment. They explained their struggle with the body and the temptations of the modern world as a difficult but necessary Haredi task and part of the current religiosity and mobilization. The students' overwhelming consent regarding the restrictions and treatments targeted at the body is particularly striking in comparison to their objections to those governing all other realms, such as work, the family, and the military, and was a rare instance of solidarity.

I began this chapter by asking why the idea of bodily restraint still is dominant in Haredi male piety. Why is it that these students, who are so critical of other aspects of their lives, agree with the concept of the evil inclination and how to counteract it? To answer these and other questions, I next turn to the feminist literature on fundamentalism. Although some differences in the model of the fundamentalist body and sexuality are apparent, the basic model as it was defined by the rabbis when Israel first became a state is now mostly accepted by members of the yeshiva world. The praxis of Torah studies is still considered the most powerful resource for men. Although body restraint requires much practice and is difficult to achieve, it is the only way that yeshiva students can maintain their dominant status in the community. Although the Israeli public at large does not appreciate these notions of Haredi studious heroism, within the Haredi world they still hold sway. Triumphing over the body and mastering the mind are still considered praiseworthy tasks and the only road to male sanctity and full piety. This is why students are reluctant to criticize, change, or even consider transforming these models of sexuality, because they represent their power and status. Compared with other resources, abstinence from sex and the control of the body still are basic categories of power and manhood in the yeshiva world. This category of piety, which is changing more rapidly in other realms, is the subject of the following chapters. The next chapter explores piety and the attitudes of yeshiva students toward work and livelihood. These illustrate the challenge to the basic assumptions of the sacred and the profane, which forms part of the transformation of traditional male piety in the yeshiva world.

4

Challenges to the Fundamentalist Denunciation of Work

Cast your burden on the Lord, and he will sustain you.
—Psalms 55:22

During a long interview with Abraham, a Lithuanian yeshiva student, about life in the study hall, he enthusiastically explained why yeshiva studies were more important than the labor market and why they were central to Haredi life. But when we asked him about the concept of work in rabbinical Judaism and the status of yeshiva students in Israel today, he criticized the current Haredi rabbinical authorities: "Some of us can study at the yeshiva hall and excel, but the demand that we all must stay [in the yeshiva] and not work is impossible. . . . The Haredi authorities are incompetent; they are afraid of change, which is why they also will destroy the future of many students."

These challenges to the traditional norms of masculine piety in the yeshiva world are the result of the younger yeshiva students' attitudes toward work. Following Max Weber, I see work and livelihood as basic components of modern society that are embedded in religious ethics and norms (Weber 1904/5), so I asked the yeshiva students to clarify their attitudes toward the Israeli marketplace and work in general.

Scholars have shown why fundamentalist groups adopt ascetic practices and withdraw from society in order to counter and reject the assumptions and products of late capitalism (Iannaccone 1998, 1465; Kuran 2004). Timur Kuran (1993, 2004) described the case of Pakistan, where the Islamic concept of charitable giving, zakat, has led to reform of the modern Pakistani banking system's policy on interest. Kuran argues that the Islamization of the banking system is designed to benefit Islamic devotees, moral individuals striving for common justice and equity. This Islamic piety is expressed through a model of pious manhood, able to rise above the constraints of the economic realm that define male power in the modern world. The religious elite uses hierarchy and power to reinforce sacredness and define the transcendental as being alienated from the economic and modern realms of entrepreneurship.

In the yeshiva world, too, excellence in studies is the most valued goal, one that promises no economic rewards. Any kind of economic involvement, such as investment or retail, belongs to the corporeal realism, the bodily and the earthbound, so occupying one's mind with business is inappropriate for men striving for piety. Accordingly, men in the working world are considered inferior to scholars in holy studies. The ideal model of the successful man is one who devotes his entire life to studying the Talmud and its exegeses.

In contrast, women are seen as naturally worldly and practical, and so they are put in charge of earthly needs, both in the home and at work. Wives are expected to support their husbands and families, and in Israel, the secular state also supports the yeshivas and the Haredi population in general.

Because the Haredi ideal model of religiosity is to withdraw from the secular sphere, it cannot include the practices and ideologies of the labor market. Even in a state that supports a capitalist market, entrepreneurship, industrialism, and commercialism, Haredi men follow this practice of withdrawal, using religious symbols and behavior to justify and deepen their rejection of work. However, even though the Hasidic, Lithuanian, and Mizrachi Haredim's concept of work varies traditionally and culturally, all Haredi sectors in Israel have accepted the traditional Lithuanian ideal of the dedicated yeshiva scholar.

Now, however, this decades-old rejection of capitalism and its modern work ethic is being challenged by Haredi students. They are in a double bind. On the one hand, they are attracted to the spiritual world of the Torah and divine guidance, with the physical and economic renunciation it entails. What was once the province of the few has become a traditional way of life, one that to a large extent defines this minority. On the other hand, the students now are protesting the ethic of total withdrawal from the profane, especially from the labor market, thereby implicitly internalizing the non-Haredi public's criticism of them: their unproductive life, poverty, backwardness, and lack of professional knowledge and training. The younger yeshiva students are uncomfortable with the ethos of economic withdrawal and exclusion from the Israeli market. So by challenging the fundamentalist models of work, they are calling for a new kind of piety, one that would combine the values of learning with the ideals of a livelihood and integration into the modern state's labor market.

While discussing work and livelihood in our interviews, most of the students told us that they had in mind a set of options (e.g., behavioral changes, job training, more choices of vocation) that would combine their work aspirations with their ideal of piety. However, in contrast to the shifts in family relations, the students' feelings about work do not seem to have been translated into practice.

Haredi Piety and Work in Israel

In a letter published in the Haredi newspaper *Hamodia*, Liraz, one of the readers and a new religious adherent, posed a question regarding work:

> I would like to know more about the Jewish attitude toward work. Presently I am faced with a difficult dilemma: On the one hand, I would very much like to abandon my formal workplace and dedicate myself only to Torah studies in the *kollel* [Talmudic seminar for married men] . . . in order to make amends for my past. I would like to study the Talmud full time. . . . I would like to obtain what I have missed by not receiving a thorough Jewish education, a sad result of my secular education in Israel. On the other hand, I am truly aware of my other religious duties; as a husband and a father, I am obliged to support my family. You must understand that my situation today is hard because earning a living takes up much of my time, and unfortunately my Torah studies are compromised. . . . I would like to learn more about two aspects: first, Jewish attitudes toward work and, second, ways to set limits between *bitahon* [trust in God] and *hishtadlut*, the endeavor that is permitted and necessary in life. (2000, 51, 8)

The newspaper's response, allegedly by a Haredi rabbi, quoted the official view of work accepted in Israel's Haredi community:

> Dear Believer, in sharp contrast to your past secular education, the Jewish faith does not view work as of high value in and of itself. . . . The socialist perception, . . . the idea that work is in fact a religious task, is not accepted in our texts today or in the writings of the sages. . . . While

Judaism has never ignored the importance of work and the necessity of labor as a central component of life, it did not regard work as a highly transcendent value. . . . Rather, it was explained as a penalty, a tax that humanity must pay for the sins of their ancestors. . . . Whereas those who have no faith see economic success as a result of individual human endeavor, the Jewish faith views hard work as a tool through which divine abundance transcends. . . . You, as a believer, must accept this notion and nothing else.

The letter writer's question reflects the continuing debate in the Haredi community between the imperative to work and the ideal of yeshiva learning. The official ruling is clear: Torah studies take priority over work. Worldly endeavors are not a value but a punishment inflicted on humankind since Adam and Eve's expulsion from Eden. Men must spend their life in intensive Torah studies even (or precisely) when they are faced with hardship or financial difficulties.

Even in the short reply to this letter, the ideology of withdrawal is interpreted as being in sharp contrast to the secular Israeli work ethic. This Haredi attitude is part of a backlash whose roots can be traced back to the Zionist revolt against the Haredi east European way of life, beginning in the late nineteenth century. The Zionists saw work, especially physical labor, as part of the creation of the new Israeli and Jewish interpretation emphasizing the utilitarian, functional, beneficial, and creative features of work (Eyali 1987).

The ideology reflected in the newspaper's response demands that members of the Haredi community stay out of both the labor market and military service. To institutionalize and justify their exemption, Haredi leaders established a new status using the Talmudic term *Torato omnuto*, "Torah study as a vocation."[1] Haredi members, as well as state institutions (especially the military and, later, the ministries of both religion and welfare), use this religious term to define the unique position of a yeshiva scholar who dedicates himself to Talmudic learning. The state's recognition thus permits the indefinite postponement of military service, the most important civil obligation in Israel. Once a young Haredi acquires this legal status, he returns to the yeshiva and is entitled to draw a stipend from the state to support his studies. If he stops studying, he will by law be eligible for military service, although this rarely happens.

According to various surveys of the Haredi community, between 46 to 60 percent of its members do not participate in the labor market, and

25 percent have part-time jobs (see Berman 1998; Dahan 1998). Members who work usually take specific jobs within a very narrow range of occupations, mainly those of teachers and clerical or administrative staff (Lupo 2003). In addition, because Haredim encourage large families, half of them live in poverty and economic distress (Berman 1998). Given their proximity to other social models, young Haredi men have come to consider themselves, and are seen by others in Israeli society, as unproductive and overly dependent on state support and on the work of others.

Despite this economic distress, yeshiva leaders have always rejected Israeli leaders' and educators' recommendations to make general and professional knowledge part of the yeshiva curriculum. The leaders' rejection has only compounded the difficulties of younger yeshiva students, who have conflicting beliefs regarding work and no skills for participating in the labor force. In addition, they lack the properties that constitute the modern work ethic: self-motivation, perception of time, competitive aspirations, and relevant technological and academic skills. Moreover, jobs available to men in the community are often defined as "enclave professions," mainly rabbinical and teaching positions, and as religious judges (*dayanim*), scribes, or heads of yeshivas. These positions are limited in number and usually pay low wages yet at the same time require a knowledge of textual studies, dedication, and leadership.

As a result of these economic pressures on the Haredi community in general and on the yeshiva world in particular, the Israeli state and a number of Haredi entrepreneurs (some of them with the support of rabbinical authorities) have created training programs to help Haredi men find work and support their large families (see Gonen 2000; Hakak 2006; Lupo 2003). This task of training Haredi men to work fulfills a strong need in the community to resolve its economic crisis.

Nonetheless, although these initiatives cater to yeshiva norms and ideals, most of them have failed and therefore have had almost no effect on the students' lives or the community. For example, the managers of some computer centers assumed that students who were used to long hours of poring over complex Gemara texts and fonts would easily adapt to working with computers and learning computer programming, information and communication technology (ICT), computer management systems, marketing, and communication. Because the yeshiva students already had developed study skills, the professional training required for suitable positions in the high-tech industry could be relatively short, they thought. But most of the training centers did not attract many yeshiva students, and those Haredi men who did attend courses came from the margins of Haredi culture (see Hakak 2006), so it had had almost no effect on their attitudes toward work and the labor market. Even though some of these centers were established with the support of Haredi leaders, they were condemned by most rabbinical authorities, who viewed ICT with suspicion. Thus, despite the difficult economic conditions, members of the community have few choices and must accept, for the most part, the traditional ideology of withdrawal and avoid all forms of training or future planning to participate in the Israeli labor market.

The economic situation of the Haredi community in Israel is unique. When comparing the Haredi community in Israel with that in the United States, Gonen (2000) found that Haredi members in the United States (both Lithuanians and Hassidic) work and participate in the labor market. But the integration of work into yeshiva studies in U.S. Haredi culture has not been successful in Israel. Members of the Haredi community in Israel view work as both an obstacle to spiritual life, which is of paramount importance in the Holy Land itself, and a danger to the enclave culture (Stadler 2002).

Investigating Work in a Nonworking Culture

Because work is a controversial issue for the Haredi community, in order to find out the students' views of work, I had to design an interview format that would enable me to ask questions that they would feel comfortable answering. I needed a method that would allow me to understand the students' religious interpretations of work. To do this, I chose, with my informant Rashi, a range of the principal texts concerning work and labor and their relationship to the ideal of devotion to the studious life and work for pay.

Rashi and I first discussed these topics and then presented them to the interviewees. By using canonical texts concerning work and livelihood, I was able to discover how the students interpreted the concept of work and how perceptions of work are reconstructed today. In other words, I interviewed the students by having them interact with texts of my choosing to which the students related as they would to any exegetical text—by applying further exegesis. I appealed to their desire to demonstrate their skills and knowledge as a way of easing the communication between us.

The interviewees interpreted a wide range of sacred sources and modern rabbinical texts, thereby enabling me to investigate diversities in their discourses about work. Throughout the interviews, I constantly inquired about the meanings and controversies derived from the texts, as well as their implications for the individual student's personal life. Because the students discussed these texts in detail, offering a range of interpretations, I was able to ask them about their own interpretations of the main aspects of their everyday life. These questions gave rise to a variety of interpretations, paradoxes, and criticisms of contemporary yeshiva norms.

To widen the scope of my analysis, I also collected numerous books, manuals, and journals, as well as children's books dealing with work-related issues.[2] Many of these texts have sections or chapters on work that relate to the problem of preparing for an occupation or learning how to deal with money matters. The popular texts published in the Haredi community also helped me understand how devotees justify their withdrawal from all forms of participation in the Israeli labor market and their personal criticism of work and piety.

The Haredi Fundamentalist Denunciation of Work

Asceticism and withdrawal from the labor market are perceived as missions that, without moving out of the communal enclave, still are difficult to accomplish, given the constant internal struggle against the evil inclination. The ascetic model offers various transcendental rewards, such as strong community ties, redemption, and the continuity of Orthodox Judaism. Yet under the economic and social pressures of the modern state, the question of how this ideal of withdrawing from profanity, and especially from work, is constituted in the community becomes more urgent, and the disturbance it causes, more visible. What are the arguments and justifications used to reinforce this ideal in the context of the modern state?

Many books for yeshiva students begin by recommending the total withdrawal from all economic activities and the dedication of oneself solely to Torah studies. In one popular book, *Son of the Torah and Yeshiva* (*Ben Torah ve'yeshiva*), the author begins by stating that a "person who considers Torah as his vocation [*Torato omnuto*] shall study all day long and abstain completely from profane work" (Schwartz 2000, 21; also see Schwartz 1978). He then exemplifies the need for withdrawing from the profane by telling the story of Rabbi Shimon Ben Yohai (a famous Jewish sage) and his followers, who are paragons of behavior for yeshiva students. Rabbi Shimon Ben Yohai "engaged with the Torah all day long, like the master artist who deals constantly with his art," implying that Torah study does not lead to learning a profession or a source of livelihood; instead, it is a vocation in itself: "The exemplary Jewish models always studied only for the sake of the divine" (Schwartz 2000, 21).

This book, like other books I examined, provides different examples of an important issue that concerns all yeshiva students who dedicate their time to studious activities: How can one survive without work? When answering this question, many Haredi writers use the Hebrew word *parnasa*, "livelihood," as opposed to the term appearing in the traditional canonical literature, *avodah*, which means both profane work, as well as worship, the work of the heart (*avodah shebalev*). These words were not chosen arbitrarily but were carefully selected to emphasize the path of the yeshiva student in Israel. By using the word *livelihood* (*parnasa*), Haredi writers separate the profane nature of work as toil from the artistic, divine, or transcendental characteristics of the labor of love, or worshiping the divine. Accordingly, toil is condemned as part of the corporeal realm (Stadler 2002). These writers often add a biblical reference to the narrative of the desert generation and the appearance of manna from heaven. In a popular instruction book for yeshiva students, *Building the World* (*Sefer binyan olam*), the (anonymous) author writes:

> Even though in Yirmiyahu's [the prophet Jeremiah's] times, there was no more manna coming from heaven, with all that, the nourishment to yeshiva students in all generations kept appearing as a miracle bound to fulfill all of their needs. . . . This is to prove to all Israel what the holiest blessed has ordered, to show all generations that the Almighty grants support only to those who dedicate their souls to diligence in studious activities. And if not always in the most superior manner as manna from heaven, his Providence exists in every generation in order to reduce his [the yeshiva student's] concern with work or the need for earning a living, livelihood. (1996, 200)

Even though contemporary times might not be as worthy of the miracle of divine manna, all yeshiva scholars are assured of a sufficiency, owing to their dedication to studious, contemplative activities. The author ends the paragraph with a claim of reassurance: As it was of old, so shall it now be: each Torah scholar will be the worthy recipient of the miraculous if he dedicates his life strictly to Torah-related activities. Studious activities make one worthy of the miraculous even in everyday life.[3] Doing ordinary, profane work thereby implies mistrust in divine Providence.

Members of the Haredi community often refer to the miracle of manna in the desert as a possible solution to their profane needs. Many of my interviewees mentioned stories about and references to miracles when we discussed conditions of economic anxiety, crisis, confusion, or moments of financial distress. During these moments, the students usually cited biblical narratives that included divine manifestation and works of wonder. For example, Hillel, a young yeshiva student from Jerusalem, explained the embodiment of manna when I asked him about abstinence from work. He was enthusiastic in his reply:

> You must understand that as explained in the traditional literature, our situation today is seen as manna from heaven. A person who has reached a high spiritual plateau, a position that is utterly dependent on God Almighty, materializes the definition of manna. This is a very high level of faith, like that of the people of the desert. You must understand that for us Haredim, the issue of manna is central to our everyday life. We ask, What is manna from heaven? Is it spiritual nourishment combined with the worldly experience? Is it worldly nourishment at all? And we say, if it were merely spiritual, it would mean that our Rabbi Moshe [Moses] never could have survived forty days and forty nights on it.

Hillel used the biblical metaphor of manna as indicative of the idealistic life expected in the Haredi community. When I asked him about the ideal life, he spoke of the possibility of being a contemplative soul fully dependent on God's divine guidance. Hillel stressed that he was willing to sacrifice everything in order to fulfill this ideal, and he used the story of manna to convince me and Rashi (who was present during this interview), that this situation was a biblical ideal.

Hillel explained that by devoting himself through his studies to the spiritual realm, the world of the Torah, he could become completely detached from all his bodily needs. Like Hillel, many students used the manna narrative to explain their experience at the yeshiva in a biblical spirit (the path to the numinous; see Otto 1917, terms). That is, detachment from the material world is considered necessary for yeshiva students to achieve full piety and maintain their position as an elite.

To reinforce the power of withdrawal, the yeshiva world has produced many popular texts regarding abstention from work and livelihood. The juxtaposition of the concept of work and the idea of the miraculous is nowadays emphasized in Haredi children's books, a new and flourishing industry in the community. Although the titles of many children's books contain the names of occupations, these occupations are from the Jewish villages of eastern Europe in the nineteenth century—carter, woodcutter, water carrier, milkman, butcher, tailor, carpenter, second-hand dealer, goatherd, fisherman, hunter—where Orthodox Jews had to work. In these popular books, dedication to Torah studies, fulfillment of the commandments, and unwavering faith carry miraculous, often material, rewards. Many Haredi books for children tell of men who left their jobs or businesses, dedicated themselves to Torah studies, and consequently were blessed by miracles and wonders. By setting the stories in the past and in a foreign land, the authors can stress the idea of Haredi sources and continuity and of the antiquity of the idea that "all of Israel" is the recipient of miraculous divine aid in times of need.

Some books contain illustrations of the blessing from heaven. in one, a righteous man (dressed traditionally) finds a jar full of gold in the sea; in another, a Haredi family is depicted in a room strewn with coins while more are raining down from the ceiling above. Such illustrations can be traced back to medieval illuminated manuscripts, such as the late-thirteenth-century Birds' Head Haggadah (folio 22v), in which two figures collect what look like multicolored coins while more round objects (and a quail) are being dropped by two symbolic hands, next to which, on both sides, appears the word *manna* in Hebrew (see Narkiss 1969, 96, plate 28).

This reference, whether or not deliberate on the artist's part, gives the viewer a visual association with manna in the drawing in the Haggadah, which is commonly reprinted in modern editions. The Birds' Head Haggadah is so named because the artist, respecting the Second Commandment, would not draw any "pictures" of beings created by God and so settled for human figures with birds' heads. In the Haredi children's books, however, this is not observed, indicating perhaps the importance of inculcating belief in divine Providence in children, even to the extent of representing human figures, and thus teaching children to rely on miracles concerning

מִסְפּוּרֵי צַדִּיקִים

כַּרְנָסָה מִן הַשָּׁמַיִם

סִפְרִיַּת מַחֲנַיִם

Figure 4.1. Cover of the Haredi children's book *Livelihood from Heaven,* one of a series of "stories of the pious." The illustration shows a miraculous shower of coins falling on a pious man and his family. Courtesy of Macahnaim Library©.

their future livelihood and to dedicate themselves to the Torah itself (see figure 4.1).

During the interviews, we frequently talked about texts and anecdotes of miraculous events, especially while discussing the necessity of working as a means of survival (see figures 4.2 and 4.3).[4] When I asked the students about the need to work in order to survive, they explained that God was the exclusive provider of earthly needs and that in their texts, the rabbis emphasized the need to abandon all forms of profane work, especially in secular modern settings. Both the rabbis and the students believe that the central tension in men's life is the contradiction between belief (*emuna*) and endeavor (*hishtadlut*). Here two images of the pious men are compared: the ascetic man who withdraws from profanity, and the active man engaged in the world and making an effort to change his own surroundings.

I asked Shimon, a young yeshiva student, to describe the ideal type of today:

> If you ask me, the ideal man in Judaism is reflected in the model of the first man: Adam. He sat all day doing nothing, believing that God would provide food for him without any effort on his part. But man is obliged to work, since this is his curse after sin, and it has to do with the compensation that man owes. Yet how much he will actually do in this world is not important. . . . It is not an effort for money, since you receive according to what you deserve, even without any effort at all . . . but you work in this world only in order to repay your transgressions.

In Shimon's view, Adam is Judaism's ideal man. He is a passive male figure: idle, he does not work, relying on God's will to fulfill his human

קְרִיאוֹת שִׂמְחָה פָּרְצוּ מִכָּל הַפִּיּוֹת:
"הַבִּיטוּ וּרְאוּ מַה נֶּהְדָּר!
הַשֵּׁם שָׁלַח לָנוּ אוֹצָר —
מַטְבְּעוֹת־זָהָב לָרֹב!
הֶאָח! כַּמָּה טוֹב!
שׁוּב לֹא נִרְעַב!
עֲשִׁירִים נִהְיֶה מֵעַכְשָׁו!"

Figure 4.2. From *The Water Carrier,* a Haredi children's book, an illustration of God sending a pious man a chest full of gold coins. Courtesy of Macahnaim Library©.

הוּא הִסְתַּכֵּל לְתוֹךְ הַמַּיִם וְרָאָה וְהִנֵּה
כְּלִי־חֶרֶס שָׁבוּר, מְכֻסֶּה עִשְׂבֵי מַיִם, מָלֵא
מַטְבְּעוֹת זָהָב וָכֶסֶף. הוּא חָפַר וְהוֹצִיא אֶת
כְּלִי־הַחֶרֶס, עָטַף אוֹתוֹ וְשָׂם אוֹתוֹ
בַּעֲגָלָתוֹ.

Figure 4.3. From *The Wood Cutter,* a Haredi children's book, an illustration of a pious man finding a jar full of silver and gold coins. Courtesy of Macahnaim Library©.

needs. He is carefree, restful, and unfruitful (see Brown 1988). My interviewees often used this interpretation of Adam and pointed out its similarity to the Haredi image of the ideal yeshiva scholar, also reflected in numerous Haredi instruction books: a masculine ascetic body striving to avoid sin and shame. The pious man is not expected to work or to engage in any physical effort. Instead, he must "repay his sin" and work for God in the study hall.

Maor states in his introduction to the Haredi book *The Believer versus the Actor* (*Hama'amin le'umat hamishtadel*):

Endeavor [*hishtadlut*] is the general word for efforts, cunning, or actions performed by man in order to improve his life, health, and economic and social condition. Endeavor is an obligation for all Jews and, according to some rabbinical figures, a commandment. The problem with endeavor is that it appears to contradict God's decree or will. . . . Different worldly endeavors appear to be useful to man in health, livelihood, and sexual and social relations. . . . That is why the individual, with his natural inclination to improve his status, is attracted to endeavor in these actions. But it must be clear to every devotee that what he receives will be according to his right, even without endeavor on his part. (1984, chap. 5)

Maor then denounces all aspects of work, which are part of the damaging logic of modernity and the Israeli marketplace, visible in the efforts and actions performed in order to improve human economic and societal conditions, in contrast to Haredi practices. Maor calls on yeshiva students not to be "men of action" in the world but to be "men of faith" seeking spiritual enrichment. He who works and strives to improve earthly conditions, Maor asserts, is an enemy of God and humanity in general, and his secular actions are sinful.

The students I interviewed reconfirmed this relation between work and penalty, also referring to the Genesis narrative. Shaul, a yeshiva student from Jerusalem, considered brilliant by his fellow students, observed: "The Haredi view would argue that work is a penalty for man's sin, a punishment. Work requires minimal involvement, so we have to reduce our engagement with these [worldly] affairs. If God provided us with everything, we all would be only players and this would be just a game."

Shaul claimed that since the days of Genesis, labor was inflicted on man as a curse, an idea that in turn contributes to the scorn for all work-related activities. Chapter 3 discussed the idea of sin embedded in men's actions. Because Adam and Eve's expulsion from the Garden of Eden to the work world was also to a barren landscape and because of the nature of the modern workplace, work is connected in Haredi society to the idea of seeing the outside world as a wilderness. That is, the workplace is a jungle requiring aggressiveness, which is fueled by sin and transgression (cf. Kimmel 1996, 55). Shaul used one of the letters of rabbinic approval printed in the foreword to Maor's book to justify this explanation:

The obligation to work for your livelihood and other earthly necessities is inflicted on man as a heavenly decree: "By the sweat of thy brow shalt thou eat bread" (Genesis 3:19). Man must see this as a tax that must be paid immediately and a curse that he cannot escape. (Maor 1984, 1)

According to this view, all worldly activities are related to the consequences of sin and are considered a burden, thereby forming a negative orientation toward the world.

In many books as well as in the interviews, this Haredi disdain for work also includes a concern for the consequences of the Holocaust. Writers and students explained that following the Holocaust, the relationship between work and learning had to be radically transformed. Because the world of the Torah was destroyed in the Holocaust, Jewish men have now been forced to reconstruct the destroyed yeshiva culture, a sacred duty of pious men that supersedes all other missions and tasks. As Shaul explained,

> Rabbis say that our generation is very unusual, and therefore we cannot learn from the experience of past generations. Because we are living in a period after the Holocaust, we are responsible for reconstructing the European Judaism that was destroyed by the Nazis. We also are living in times of secularization. Because most Jewish people do not practice religion, it has become our obligation to study.

Here Shaul is repeating the arguments made in many books meant for yeshiva students that discuss the Holocaust and the importance of rebuilding the institutions that housed the Torah and Judaism. By using the Holocaust as an explanation and motivation, the rabbis have added an existential, functional mode of reasoning that stresses the transcendental rewards for adherents of Haredi fundamentalism.

Students' Critiques of the Haredi Denunciation of Work

The denunciation of work has been a basic component of piety since the beginning of Haredi fundamentalism in Israel. When I asked the students who should enter the workforce, they cited women and foreign workers as possible alternatives to masculine labor. Even though contemporary Haredi texts regard work as an obstacle to redemption, most of the traditional Jewish canon has generally honored and valued it (Eyali 1987). Throughout history, the individual was thought to be invigorated by his involvement in worldly affairs and to be obliged to earn his own livelihood. The sages spent much of their time writing about the value of work, especially manual work, and the rabbis viewed work as an integral part of life and a place where Jewish ethical concerns could be realized (Eyali 1987). Nonetheless, the Haredi leadership, like that of most fundamentalist movements, chose to emphasize marginal interpretations of the tradition when denouncing work (Stadler 2002).

Yeshiva students are aware of the more traditional canonical interpretations of work as being valuable and necessary. But they also accept the notion that they live in a unique historical period that requires different forms of religious devotion. Although the students did acknowledge the centrality of the Haredi models, they also expressed frustration, distress, and apprehension over this subject. Most of their criticism was of the community's current leaders and of what students see as these leaders' inability to instigate changes.

Shlomo was studying at a yeshiva in Jerusalem when I interviewed him. When I asked him about the yeshiva students' renunciation of work, he criticized the religious elite and emphasized the need to change the community's interpretation of work:

> Our leaders don't want to create alternatives. . . . They would prefer that we experience distress and confusion, but they will not try to make changes or reform our situation. This is why I think that changing the yeshiva ideal is not a task for regular people but only for a great leader. . . . Let me tell you why. Because today changes would be very dangerous, and our leaders are well aware of this. . . . Consequently, they are afraid . . . afraid to change and destroy the community . . . destroy what our founders created. . . . This is why they prefer to preserve the situation as it is . . . and this is why many problems arise, for example, economic distress, educational problems. . . . This is why we have problems with students who can't deal with the yeshiva lifestyle, who cannot deal with this ideal, but then cannot look for work in the Israeli market.

During the interview, Shlomo claimed that the current leaders of the Haredi community were not capable of reform and thus were fully responsible for the economic plight and condition of yeshiva students like himself. He expressed his frustration with his own economic future and was reluctant to rely on family support, state stipends, or women's work. Shlomo was the first to describe the rabbis' fear of changes in the area of work, pointing to a problem that many students raised: the inability of many students to achieve the pious ideal demanded by the yeshivas leaders, and the limited options that yeshiva ideology offers them. Interestingly, in his critical remarks, Shlomo and others did not use biblical or exegetical parallels.

Many interviewees expressed a fear of poverty and of a future of even greater hardship and dependency. They felt that this problem was part of the rigid interpretation of yeshiva ideals that provides no solution for their current financial needs. The yeshiva students claim that these demands for strict conformity to the Haredi work norms have resulted in unbearable conditions for Haredi families. During the interviews students expressed great concern about their future families and hoped that their leaders could find practical solutions to the problems of not having a livelihood. Pinhas, a yeshiva student from Jerusalem, noted the tension between yeshiva piety and work:

> In previous generations, a rabbi with five sons could send one of them to the yeshiva and the others to work, and each one could find his way. . . . One might be a shoemaker, one a glazier, and another a doctor. . . . Today that is impossible. . . . The truth is that the Torah does not say that everyone must sit and study all day long, from morning to night. . . . It is true that nowadays we, the Haredi public, are a minority that is forced to take on the burden of Judaism because many people have left, but we pay a high price for this load, we pay too much for this ideal, we send all our men to the yeshiva, knowing that only one will succeed.

Pinhas was considered one of the best students in his yeshiva, trying to fulfill the model of piety and spend most of his time at the yeshiva hall. But when I asked him about his future profession and how he planned to support his family, he rejected the yeshiva's norms. First he laid out what he viewed as the community leaders' extreme interpretation of the community today with regard to work and expressed his discontent with them. Pinhas then singled out yeshiva asceticism as an impossible goal that took a high toll on the students. The fact that the Haredi minority had to assume by itself the burden of Judaism seemed unrealistic to him. Pinhas compared this situation with that of men sent to be killed in war, of whom only a few would return. He continued with a reflection on the yeshiva masculinity by defining current yeshiva piety as a sacrifice:

> We're talking about an ideal that belongs to a traditional worldview: a view that will not let the individual face his life alone, a culture that protects its members by asking young men to sit in the yeshiva. . . .This is how they defend you from the streets. . . .They just help you to escape

reality; . . . they ask for isolation, blindness; they ask you not to read, not to know, not to ask. . . . That's why work is considered going out to the streets . . . and this is forbidden, he must abstain from work . . . not because of the ideal to study, but because of fear, from the streets, secularity, and secular institutions.

Many of my interviewees made this criticism. Pinhas regarded yeshiva piety as deprivation, a sacrifice with few rewards for students. Although he recognized the traditional transcendental rewards of yeshiva asceticism and its contribution to maintaining Judaism, he complained of the isolation from Israeli civic life and culture. Pinhas maintained that the leaders of the yeshiva world were so occupied with keeping its boundaries "pure" that they had failed to address the changing needs and economic anxieties of most members. This left many in this generation trapped without options, which many interviewees described as the dangerous trap of yeshiva life, a complicated problem with no solution in sight. In his criticism, Pinhas contended that rabbis and leaders of the yeshiva world forbade work and participation in the secular workforce for the wrong reasons: "not because of the ideal to study," whose motivation was a theological necessity for piety, but in order to reinforce the walls of the enclave in "isolation," "blindness," and "fear."

One of the most common problems that the interviewees brought up was the lack of secular training or planning for the future. Yosef, a yeshiva student from Jerusalem, pointed out the limitations for students like himself:

Today, you can't go out and simply study law or medicine; a yeshiva student can find only illegal work [unreported income] in temporary jobs. He cannot turn to any professional or academic institution, as it would be considered a sin by the Haredi rabbis . . . if he decided to do it. . . . It would be like abandoning the community, . . . as it would mean that he was no longer a member of the Haredi community.

Work is thus interpreted as a sin, penalty, or profanation, and studying material other than sacred studies is an exclusionary act of desertion. Yosef spoke of an existential dilemma with regard to work. Even if a student wanted to work or study outside the yeshiva, he could not, as the state stipend is granted only to full-time yeshiva studies, a status that does not allow men to work legally. Therefore, most of the work possibilities available to yeshiva students are marginal, temporary, and low-skilled jobs. Consequently, in contrast to his elite status in Haredi society, the ye-shiva scholar finds himself at the bottom of Israel's hierarchy of work and professions.

Yosef, like many other students I interviewed, felt that it was the de-liberate opposition by Haredi leaders that was preventing students from learning about and, in some measure, participating in other fields. He seemed to be suggesting that they needed to pay attention to the students' demands and provide them with marketable skills and knowledge. But Yosef doubted that this would ever happen, as it would mean abandon-ing the enclave and destroying the yeshiva. Like many others, he viewed the current Haredi economic situation as an impasse between an ideology emphasizing isolation, on the one hand, and a need to survive economi-cally, on the other. Students did turn to their rabbis for help, but as they explained, the rabbis were afraid to change this attitude toward work, as it might destroy the community and its already fragile borders.

When I asked Naftali about this tension between piety and livelihood, he accused the rabbis of working against the youngest generation. He claimed that the rabbis' views of strict piety limited all possible access to the labor market, not because of pious aspirations, but because of fear of losing control and power over men in the community. Banning work and secular knowledge was a way to maintain power over the youngest gen-erations. This is also how Naftali explained the ban against computers and the Internet in Haredi homes: "Why do you think they [the religious au-thorities] fight the use of computers in the community . . . ? Because they are afraid of losing the control they have now over yeshiva students. . . . Every profession other than being a teacher, scribe, or rabbi is forbidden because of the same reason, the fear of losing control."

According to Naftali, computers, seen as a route to freedom, are pro-hibited because of the rabbis' fear of what the yeshiva students would do if they were not restrained. Restrictions on piety are interpreted as the rab-bis' way of controlling the students. The fear is thus explained as deriving not from technology and its uses per se but from the freedom, autonomy, and choice that technology offered to young men.

In many interviews, the students described this situation as causing impossible tensions for them. Shlomo spelled out what it was like to try to provide for a family with no professional training:

> You begin your professional life as a teacher; you need money, so you
> work "illegally;" you do not report to anyone. But then you reach the age

of thirty-five, thirty-seven, and you already have at least five children, so you are exempted from the army and you are prepared to work and you need to support your family . . . but you have no professional training or knowledge. [Your] yeshiva education did not provide you with any of these skills . . . so you look for shortcuts that can give you the education you need: short-term computer training, courses for career retraining, and so forth.

Students see the constraints of work and piety as not only limiting their life decisions but also having an immediate effect on them. By not permitting work and training at the yeshiva, the students are indirectly led to, for instance, illegal work and makeshift training. Many students were aware of this and suggested possible solutions that the religious authorities could offer to help them overcome their economic difficulties. As Moshe suggested:

If you offer them [yeshiva students] work that allows them to study, they will probably take it. . . . Our leaders can discuss this with the minister of labor and find a good solution for Haredi men. . . . They can work in the yeshivas; they can use computers or microscopes or something; and just as when they sit and learn [the Torah], they can work and make a living. . . . In that way they can start off the morning with a prayer and then work.

Moshe listed yeshiva students' various opportunities to work in the Israeli labor market, especially in computers or science. He recommended that Haredi leaders discuss these problems with the relevant state representatives.

From these narratives, we may infer that the younger generation is no longer satisfied with the transcendental rewards of the fundamentalist yeshiva. Many students challenged the ideal of male asceticism and protested their exclusion from this-worldly rewards. They expressed a strong desire to work and to provide for their current or future families. They were uncomfortable with the need to rely on state stipends and charity and even were worried about their future. They pleaded with their leaders to be more active and reinterpret work to suit their new demands. In the students' view, as an institution the yeshiva had to change in order to give the students opportunities to incorporate religious values in their work world or to choose other means of fulfilling the Haredi life.

Yeshiva students worry that their education will not enable them to join the labor market and that they have no alternative but to remain in the yeshiva or look for positions in their community as teachers or other religious-based positions (e.g. religious judges, kosher food supervisors). Whereas the traditional thinking was based on surviving without working, justifying this position by their yeshivas' unique historical position, the younger generation today wants to combine religious work with a livelihood, in opposition to the teachings inculcated in them since childhood and without seeing them as incompatible.

But how can a yeshiva student be prepared for the labor market if he studies only the Talmud most of his life? And how can the yeshiva change? The justification for declining work in favor of studying still is powerful and dominant in the community. Although repeatedly asked, students could not come up with many practical solutions. More important, I did not see these criticisms materialize into a groundswell for any kind of reform.

Conclusion

In the yeshiva world, work is a source of tension and criticism. The denunciation of work is thus a central feature of Haredi piety, and its structure remains constant: work is an obstacle to yeshiva studies, which alone can provide the path to redemption. Work thus exhibits a distrust of divine oversight. The rabbis have reinforced the withdrawal from economically productive activity through the use of such canonical texts as "Cast your burden on the Lord, and he will sustain you" (Psalms 55:22). Haredi ideology denounces work, and by forgoing the option to be productive, male members are controlled by the rabbis, and community boundaries are protected and reinforced, which results in the students' economic dependence, physical passivity, and isolation from Israeli society.

The Haredi denunciation of work is currently being contested by a new generation of yeshiva students who are resisting the traditional model of piety rooted in a text-based male asceticism and the founders' otherworldly orientation. That is, students are questioning the viability of the Haredi masculine model for everyday life in contemporary Israel and its continuity.

Despite their criticism and discontent, the students have not yet offered any alternatives. In contrast to other areas discussed in this book, such as military service, volunteerism, and gender roles, students have few solutions to this predicament. Although they acknowledge that there are few economic options, they have not been able to propose a solution that combines both material needs and religious piety. When I asked the students about alternatives to yeshiva studies and how they viewed the possibilities of integrating professional studies into the yeshiva's curriculum, they evinced discomfort. Going to work would be the end of their role as the interpreters and protectors of the Jewish faith and of their privileged status. It would be a radical departure from generations of belief and practice and be a rebellion of sorts against Haredi solidarity. This may be why the students have shown so little willingness to acquire professional skills, just as they seem indifferent to the most prestigious professions and jobs in the Israeli labor market.

The students have yet to offer solutions that could change the Haredis' current attitude toward work and that would alleviate their personal and family hardship. Until they do, therefore, yeshiva students will report feeling trapped, remaining faithful to the denunciation of work promulgated by the founding rabbis of the contemporary Haredi community and loyally awaiting initiatives from their rabbis and leaders. The next chapter describes a different model of piety being offered by yeshiva men in their attitudes toward the military, combat soldiers, and militarism.

5

The Idealization of
Soldiers' Masculinity

And the officers shall speak unto the people, saying: Who is the
man who has built a new house and has not begun living in it?
Let him go and return to his house lest he die in the battle and
another man begin living in it.

—Deuteronomy 20:5–7

In contrast to the practices of withdrawal associated with
work, a model of piety is being constituted in the yeshiva that includes an
idealization of soldierhood and this worldliness.

The Haredi disapproval of military service in Israel is a modern development, formulated by the community's founding fathers during the
post–World War II establishment of the community in Israel. Military
service is compulsory for most Jewish Israelis over the age of eighteen,
except for members of the Haredi community. And as explained in chapter 4, during the three years when most Israeli men construct their sense
of identity and selfhood through military training and war (Ben-Ari 1998,
58; Ben-Ari and Lomsky-Feder 2000), Haredi men reinforce their body
discipline and mortification through Talmudic training and yeshiva socialization. To them, true Jewish sacrifice and piety can be achieved only
in the yeshiva and not through interference in God's plans, as in affairs
of state. This Haredi resistance to military service is one of the tools by
which the community maintains its ideology and practice of separation
from state affairs, which is a key principle of fundamentalist ideology in
general (Ammerman 1987, 3). The Haredis' rejection of military service
also is part of their general denial of the Israeli secular state and its institutions (Almond, Appleby, and Sivan 2003; Eisenstadt 2000).

This rejection of military service in the Israeli Defense Forces has led to frustration and resistance. Through their reflections on the model of the combat soldier, young Haredi students have reconstructed their model of piety and fundamentalism, and contrary to the traditional view of yeshiva piety, they have expressed a desire to participate in the military and be part of the state's renowned band of warriors. Accordingly, yeshiva students reject the rhetoric of exclusion and instead subscribe to a piety with inclusive hegemonic images, practices, and models of masculinity taken from the dominant secular and Zionist culture.

Images and models of soldierhood are central to Israeli culture. Israeli men are expected to fight or to be prepared to fight, to enlist for military service, and to undergo military training, renewed periodically throughout their adult life in the reserves (Ben-Ari 1998; Morgan 1994, 166). In non–Haredi (including religious) Israeli society, Jewish male identity is formed by their service in the military and by the language of war and struggle, making the IDF a means of achieving and affirming manhood (Ben-Ari 1998, 112).

Even before the Israeli state was created, scholars claim, the demands for heroism, valor, and self-sacrifice were reinforced by leaders and presented as a contrast to the image of the helpless, effete Jew of the Diaspora. Combat was glorified, and strength, courage, endurance, duty, male fraternity, risk taking, and heroic sacrifice became part of the narrative of legitimizing and building the Jewish nation (Ben-Ari and Lomsky-Feder, 2000). The frequent wars and terrorist attacks in Israel became "objective" support for these qualities but also occasioned a counterreading, an exchange of cause and effect, leading to criticism and pacifistic worldviews. The Second Lebanon War (the official Israeli title) in the summer of 2006 and its political consequences reinforced these militaristic ideals of heroism and security politics in all aspects of Israeli life.

Yeshiva piety was constructed as a response to this Zionist ideology, which created the image of the diasporic Jew as its Other. Although yeshiva piety was constructed as an exception in Israel—a reaffirmation of the excluded Zionist Other—by now militarism has infiltrated and influenced it. According to the official Haredi view, the military is dangerous and contaminated. Haredi leaders were concerned that service in the military would undermine the ideals of ascetic yeshiva life, blur community boundaries, and even threaten the existence of the Haredi community. Therefore, members who defy these strictures and join the military are seen as all but lost, undoubtedly exposed to temptation, and defeated by the transgressive nature of modernity and secularization. Until recently, breaking away from the fundamentalist enclave to join the military was considered a violation of the sacred, a sin that would ultimately result in the eradication of the Haredi community and Judaism at large.

The exemption from military service granted to Haredi members is a controversial issue in Israel. In a society with a strong military ethos, in which the army is a central force that influences the country's economy, politics, and culture, outsiders see the Haredis' refusal to serve in the military as exclusionary, anti-Zionist, and antistate. Most of the Israeli public actively opposes this exemption, rejects its theological justifications, and protests its expansion and institutionalization (Stadler and Ben-Ari 2003). The political and theological representatives of the community, loyal to the basic Haredi separatist ideology and principles of fundamentalism, resist all political and civil initiatives to alter this agreement with the state. Given this conflict, young Haredim have constructed new models that combine piety and manhood, idealize soldierhood, and reflect a yearning to participate fully in Israeli society.

Haredi Military Exemption in Israel

Jewish law (*halakha*) recognizes a number of categories of war and the conditions under which exemptions from military service may be obtained (Bleich 1983, 3). But in the rabbinical tradition, there are no theories of war (Walzer 1996, 95), and war has only rarely been the subject of Jewish critical and theological reflection. According to Michael Walzer, this situation is a consequence of the meaning of exile: "Historically, Jews are the victims, not the agents, of war, without a state or an army, they are also not the theorists of war" (1996, 96). In modern Israel, the citizens, mostly Jews, have needed to establish a large regular and reservist army in order to protect themselves. The situation in Israel thus necessitated a modern rabbinical reformulation of the requirement to serve in the military and defend the Jewish state. The question of the Haredis' participation in the military and their relations with the nation-state have been the subject of much debate at various periods, most notably during and immediately after the 1948 war for the establishment of the Israeli state. In contrast to other Jewish groups in Israel, especially the Zionist religious sects, Haredi leaders decided that in order to revive and reinforce the Haredi culture after the Holocaust, they must keep their members in the yeshiva and out of the army. The Haredi ideal of masculinity and piety thus could be attained only through a life of abstinence, ritual, and profound study, rather than by fighting in wars and otherwise defending the secular state.[1] During the 1948 war itself, however, Haredim fought shoulder to shoulder with other soldiers in the defense of Jerusalem, which was accepted because of the exigencies of the times.

After the state of Israel was established, Haredi leaders led the struggle against military service for yeshiva students in particular and for Haredis in general. Drafting Haredi men into the military was a controversial issue, and the Hazon Ish asked David Ben-Gurion, then the prime minister, also to exempt Haredi women from military service.[2] Haredi leaders argued that in addition to protecting itself, the Jewish state had a duty to reconstruct the world of the yeshivas and to revive the Haredi community, which had been almost entirely destroyed in the Holocaust (see Ilan 1999, 7). Ben-Gurion granted a postponement to four hundred Haredi yeshiva students, which eventually led to a permanent exemption.[3] Since the decision to exclude the Haredi entire community, both men and women, from the military, the recruitment of Haredi youth has been a constant source of debate (Stadler and Ben-Ari 2003). Then the reinforcement of yeshiva culture during the 1950s and 1960s further deepened the tensions and conflicts between Haredim and non-Haredim on issues of the military in particular and on the Haredis' reluctance to participate in civic duties in general.[4]

The exemption of Haredim from the military is one of the main and most complex issues dividing Haredi and non-Haredi society in Israel. As Stuart Cohen (1997, 1999, 396) notes, the primary importance of Haredi exclusion is symbolic: when large numbers of Haredim choose not to participate in what is regarded as the most significant of all national duties in Israel, they reinforce their marginal status, leading to resentment by all Israelis whose family members do serve in the military.

After the elections of 1977, which brought a right-wing, traditionalist coalition to power for the first time in the country's history, Haredim became more involved in the government, and the contradiction between state duties and community interests came to the fore (M. Friedman 1993). On the one hand, Haredi leaders demanded exemption from military service and other civic duties, while on the other hand, rabbis sought active intervention in all state affairs. During the 1990s, resentment of the Haredis' refusal to join the military mounted, resulting in the establishment of the Tal Committee in August 1999 to reconsider the Haredi exemption. In addition, the NACHAL Haredi, a special combat unit made up of Haredi men, was created as an option for Haredi men who wished to join the army and still maintain their ultra-Orthodox lifestyle (Drori 2005; Hakak 2003).[5] This segregated battalion, formed with the blessing of some rabbis and with the dire warnings of others, inducts about sixty Haredi men a year, mainly yeshiva dropouts, whose dietary and religious needs are supplied by their rabbis.

Several political parties oppose what they see as the state's overly generous attitude toward the Haredim and the yeshivas. In 2003, the newly formed Shinui Party became the third largest in the Knesset, elected on a platform that targeted what it considered the state's preferential treatment of the Haredi sector and yeshiva institutions. Shinui's position was that because Haredim are not Zionists, do not spend three years serving their country, and do not risk their lives, the state should reduce its support of the Haredi community, particularly of the educational system, cut back the stipends for yeshiva students, and abolish the military exemption. Shinui's success was short-lived, however. Remaining true to its founding principles, the party refused to compromise, soon found itself in the political wilderness, and vanished in the following elections.

Currently, yeshiva students in Israel comprise a population of more than seventy thousand (see Schiffer 1998, 11), and the Tal Committee estimated that these numbers would rise (Ilan 2000, 340).[6] Accordingly, the committee ruled that Haredi yeshiva students decide at the age of twenty-four whether they wished to remain in the yeshiva or leave and obtain employment after a short period of military or civic service.[7] Most Haredi authorities regarded these recommendations as catastrophic and threatening the community's very existence. To date, the Tal Committee has had only limited success, and only a few Haredi men have been recruited (Drori 2005).

After these recommendations were made public, most Haredi authorities called on yeshiva students to devote themselves exclusively to their sacred duties alone and to disregard the country's appeals. Posters (*pashkevils*) in Haredi neighborhoods reminded yeshiva students that the community's principles opposed the state's demands. The following is an example:

> The loud cry of the boys' souls, seduced into extermination in the army, rises to heaven. Inconsolable parents cry and mourn the souls of their trapped beloved sons. Heaven calls on us to act with all our strength for the sake of the souls of Israel, so that they will not be destroyed in the army.

The official instructions to yeshiva students were clearly stated and distributed through a popular booklet entitled *The Tal Law: A Trap for the People of Torah*.[8] In it, the rabbis explain that Haredi men are obligated to God alone, not to the state or its agents, which constantly "plot against the fortress of Torah" (2001, 4). This book, and other publications, stresses that students of the Torah must purify their souls through the Torah alone and "not . . . fall into the evil hands of those seeking to destroy Judaism" (see Y. Cohen 1993).

Soldiers of the Lord: The Fundamentalist Ideal

In 2001, while walking through the streets of Me'ah She'arim, a Haredi neighborhood in Jerusalem, I came upon a huge poster saying: "Commit suicide! Be all that you can be in the NACHAL [the Haredi unit]."[9] The farther I walked in the neighborhood, the more posters and signs I saw opposing yeshiva students' enlistment in the Israeli army. Other posters declared: "Yeshiva youngsters are being killed in the army"; "A holocaust is at our doorstep"; "We should draft all members of our community to save our boys from death in the army!" These posters were portraying the military as a superfluous realm of action that would bring illness and sin, in sharp contrast to the sacredness of yeshiva life. A detailed explanation was given in the Haredi poster entitled "Captured by the Words of the Blessed Torah": "This afternoon, dozens of yeshiva students went out to oppose the impurity of the instigators that seduce young Haredi boys into joining the army." The poster describes the state's fraudulent drafting of students and the naïveté of the young Haredim who are tempted to enroll as "mercenaries of apostasy":

> When our students arrived at their destination, they were shocked! They watched innocent Haredi boys being put in trucks that were about to transport them to the "gas chambers" of the "NACHAL" to be exterminated. The students who saw this pleaded with the instigators to have mercy and spare the boys' souls, and begged the boys not to be tempted to sin. One of the boys consented and even got into a taxi to escape their hands, but these evil minds stopped the taxi and took the boy and his belongings back to the truck again.

In this dramatic description, the symbols of the Holocaust are used to show military enlistment as an act of coercion against Haredim. The army is compared with the Nazi concentration camps, and the drafting of Haredi boys is compared with the Nazis' methods of exterminating Jews: Haredi texts commonly use terms of deception, gas chambers, and human transports to describe the state's intervention in their world.

This poster concludes with another allusion to the Holocaust. The yeshiva students who followed the "innocent" boys to their military base watched them from a distance and commented:

> It is enough to see the conditions of the boys who are already in the army, to understand the meaning of contamination, and the abyss into which they have fallen. The Haredi community in Israel will not sit back while its purity is tested and watches the sacred being violated.

The announcement ends with a general call to all Haredim to reject the decree and struggle against the enlistment of yeshiva students.

Although posters usually reflect Haredi sentiment, they do not show the variety of Haredi positions on the issue of military service. In order to further understand the meanings of the fundamentalist rejection of military service, I looked at popular instruction books that the community's rabbis distribute to yeshiva students. These manuals instruct students in the behavior and moral standards required of them in the yeshiva world and community. Because they focus chiefly on the obligation of all male members to study the Torah, these books rarely deal directly with questions regarding the army or military service. Generally, though, the books reinforce the fundamentalist ideology of asceticism in order to defend the enclave against the ills of modernity. Nevertheless, they do deal at least indirectly with military issues and tell the community members how to respond appropriately. In these books, students, *bnei Torah*, are defined as other-worldly soldiers, that is, spiritual warriors of the Israeli people who protect the Jewish people and enhance its spiritual aspects (Stadler and Ben-Ari 2003).

The writers of these yeshiva manuals maintain that for believers, the Israeli soldier is not a valid model, yet they compare the ascetic endeavor with the tasks of the combat soldier. Nonetheless, the sacred task fulfilled by Torah study in the yeshiva must be clearly separated from earthly endeavors. Because joining the military implies acceptance of modernity and secularization, it is a sin and thus an agent of destruction. The authors of moral instruction books condemn participation in military activities because war encourages war; the only way to halt this vicious circle is to study the Torah.

For example, in the book *The Believer versus the Actor* (*Hama'amin le'umat hamishtadel*), Rabbi Menachem Zeev Maor writes:

> The only way to prevent Israel from fighting with the Gentiles is by study-ing the Torah. Doing this reduces the chances of Heaven's decreeing war, so no harm will be done. Conversely, becoming a soldier and fighting in the army, especially if this comes at the expense of studying the Torah, will not help win the war because wars are actually decided by God. En-emies are sent or held back by God. (1984, chap. 8)

Here avoiding war depends on religious devotion and awe, which are the products of male yeshiva asceticism. Any distraction from their sacred work leads to disease, and profanation results in war and disaster for the Jewish people. The religious authorities defined the first Gulf War as "a divine rebuke for the secular arrogance of contemporary Israel. . . . God was reminding Israel that its rightful role is not waging war but having faith in the eternal protective power of God" (Selengut 1994, 246). This rationale, emphasizing God's intervention, explains Iraq's reluctance to at-tack Israel in the second Gulf War. "Drafting 'Bnei Torah' into the Israeli armed forces, forcing them to give up full-time study, would bring disas-ter upon the Jewish state" (Selengut 1994, 245). It is important to note that the Haredi explanation of war as resulting from the abandonment of To-rah studies does not erode Haredi support for intensive military activity in the occupied territories, and the general Haredi approval of the army's actions during the intifadas and the recent war in Lebanon.

The militaristic discourse of the secular majority has infiltrated Haredi rhetoric. The rabbis themselves are familiar with the criticism regarding the religious exemption from military duties, yet at the same time they understand the difficulties of persuading young Haredi boys to fulfill a religious model that is other-worldly in nature and has few physical or earthly rewards. They compensate for this contradiction by creating a model of the heroic yeshiva student based on a secular image of an Is-raeli combat soldier. Haredi writers equate the importance of the asceti-cism required by the Jewish tradition with the popular image of the Israeli soldier to claim that both models are equally important. The hard work of the student, overcoming the evil inclination and living a pure life, is like that of the soldier preparing to defend the Jewish state. Both yeshiva students and combat soldiers are represented as active agents of Judaism who are constantly engaged with the protection and well-being of the Jewish people; both male fraternities are equally devoted to their mission and willing to sacrifice themselves for the Jewish people and the state. In fact, the yeshiva student's struggle against the evil inclination is described as even more difficult than being a soldier.

For example, in the *Guide for Yeshiva Students* (*Sefer hadracha le-ven yeshiva*), a popular manual for yeshiva students, Aharon Melovitzky describes the war of the *ben Torah* against the evil inclination as the most difficult and courageous war of all:

> The temptation of lust is lurking at your door day and night, every hour, knowing that when it captures you in the net of passion, you will be completely controlled by it, and you will be like a prisoner captured in its hands, . . . since its wish is to confuse and humiliate you, to depress you until you despair of your loss of all the things spiritual and until you have concluded that all your efforts were in vain. (1994, 196)

Haredi rabbis describe the army—the site of the ultimate profanity and unruliness—as a device used by the state to seduce students into abandoning the community and destroying its boundaries. By joining the army, they fear, Haredi men will become dangerously influenced by primitive instincts (Rotundo 1993, 232). The real hero is he who overcomes his passions: he is mature, a guardian of boundaries, a person who values reason and order over unregulated passion and who puts duty before pleasure, the safety of the community, and the continuity of the Jewish people before his own desires which, he recognizes, can be overcome. Thus the military imagery is used not merely for its forceful evocation of maleness but also for its strong ties to coming of age in a secular society. For most Jewish men in Israel, the military is an image of adulthood and a common rite of passage into adulthood. The absence of this experience for young Haredi men therefore implies, for themselves and for others, that they have not yet matured.

The use of military language and images to fortify the fundamentalist culture can also be found in many other fundamentalist groups. For instance, groups like "Marines for Christ" and "Be a Champion for Jesus" reinforce the Christian fundamentalist enclave culture and the glorification of God in everyday life (see Almond, Appleby, and Sivan 2003, 44). Yet even this ascetic fundamentalism is changing as well.

Contesting Ascetic Fundamentalism

Although prohibitions against military service are strong, the Haredis' use of military practices and images have been central to their view of piety since the establishment of their community in Israel. In my interviews with yeshiva students, their differing attitudes soon became apparent: many of them expressed doubts about the fundamentalist model of yeshiva religiosity, the ideal of abstinence, and the exemption from military service. Many interviewees did not object to the military on conceptual, religious, or moral grounds, and many of them, both young and old, often spoke of their great interest in the Israeli Defense Forces' achievements and activities and evinced substantial knowledge of the army's structure, functions, and courses and its units, bases, and commanders. Many knew all the details about Israel's wars. Even as the mystique enveloping the army has largely been penetrated and dispersed by the larger Israeli society, young Haredim criticize their own exemption and claim a willingness to participate in military activities and wars, for a variety of reasons (see Ben-Ari and Lomsky-Feder 2000; Kimmerling 1979, 22–41; Sasson-Levy 2006).

Although when I first started this project, I did not directly address military issues, most of the interviewees raised the subject themselves, many speaking at length about the army, their reasons for not joining, the justifications offered by the rabbis, and their own opinions about these issues. Their comments revealed their uncertainty about the choices that had been made for them.

In fact, the students disapproved of several aspects of the Haredi world: the dire financial situation of Haredi families, their exclusion from the army and thus from opportunities in the labor market, the structure of the yeshivas, their obligation to study constantly, and the current community leadership. The students' main criticisms focused on the demand of the founding Haredi generation that they dedicate themselves to Torah studies, accept a humble existence, and remain celibate until marriage. The young yeshiva men questioned the viability of the original model for everyday life in contemporary Israel and argued against this on many levels.

Many students felt that for the original founders of the yeshiva world in Israel, the asceticism and piety required of them might have been acceptable but that they were no longer possible today. Although the interviewees accepted the tenets of the yeshiva-based religiosity, they resented being required to lead entirely disciplined lives without any alternatives or personal choices. As Shlomo, a yeshiva student from Jerusalem, told me:

> They [the Haredi authorities] have built a society with very unrealistic values. It may be all right for a specific few, a few ascetics who enter a monastery and also decide not to marry. . . . But to say that everybody in a society, without discrimination, should study . . . and that abstinence is part of this ideal, is simply not realistic. This is not what is written in the scriptures, and it is not suitable for humans.

In a roundabout way—and intentionally so in my view—yet expressing himself very clearly in his choice of words in Hebrew (which depends heavily on quotations from and allusions to sacred texts), Shlomo is referring to the fact that Judaism strongly emphasizes the virtues of married life, and by requiring young men to remain celibate, the rabbis might be leading students dangerously close to the Christian model of piety or to those Jewish ascetics whose extreme abstention is condemned in the scriptures. Celibacy may be acceptable to some, but not all, Shlomo insisted, for as others mentioned as well, not every person can control his body and overcome his own evil inclination. Shlomo explained that the yeshiva's strict requirements do not suit all men and that the cost of forcing this way of life on yeshiva students could ultimately endanger the community of faith. Shlomo recognized that beyond questions of celibacy, the current arrangement was not for everyone:

> When you stop to think about it, it is horrible that parents may recognize that their son might not be an outstanding student of the Talmud or become an exemplary rabbi. But they nevertheless feel obligated to send him to the yeshiva, because perhaps out of the thousands who study, he might become one of the few who are chosen. I am not willing to pay this price. . . . Maybe as a leader, these things look right, but as an individual, if I recognize it in myself, I should get up and leave.

It seems that for Shlomo, the yeshiva model is both a personal burden and a disservice to the community. Moreover, the founders and current leaders are not considering the requirements of the country. Indeed, Shlomo portrayed himself as trapped in this model of yeshiva piety. Although he was happy living according to the ideal, he was paying a price and sometimes wanted to leave. This contradiction reveals the lack of alternatives for masculine virtuosity in the community. Although Shlomo and others like him do not particularly want to leave the community, they have very few professional options within it. Shlomo mentioned the army as an alternative, stressing it as a wider Israeli version of masculine strength, one that, in his eyes, was preferable and could include, if possible, heroism under fire. Shlomo complained that in contrast, in the yeshiva world there was only one path and only one model of piety.

Chanoch, an eighteen-year-old student, explained this when we asked him about the army:

> Some of us actually have a more positive attitude [toward the army], but you will not hear much about it in the media. You will hear it more in face-to-face interviews with public Haredi figures. These leaders, however, will not express this view in public because they do not want their words to become ammunition in the hands of those in the secular society who want to fight us. We also have a problem with the public with young people who are not amenable to studying. This same dilemma is debated in the Babylonian Talmud about young men who study the Torah but see no blessing in their studies. The Talmudic rabbis resolved this issue by deciding that five years of study was the limit and that those who were not suited for it should get up and leave the whole thing.

The interviewees reiterated the concern that most Haredi youth are not suited to yeshiva life. They argued that these young men should not fight their own inclinations but, rather, enlist in the army. For example, Aaron hinted at an alternative, well-established interpretation in Judaism:

> Today, if we send all the young boys of the next generation to the army and to work and require only that they keep kosher, I am not sure how large a percentage would remain [in the yeshivas]. Why? Because despite what most people think, Judaism is not just about abstract study but is actually a very practical religion. . . . I mean, they [the Jewish sages] understood the attraction to the carnal . . . that man is a material creature, and that a religious person is attracted in exactly the same way as a

secular person is to exactly the same things, right? And today the temptation is so great the walls have to be fortified.

In sum, these interviewees are caught in a contradiction of their own
making: they believe that the ascetic model is the ideal one for men to follow as Jews today, even though they recognize that this ideal is impossible
to realize and that their attempts to live accordingly only frustrates and
adds stress to their daily lives. Aaron suggested an alternative approach,
what the Haredim call "practical Judaism." This allows yeshiva students
to relate to the secular world and to create a balance between the Haredi
rabbis' definitions of the sacred and the profane.

The students' criticism of the yeshiva authorities and the masculine ascetic model in favor of a military image and their declared desire to serve
in the army is part of a wider trend to change the community's definitions of religiosity. In our interviews, these students expressed a yearning for a change in their religious experience and in their participation
in and connection with all that is physical, material, and corporeal. They
imagined that the army would allow them to experience these forbidden
dimensions of life and to test alternative models of behavior. Their critical
language reveals a tension between the fundamentalist ideal of asceticism,
piety, and withdrawal and the desire to fulfill a model of soldierhood and
this-worldly religiosity. Their rhetoric blends the charismatic features of
yeshiva fundamentalism with various militaristic symbols and practices.
Thus, although most of my interviewees perceived the army as an arena of
transgression that stood in opposition to the sacred, they also regarded it
as a possible site for constructing a new model of Haredi heroism and for
practicing novel piety.

Soldierhood and Piety

Along with the students' fantasies of alternative Haredi piety, soldierhood
may be extended in unexpected directions. While Shlomo was talking
about the army, he remarked that his attitude was not exceptional: one
had only to look at the costumes the children wore in the Purim festival.[10]
Purim, which is celebrated in the spring, is the most joyous Jewish holiday
of the year, during which children dress up, thereby allowing a glimpse
into the Haredim's fantasies and wishes (see Heilman 1992; Jacobs 1971,
1390–95). I followed Shlomo's suggestion, and since Purim 2002 I have
been visiting Mea She'arim during the celebrations and photographing

Figure 5.1. A boy dressed up as a soldier, Jerusalem, Purim 2006.

Haredi costumes. In 2005, the most popular costumes worn by Haredi children were those of soldiers, police officers, and members of the rapid-response medical units, ZAKA[11] or Hatzolah Israel,[12] in their yellow or orange outfits. I noticed that the children dressed in green soldier uniforms made sure that they wore red army shoes, red berets, and other symbols that would identify them as miniature Israeli paratroopers. It was ironic to see a Haredi father, dressed in traditional garb, holding the hand of his little boy, dressed up as a combat soldier and representing one of this society's greatest prohibitions (see figures 5.1 and 5.2). The streets were filled with little boys representing the Haredi community's greatest conflict: the fear of secular Israel and the attraction to it, through fantasies about the carnal masculinity of soldiers (Stadler 2007).

While discussing issues relating to the military, many of the interviewees revealed their ambivalence. For example, Shimon, a student from a yeshiva in Jerusalem, feared that the students might actually be allowed to join the military. During an interview with Shimon at his parents' house in Jerusalem, he said he was worried that good students would prefer vigorous activity and liberation to the constraints of yeshiva life:

In the long term, this can harm Haredi education very, very much. . . . How will the rabbis decide who deserves to study and remain in the yeshiva and who is not proficient enough and should instead go into the army? I can

Figure 5.2. A boy dressed up as a soldier, Jerusalem, Purim 2006.

imagine a situation in which, for instance, the rabbis devise tests to determine the suitability of young men for yeshiva life. Perhaps someone who might be a very good student but prefers to go into the military will deliberately flunk the yeshiva exams in order to be free to join the army. But this is illogical and impractical. . . . All in all, the yeshiva is a very demanding institution, and everyone who doesn't succeed in his studies will know that he has the option of leaving everything and going into the army.

Shimon's own fascination with everything connected to the army led him to describe the yeshiva as less attractive to young men than army life. At the beginning of our conversation, Eli, another student from Jerusalem, confirmed his full commitment to the yeshiva. But later in the interview, while talking anxiously about the yeshiva's constraints and pressure, he spoke of a longing to undergo military training. While I was sitting with Eli near his yeshiva, he suddenly blurted out:

> You know we are just like anybody else; we want to be in the world; we have the same amount of energy as others. The boys at the yeshiva are full of energy and simply do not have where to vent it. . . . If we all joined the army, it would make it stronger, and the Jewish nation would have a better army.

Surprised by this declaration, a statement that contradicted the world-view he had maintained until that moment, I asked, "So why don't they [the leaders of the yeshiva world] do something about this?" Eli lowered his eyes and said: "Well, they know that the minute they recruit from the yeshiva world, all the country's recruiting offices will be flooded with yeshiva students wanting to enlist."

Yeshiva students' fantasies about the army are represented by a narrative glorifying Israeli combat soldiers and wars. Those interviewees who expressed a wish to enlist saw only one possibility: becoming a combat soldier (even though there are many other, perhaps more suitable, options for them in the IDF). When students say they want to join the army, they are hoping that by becoming soldiers, they will fulfill the hegemonic model of Israeli masculinity: a soldier who is tested in his soldierhood as a symbol of his manhood, and he goes into combat to prove his courage and heroism (see Ben-Ari 1998; Lomsky-Feder and Rapoport 2003; Sasson-Levi 2002, 2006). In this view, the primary trial of men is that of mastering stressful situations, especially during a battle (Ben-Ari 1998, 113).

The contradictions in these interviews are clear. Even though the students fantasize about becoming "real men" by participating in military life, few of them actually try to fulfill these dreams. Although they strongly criticize the yeshiva, they nevertheless accept the rabbis' ideals of the *ben Torah* and remain in the yeshiva.

To better understand the use of military symbols in their piety, I also analyzed Haredi films, audiotapes, and videotapes that focused on the military. Like other fundamentalist groups, the Haredim use films, audiotapes, and videotapes to spread their ideas and values (Caplan 1997).[13] The Haredi films offered two views of the army, as a site of sin, hedonism, physical release, and risk and also as a location in which yeshiva students might pursue alternative expressions of religious devotion.

In the popular Haredi video *Soldiers without Uniforms*,[14] the military, which is usually perceived as a strict and harsh institution, is shown as a wilderness in which young men are free to be adventurous and wild. The film depicts the story of a yeshiva student who is forced to enlist and joins a special combat unit. Here the Haredi desire to participate in the army materializes: the yeshiva student turns out to be an excellent combat soldier who achieves a high rank and learns sophisticated military techniques. Over the course of the film the yeshiva ascetic is transformed into an experienced combat warrior who nonetheless remains a pious man. He is presented as easily being able to perform difficult tasks and fulfill all army obligations. The message in this film is clear: because socialization into yeshiva life is arduous and demanding, it also prepares young men, both spiritually and physically, to serve as combat soldiers. The film tackles head-on the widespread desire to belong to the secular-military collective by showing what a yeshiva student can achieve there. But at the time it constantly suggests that in contrast to yeshiva training, performing in army combat units is easy. Many yeshiva students I interviewed implied that yeshiva socialization is actually a good place to gain the discipline and strength required in military life.[15] Because yeshiva training involves the discipline, control, and mortification of the body, it is like army training.

Secret Mission in Damascus is another example of wish-fulfillment entertainment connecting the ideal of Haredi asceticism with the life of the combat soldier. Uri, the main character, fulfills these two ideals: he is fully dedicated to his yeshiva studies while also being a soldier and warrior. In the film he undergoes extensive physical training, weapons drills, and karate exercises, as well as spending time in the intensive learning and performance of Jewish commandments. In another film, *The Jew from Beit Jala* (n.d.), the Haredi student is a security officer who investigates terrorists and bombings in Israel. In one of the scenes, while commanding a special mission in Beit Jala (an Arab village near Jerusalem), he finds an ex-Jew who allegedly converted to Islam. After this scene, the film shifts its focus. Now, though remaining a member of the elite army group, the Haredi student devotes his time to the holier task of helping this man find his way back to Judaism. In both these films, the main characters fulfill two masculine models by being the most dedicated students at the yeshiva and the best soldiers in their combat units.

Both my interviews and text analyses showed that the yearning to become a combat soldier was the ultimate fantasy of young Haredi ascetics,

Figure 5.3. The DVD cover for the Haredi film *Soldiers without Uniforms,* about the trials and successes of a yeshiva student in the army. Courtesy of Avi Greenberg from Greentec Marketing LTD, Bnei Brak.

permitting them to escape from the yeshiva's constraints and pious norms, an imaginary alternative possibility for courageous and sacrificial masculinity. This twofold model contains militaristic features as well as possibilities of trying out alternative modes of religiosity and piety. In these films, the student overcomes all carnal impediments, enters the secular realm, and emerges unscathed without sinning, indeed with his Haredi identity and piety fortified. In *Soldiers without Uniforms,* the Haredi elite fighter must survive grueling basic training and physical hardship. Military discipline involves difficult training and deprivation of food and sleep, which are physical challenges that yeshiva students face daily (see figure 5.3).

Military training also is portrayed as relatively easy compared with the real tasks required of the Jewish soldier: performing all religious commandments with full devotion and perfection in the context of the army and under modern, secular circumstances. The film shows the protagonist's military training as a religious trial of faith and manhood. When he tells the head of his Lithuanian yeshiva how difficult the army is, the rabbi answers: "I understand the difficult trial you are facing. You know, though, that you must make sure that in public you keep the Lord's name sacred and uphold all commandments. . . . It is a religious trial, I know, yet you must be strong."

The possibility of strengthening one's religion through military service also was mentioned in most of the interviews. Here, again, the students regarded the army as not only a site of impurity and sin but also a potential site for religious trials and examination.

Military service offers an alternative route to manhood, one that is tempting to yeshiva students, as it embellished with the fantasies bred by prohibition. These fantasies allow yeshiva students to enter worlds and identities that are forbidden, wild, impure, threatening, and hostile. They allow *bnei Torah* to think about their abilities to control their bodies and souls in a world that is unreal for them, and they expose a yearning for a new model of behavior emphasizing active masculinity, sacrifice, soldierhood, and civic participation.

Conclusion

What is the meaning of the students' passion for the military and their religious aspiration to an alternative piety? What is the meaning of the yeshiva students' fantasies about joining the military and becoming heroic combat soldiers? Young yeshiva students no longer will accept separatism accompanied by an antisecular ideology and an inward-facing model. Although the younger students and rabbis were brought up in these separatist communities and were expected to follow the model of the founding fathers, in contrast to the earlier generations, the young men I interviewed grew up in the state of Israel and accept its existence. They are forced toward change by external pressures such as terrorism, war, and political demands, as well as by internal pressures such as population growth and the "one size fits all" educational approach.

Bnei Torah are caught between contemporary, secular Israel and the Haredi establishment's strong insistence on realizing the ideology of yeshiva scholarship for purposes of control and as part of the Haredi politics of piety. But this situation has become problematic in their narratives because the younger generation wants to fulfill, as equal citizens, the ideals of study and simultaneously participate in the institutions of the state. For the younger yeshiva students, other-worldly, metaphysically oriented activities are not always fulfilling. This in turn has created fertile ground for the emerging opposition of younger *bnei Torah* to the existing models of scriptural fundamentalism and other-worldly masculinity. When discussing the military and soldierhood, the students challenged the existing structures and meanings of Haredi institutions. Their fascination with military service was directed at a specific aspect of their upbringing—their desire to sacrifice themselves for the nation—through legitimate state models like the army, just as they perceive themselves doing "in the tent of Torah."

Clearly, piety, soldierhood, and nationalism are linked. My analysis in this chapter reveals a longing both to participate in the wider society and to fulfill a courageous model of religiosity, one that offers different paths to religious experience and national commitment and the construction of new forms of Haredi piety. The students' desire to take part in military activities is a yearning for a more active, energetic and stimulating religiosity (Aran, Stadler, and Ben-Ari 2008, 1–2). Through their desire to join the army, these students express also their desire for social and civil integration and, by meeting the army's challenges, to establish new models of corporeal, this-worldly sacrificial piety, which still will follow the yeshiva model by being equally heroic.

In contrast to the studious practices elevated in the community, military practices are not intellectual, ascetic, theoretical, or textual. In their fantasies, yeshiva students yearn for active physical challenges and sacrifices through which they can develop a heroic charismatic religiosity, free from the traditional authorities and the textual constraints of fundamentalism. This longing indicates the possibility of transformation within the scriptural and ascetic features of the community and a movement toward worldly involvement. These opportunities for change also are evident in the massive support for the Israeli force's actions in the occupied territories and the recent vast Haredi enrollment in various defense and aid organizations, such as the Civil National Guard, the Israeli Red Cross, the police, and most visibly, the volunteer Haredi organizations such as Yad Sarah, a charitable association centering on health and social welfare, and ZAKA, an acronym for the Haredi Disaster Victim Identification Teams, which is discussed in chapter 8. In this way, the Haredi community has adopted technology and consumerism and become active in politics, even though its reliance on rabbis and their interpretations of piety and sacred texts is total. The Haredis' participation in army practices and soldierhood therefore are unlikely to be accepted any time soon.

The next chapter explores the challenges confronting piety and religious experience through the changing interpretation of gender roles and the meaning of fatherhood. In contrast to the previously examined areas of sexuality, work, and the military, the new ideas challenging gender have indeed been translated into practices of new masculine piety.

6

The Domestication
of Masculine Piety

Therefore shall a man leave his father and his mother, and shall
cleave unto his wife: and they shall be one flesh.
—Genesis 2:24

In the yeshiva community, the challenges to traditional norms
of masculine piety are directly influencing and affecting the relationship
between husband and wife. Accordingly, scholars studying the influence
of contemporary feminism on fundamentalist groups and piety have
found new gender models and greater egalitarianism (Brasher 1998; Griffith 1997; Mahmood 2005; Stacey 1990). In addition, anthropologists of
fundamentalism and gender have highlighted women's discontent with
their roles as exclusively wives and mothers and have shown that they are
becoming agents of protest and transformation within these groups (Abu-
Lughod 1986; El-Or 1993a, 1993b, 62, 2006; Griffith 1997; Mahmood 2005,
153–88). For example, Mahmood investigated women's mosque movements in Egypt as agents of both transformation and the construction of
new forms of female piety.

Few studies, however, have analyzed these questions from the viewpoint of men's desire to change the existing fundamentalist-based models
of religiosity, and they have not studied the resistance of the dominant
elite men and how they are trying to rethink and change models of behavior. A parallel example of my examination of new forms of masculine
piety can be found in *The Promise Keepers* (2004), Bartkowski's analysis
of how fundamentalist Christian males are reconstructing their religiosity. Bartkowski claims that evangelist men are trying to replace the conservative notion of "godly masculinity," which used to be based on an

"instrumentalist" definition of manhood and is characterized by aggression, rationality, and achievement. In turn, this model of (Christian) piety is based on the concept of an "expressive masculinity" that encourages greater male participation in family life, with an emphasis on the expression of feelings and greater gender egalitarianism. Bartkowski relies also on previous analyses of male resistance to the conventional and traditional familial roles as protectors and breadwinners (see Ehrenreich 1983; Kimmel 1996, 256; Williams 2001, 4).

Despite the yeshiva's traditional expectation that students maintain a high level of asceticism, even in their relationship with their wife, young Haredi men now are reinterpreting family and gender. Young yeshiva men and a new generation of writers are using a discourse of domestication and have initiated a movement encouraging men to form closer relationships with their families. In these instances, the men serve as teachers and therapists for their wives and children. In manuals for students, husbands are instructed to enhance their wife's well-being by addressing her frustrations and grievances. Such expressions of emotional support are part of the new ideals of manhood and piety, replacing the separation and isolation of Haredi men from their wives and families. New Haredi writers are defining and comparing the new gender roles in the family with those of the yeshiva ideal. This chapter explores the feelings of young yeshiva students about this model and how they are reconstructing new relationships in the family, as well as their feelings about fatherhood and piety.

I found the information for this chapter in the books and audiocassettes produced by the younger generation of Haredim since the 1980s. In the "old" model of yeshiva fundamentalism, rabbis instructed men to let their wife take care of family obligations. Now, however, popular texts instruct young yeshiva scholars to combine their studies with their family tasks and functions and to offer physical aid and emotional support to their wives and children. These new books and CDs include popular psychological texts on human nature in general and on women's anatomy, biology, and psychology in particular. Many instruction books contain psychological profiles of women and discuss women's ambitions and desires. Rather then emphasizing the closed men's world of the yeshiva and the male bonds separating it from their wives' worlds, the new discourse promotes unity and companionship between the sexes. This process of domestication also redefines the ideal of fatherhood and engagement in an emotionally involved relationship with the children, the family, and the community.

The Triple Bond: Men, Women, and the Torah

As are other fundamentalist groups, the Haredi community is oriented toward family life. Haredi children are encouraged to marry at a relatively young age and to have large families. In 2000, the average age of marriage for Haredim was 21.3, compared with 27.2 for Israel's population as a whole. The Haredis' birthrate is very high, with 7.7 children per family, compared with 2.6 for the general Israeli population (Gurovich and Cohen-Kastro 2004, 37).

Nonetheless, despite the centrality of the family, the gender separation in the Haredi community is extreme, as reflected in the discourse and imagery constructed by its leaders (see Bartkowski 2000, 40; El-Or 1993a; Jenkins 2005; Messner 1997). The official view describes the separate roles in the community and the family by pointing to the parents' differing emotional relationships with their children and the children's needs, and it asserts that images of the body and of bodily pollution are detrimental to study and the achievement of piety. More practically, though, the various educational organizations and cooperatives do answer the vast demand for child care and preschool.

As in other fundamentalist groups such as the evangelical movements in the United States and the Islamic revival movements (Griffith 1997; Mahmood 2005; Neitz 1987), marriage is one of the bases for a strict, moral, religious life. Haredi marriage is endogamic and thus shaped by various constraints. Strict taboos limit men's contact—visual, aural, and tactile—not only with women in general but also within their own family and with their own wives. The rabbis in Israel have added to and strengthened these limitations with a comprehensive system of taboos to avoid the growing danger of secularization and the ills of the modern Zionist state.

Haredi leaders view women's tasks as earthly concerns, utterly different from their husbands' sacred duties. In all religious and intellectual aspects, therefore, women are regarded as inferior. Yeshiva students are spiritual beings and their studious tendencies are their only route to salvation. In contrast, women function only as assistants to their husbands in helping them in their transcendence and, by this means, obtain their own transcendence. This gender division, based on the Torah as "the function modality by which male dominance over woman is secure in rabbinic discourse, thus fulfilling the functions that physical domination secures in various other cultures' formation," is a constant in the Jewish tradition (Boyarin 1997, 156).

Gender separation thus is the denial of women's access to the yeshiva world and the scriptures. In Israel, Haredi women are educated separately in the Beit Ya'akov (House of Jacob) educational system, which originated in Poland after World War II. Its aim is to train Israeli Haredi women to raise their children, find a job, and enable their future husbands to be devote themselves completely to their yeshiva studies (Caplan 2003a, 78; El-Or 1993b, 586; M. Friedman 1988, 22). Women are expected to have many children and to educate and provide for them as well as for their husband. Haredi men's tasks do not include breadwinning and protection; rather, they are required to devote themselves solely and exclusively to transcendental activities. To emphasize this need for separating the sexes, many books and pamphlets explain the dangers that women pose.

Women are portrayed as associated with prohibitions, cultural pollution, and temptation because of their immodest dress and expressions of sexuality (see Biale 1988, 217; Wagner 1998, 78). Unlike men, women fulfill most of their religious aspirations and gain their spiritual rewards through routine domestic tasks. For women, housework, cooking, cleaning, and raising and educating the children are considered to be God's work and so are considered complementary to, but distinct from, the intellectual work and rewards of yeshiva men. In the Haredi view, women's work—that is, fulfilling the basic needs of their children and husbands—ensures their share in the rewards of the world to come (cf. Boyarin 1997, 153). This gendered division of labor is related to a traditional religious ideology that was accepted in other historical periods but has taken an extreme form in the current Haredi rhetoric (Wagner 1998). This sanctification of women's work also is underscored in other fundamentalist groups, such as the evangelical Christians in the United States (Gallagher 2003, 105).

This twofold image of women makes them, on the one hand, "polluted providers," who facilitate men's religious functions as yeshiva scholars by providing for the family's worldly needs. But on the other hand, women are a constant source of temptation and contamination. These restrictions on women's permissible activities and the warning against the evil they embody—which also is part of men's struggle against the evil inclination—reinforces this separation and valorizes the sacredness of men.

Haredi texts reinforce the importance of this gender division of tasks and obligations and their separation in everyday life. For example, in the popular booklet *The Happiness of the Wife of a Yeshiva Scholar* (*Oshra shel eshet talmid hacham*), the author, Rabbi Wegshel, explains: "The Haredi woman should be modest; she should cover herself from other people; and her eyes should always be looking down and her voice gentle. . . . Women's ambitions should be concentrated only in house affairs: to raise children and provide for their studious husbands" (1998, 78–80).

Along with the separation of tasks and obligations, books, pamphlets, and posters (*pashkevils*) stress the strong ideology of modesty. Women are urged to stay at home and carry out the various tasks of mothers and homemakers, which are assumed to be the sources of women's happiness. To reinforce these notions, writers use a repertoire of words—happiness, joy, fulfillment, cheerfulness, delight, enjoyment, satisfaction—together with detailed descriptions of domestic tasks.

Many texts advise men and women to remain in their respective spheres and, most of the time, to mix with only members of the same sex. This separation and isolation of the sexes is maintained through a strictly rein-forced ideology of modesty for both sides. Modesty is achieved by means of taboos related to encounters between the sexes and the approach to the body. Women's pollution is perceived to be magnified by the forces of mo-dernity and its features. In turn, secularization is said to be the creation of new spheres of pollution, which increase the opportunities for sinning and therefore require greater vigilance by Haredi men and women. Among the many aspects of life that are perceived to have a uniquely demonic nature, encounters between men and women are paramount. Therefore, both women and men are directed to avoid any unnecessary relationships or encounters outside their respective spheres. The idea of pollution is con-nected to being outside one's accepted gendered place. This is why manu-als for men emphasize the importance of being attached to a particular yeshiva, a self-sufficient institution that provides shelter and knowledge as well as protection from the secular and female worlds. Students are kept away from women and from the profligate secular spaces, which are likely to pollute men and endanger the sacredness of males.

Of the many taboos and prohibitions discussed in manuals, books, and publications, the one that poses the most dilemmas is women going out to work. This is because women are usually seen as being at risk and as susceptible to seduction, and so they are advised to abide by the strictest norms of modesty, whether at home or at work.

Women's isolation in the house is often justified by describing their tasks as religiously rewarding. The sanctification of daily work is a com-mon discourse in these writings. All difficulties in the house are smoothed over by saying it is for God's sake (*leshem Shamaim*, i.e., with no immediate reward). Daily tasks should be performed in the correct spirit or intention and with joy and grace so as to find a transcendental aspect in the mundane. These rewards are also explained as tools to strengthen women's motivation and satisfaction:

> Women know at the bottom of their hearts that their work has a purpose. . . . They know that their work is never in vain. . . . Even when she has a difficult child and might think about escaping from the chores in the house, when she learns that all her doings are for God's sake [*leshem Shamaim*], she will be happy to accept them because they have grace, her work has a reward, and it is the work of God. (Weshgel 1998, 1–2)

This text and others like it define the ideal woman as diligent, dedicated, and swayed by emotion, whereas the ideal man is defined as studious and rational. In the popular 1980s Haredi book *A Faithful Home* (*Bayit neeman*), Hertzman describes the reward and fulfillment of pious Haredi manhood:

> Man desires to transcend. His flesh, made of earth, wishes to elevate to the level of sacred flesh, and when his body is sanctified and rises up, it becomes the spirit of life, a soul that aspires to finally unite with its creator. . . . At this moment heavenly joy is infinite. . . . Because this is the purpose of the creation of men, to transform, the substance transformed takes the true shape. . . . This is realized solely through Torah toil. (1982, 13)

For Hertzman, male piety is the actual bodily transcendence and spiritual union with the Creator, which can be achieved only through dedication to Torah studies and only within the safety of the yeshiva hall, described as a thick defensive wall separating men's bodies from the world. This is a common metaphor. For example, in *The Soul of the Yeshiva* (*Nefesh ha-yeshiva*), Yaakov Friedman refers to a notion that appeared in numerous interviews:

> A thick wall separates the world of the yeshiva from the world outside. It is a wall that brings pleasure as well as emotional pain, longing; it is a wall of inner feelings which a stranger cannot understand! This is the wall that separates the bent back and sparkling eyes of the one who was blessed by the Torah. (1997, 17)

Such writings emphasize male scholasticism, asceticism, isolation from women, and exclusion from state duties and participation in civil society. Haredi manhood is characterized by total devotion to the yeshiva, its masculine fraternity and canonical wisdom. To succeed in this realm requires the suppression of sexual desire, so yeshiva students must limit their contacts with women, including their wife.

Even the sexual relations of husband and wife are subject to strict rules so as to avoid pollution, a further indication of the need to isolate men and protect them from interruptions to their studies. The techniques they use, such as memorizing sacred texts, are part of the practices intended to protect men from thinking about their physical desires.

Despite the masculine ideal of asceticism and withdrawal, the rabbis have fortified the patriarchal structure of the family, in which men also are the heads of their households. In contrast to fundamentalist groups in which men acquire power from both their religious authority and their professional status, as indeed was the case in Jewish communities in eastern Europe before World War II, today in Haredi culture men are deliberately excluded from the labor market and other sources of status. This has created tension between the masculinity of the yeshiva and the position of men in the family.

In Bartkowski's analysis of the evangelical Promise Keepers, manhood is characterized by courage and decisiveness in the workaday world, thus emphasizing men's position and power in the home and family (2000, 35–36). Haredi fundamentalist discourse, however, defines masculinity and piety solely through the lens of excellence in the study hall and through ideals such as asceticism and withdrawal. Contrary to the ideals of courage, toughness, ruthlessness, and decision making in daily affairs, as in other fundamentalist settings (e.g., Messner 1997,26), Haredi rabbis create passive qualities of masculinity like nonproductivity and submission. The ascetic ideal of withdrawal and the dominant status in the home, once seen as natural extensions of each other, have now been problematized as being in tension with each other, which is one of the principal criticisms I heard in the interviews.

Masculinity, Emotions, and Family Therapy

In contrast to the fundamentalist yeshiva model of masculinity described earlier, my analyses of the interviews and the most recent manuals revealed a surprising shift. In these new narratives, men are called to return to the home, become teachers in the family, and bring the yeshiva atmosphere into

Figure 6.1. A Haredi father with a baby carriage, browsing through books.

their houses. Men now are encouraged to learn about their wives' emotions and to provide emotional support for their children. This shift challenges both traditional ideas about the place of the yeshiva, masculine roles in the community, and Haredi piety, as well as scholarly notions about the stability of such traditional structures (see figure 6.1). Next I explain this shift by looking at the yeshiva student as a home teacher and as a therapist.

Bringing Home the Spirit of the Yeshiva

As I walk through the alleys of Mea She'arim in the mornings and afternoons, I see new models of fatherhood. Men are pushing baby carriages and taking children to or from school and preschool. Waiting rooms, clinics, groceries, supermarkets, and playgrounds are full of Haredi men and their many children. This transformation, so visible in everyday Haredi life, is discussed in many new yeshiva guidebooks and also emerged as a central theme in the interviews.

Some of the manuals for yeshiva students advise men to forgo the solitude of the yeshiva and bring the Talmudic wisdom into their homes. They are suggesting that students use the textual and interpretive skills they learned at the yeshiva to reinforce their position at home and teach their wives and children the norms and ethics of the Torah. In addition, women are viewed not as opposing forces to men but instead are infantilized and categorized with the children as pupils.

In a popular instruction book for yeshiva students, *A Note of Guidance to Yeshiva Students* (*Maamarei hadracha le'avrechim*) the author, Shmuel Wolbe, encourages his students to spend more time at home and to study in the presence of their children and wives (1989, 19–20). Rather then strengthening men's isolation and dedication to the yeshiva fraternity, Wolbe stresses their teaching and guiding at home as an important male duty. The position of "home teacher" is explained as a moral religious task and, in psychological terms, as a way to spend "quality time" with the children. In the popular book *Spend Your Life with the Woman You Love* (*Re'e hayim*), the author, Hayim Meir Halevi Vazner, addresses men's relationships with women and family life. The title of his book is borrowed from Ecclesiastes 9:9: "Live joyfully with the wife you love, through all the fleeting days of the life that God has given you under the sun." Vazner opens the first chapter with the following argument:

> Every man in Israel must know that most of the problems and turmoil in the house are caused by men either directly or indirectly, or we know that at least men could have prevented them . . . because the husband has persevered and is immersed in his studies and because he dwells in the world of the Torah. . . . All that is related to religious matters prepares and trains him to pour this goodness into the house . . . because Torah brings joy and grace. . . . All the treasures that the student learns in the study hall he must bring home. . . . He must be happy and kind and extend his psychological fulfillment to his wife and children. . . . Because men, women, and the Torah are connected and empower one another in a triple bond, when there is happiness in this bond and the wish to build

a house is based on the Torah, all this kindness grows and blossoms and is based on a sense of awe. (1986, 9)

While the link between piety and Torah studies is familiar, Vazner replaces the emphasis on the yeshiva by arguing that learning is not a practice confined to the yeshiva but should be extended to the domestic sphere as part of the father's tasks. He should do this in order to reinforce his authority, which he does through the authority of Torah, to which he has sole access within the family. Torah learning in the house also increases sacredness. In the new discourse, students can take to their homes what they have learned about piety at the yeshiva. Studying at home with wife and children present while directly encouraging and supervising pious activities can contribute to the family as well as to the student.

Men also are encouraged to offer emotional aid and to concentrate on the emotional bond with their wives, to listen to their needs and support them openly. Contrary to the older model of piety, which sees the yeshiva as the only institution that can defend and maintain the enclave of ultra-Orthodox Judaism, the new concept of the yeshiva sees part of its function as teaching the students how to deal with family and emotional matters. The knowledge and wisdom of the Torah can give a man the necessary skills to hold a family together, raise children properly, and share domestic burdens with his wife. Armed with this wisdom, men are invited into what was the traditional domain of women: raising and educating children and looking after the family's physical needs.

Yeshiva Students as Therapists

The new discourse tells yeshiva students to take therapeutic action. In contrast to fundamentalist ideals emphasizing the total separation of the sexes and the ideal of ascetic piety, men now are advised to befriend and become emotionally close to their wives, to pay attention to their needs, and to help with the great amount of housework required in large families.

Haredi manuals advise also that a man take responsibility for his wife's and children's emotions. Popular psychological rhetoric about emotional support in the family uses biblical references to the sacredness of marriage and the family to assure their readers that there is scriptural precedent for the advice. In Haim Friedlander's book *And Thou Shalt Know That Thy Tent Is in Peace* (*Veyadta ki shalom ohalecha*)[1] a manual for yeshiva students, the author advises the bridegroom to prepare for his family tasks:

To create a pleasant home, the bridegroom must prepare himself thoroughly in advance. He must learn about his future position as a husband and a father. He must recognize his obligations to his wife and learn about her emotional needs and about the female nature . . . and her expectations from him as a man and as a father. . . . He also must be aware of her fears, difficulties, and obstacles, if this is possible, in order to prevent any tensions in advance. . . . And if obstacles appear, he must be ready to make an effort to resolve them. (1986, 1–2)

The general assumption expressed in these writings is that women are commanded to give birth to children and that by doing so, they will have fulfilled much of their divinely ordained destiny. But with so many children and domestic obligations, they are emotionally and religiously frail. Here again, popular psychological rhetoric is used to describe feminine emotional instability and the obstacles that can result from female frustration with the Haredi culture. In contrast to the founding fathers' norm of completely separating men's and women's worlds, the younger writers now advise ways a man can help his wife get over her frustrations. The most popular recommendation is to try to make women happy.

In the manual *Observations for Avrechim* [i.e., married yeshiva students] (*Pirkei heara le avrechim*), Rabbi Shlomo Hacohen Eisenblat describes marital frustrations:

When men realize that women are full of complaints against them, . . . their feelings cool, [and] . . . the gaps between them grow. . . . In order to fix this emotional escalation, men must make their emotions healthy again. . . . Men must create an atmosphere of joy; [a husband must] smile at his wife, help her, encourage her, and make jokes in order to make her happy. (1983, 26)

Like Eisenblat, many writers and interviewees claim that men are responsible for women's happiness, should allow them to vent their frustrations, and try to support them. Using popular psychological reasoning, male authors explain that the wife's happiness is a sign of self-realization and is important to the stability of the Haredi family. This should not be mistaken as a feminist view, since the main function of the husband at home is guiding his wife's behavior and inculcating morals, and always reinforcing male piety.

Men are constantly advised to be open, to listen to their wives, and to be attuned to their feelings. Husbands should be prepared to communicate with their wives on an emotional level as well as a practical one, and to provide theologically and psychologically applicable wisdom from the teachings of the Torah and related scriptures.

In sum, men are encouraged to become lay therapists in their families. The performance of the yeshiva student as therapist is regarded as essential to the success of their marriage and to women's happiness, whereas the previous model emphasized, for men, full dedication and withdrawal from women and family and, for women, sacrifice for the sake of men's piety. The most recent writings advise men to take time off from the yeshiva to help their wives, even at the expense of studies. Nurturing a wife's positive outlook on life will benefit the husband in the long run, as Rabbi Eisenblat explains:

> When you feel the need to help [your wife], do not proceed with studies like a blind man. . . . You must take the time you need to help her; you must take her for walks and spend time with her, because a little *bitul Torah* [i.e., not studying] will save much more time in the future and the deterioration of goodwill resulting from a bad atmosphere. . . . So he must take upon himself the task of clearing the air as well as guiding his wife, encouraging her, and gently asking her to behave in a positive way and to smile more, and also to find the right moment to discuss with her ways in which he can improve her spirit and their situation. (1983, 26)

This writer is encouraging students to postpone their spiritual obligations in support of a wife and to become involved in her duties and responsibilities, thus contradicting the previous emphasis on the division of roles and physical separation. The reintegration of men into the household is explained as their new mission to save the family. Indeed, one of the fears that the students expressed in their writing and interviews is what they see as the collapse of the Haredi family, both economically and emotionally. This fear is echoed in many texts. For example, in *Spend Your Life with the Woman You Love*, Haim Vazner alludes to the current situation:

> To understand the changes in both [the husband's and wife's] lives [after marriage], their habits, the need to learn how to help with the many domestic tasks, . . . the most important thing is to understand the wife's soul and emotional needs. . . . If a man studies through the Talmud how to

prepare his soul according to the Torah, he will succeed and will reduce the potential tensions and conflicts that are, unfortunately, the reality in some homes today. (1986, 46)

Some of the writers acknowledge the pressure on women to raise and support large families and realize that they must change the traditional model and division of work in the family. Whereas the life of the community and the family used to revolve around the men's activity at the yeshiva, and men expected their wives to support them, now men are encouraged to return home in order to actively help and support their large families. This is a seeming inversion of the biblical narrative of woman's creation as "helpmate" to her man (Genesis 2:18), since now men (supposedly) have become helpmates to their women. But in "protecting" or "reinforcing" the fragile family, men's intervention does not give up the privileges of their studious piety but provides a practical realm in which to apply what they have learned.

The responsibility for maintaining the family is no longer solely the mother's but now should be shared with men. For example, in *Observations for Avrechim* (*Pirkey heara le avrechim*), a guide for married scholars, Rabbi Eisenblat writes in the introduction:

> Many people see marriage as a routine. Some are satisfied with less and are not aware of the happiness that they can gain only if they work and have the right attitude. Some are entangled in difficulties, and some are disappointed by their wives' inability to understand them. This is the reason I have written this book. You must understand that if you have the right attitude and patience, you can solve all your problems. By understanding the female point of view, men can bring goodness into the home and can help her overcome her problems and enjoy a happy marriage. (1983, 1)

The opening gets straight to the point: the anxiety about the breakup of the traditional Haredi family. The idea of routine in marriage, together with such terms as *disappointment* and *tensions in the family*, is taken from a modern, therapeutical discourse of family crisis. The word *love* is not used, nor is it necessarily a condition for marriage in the Haredi community, in which arranged marriages still are the norm. Writers do, though, refer to concepts like happiness, satisfaction, and positive attitudes as the rewards of a (happy) marriage. Here men are encouraged to use their emotional resources and Talmudic wisdom to strengthen the family mentally and emotionally as well as spiritually. Men are now challenging the rational model of the detached scholar (Boyarin 1997, 152), and a new, emotionally involved model is gathering momentum.

In *Spend Your Life with the Woman You Love*, Vazner explains how women's frustration is reinforced by domestic work, and he advises yeshiva students how they should behave at home:

> Men should pay attention to their asceticism and how it affects their family. . . . Of course, men aspire to rise up and unite with God, but they also must pay attention to their family and their needs. . . . It is clear that when men find satisfaction in their studies and the more of their physical and spiritual needs are fulfilled by the Torah, the more relaxed and pleased they will be with God's work. . . . Study satisfies most of their desires and lust, but what about their wives!? Their wives cannot enjoy this unique spiritual satisfaction; they cannot taste the sweetness of the Torah; they must remain on the level of flesh and blood. . . . They can enjoy only earthly goods. (1986, 45)

The author makes the rationalist claim that because the Torah satisfies all desires and women are excluded from the life of the Torah, it follows that they must be dissatisfied with all levels of their lives. Men must pay attention to this frustration and find ways of addressing it. What the book strongly implies, then, in startling contrast to earlier works, is that the traditional idea that men dedicate their body and soul exclusively to the Torah has negative effects on both women and the functioning of the family. Haredi women are left unfulfilled by their husband's asceticism, which produces discontent and frustration, says Vazner. Men must provide emotional and spiritual sustenance for their wives to help them overcome their lack, their emptiness. Failure to do so can be fatal to the marriage:

> Men who transcend through their study and dedication can easily find themselves renouncing completely all aspects of mundane life and earthly obligations, . . . leaving his wife behind, far away. . . . If he ignores this condition, a great gap will open between them. All this can happen to a man if he ignores his family. Therefore he must talk often with his wife and listen to her needs, because if he does not, their separate worlds can produce depression and a lack of joy, and eventually both of them will become unhappy and dissatisfied. (Vazner 1986, 45)

Such texts warn Haredi men of women's dissatisfaction, whose source is the husband's overinvolvement in yeshiva asceticism, to the detriment of the relationship. The renunciation that traditionally was at the heart of Haredi fundamentalist piety has now come to endanger the institution of the family itself. The marital gap that Vazner mentions is interpreted as especially dangerous to men. Writers advise students about how to avoid these risky situations, counseling them to pay attention to their wives and even to temporarily abandon their Torah studies and the yeshiva's ethics. Students should communicate with their wives often, to educate them and help them fulfill their spiritual needs, and, no less important, to compliment them often. The students are warned that women can fall into deep depression and dissatisfaction if their husbands ignore them in the name of asceticism.

It is important to note that even though the attitude toward male behavior is different in these books and manuals, the ideal Haredi woman has not changed. Women are still defined by writers through the use of traditional features and canonical Jewish texts, and the female attributes of worldliness, productivity, and inferiority still are central in books for yeshiva students. I found that in the texts and interviews, only manhood had been redefined. Male piety now is based not only on concepts of yeshiva otherworldliness but also on new ideals of fatherhood in which men participate in the family, support their wife, and help her with her domestic tasks. The writings imply a fear of losing control and power over the mundane, especially women. Although the obligation to study is part of male piety and thus the source of men's power, another source is their control over the family, particularly through income. Because men must remain in the yeshiva and, in any case, the labor market open to them is limited, they cannot control their family by economic means and so must use means of emotional involvement and care.

Women's dominance in the work world is a source of tension and friction in the family. It was criticized many times during the interviews and is a subject of criticism in writing as well. Students express frustration at being denied the role of breadwinner and find themselves in a dilemma: by the rules of the community, they are obliged to study, and by Jewish law, they are obliged to provide for their families.

When I asked how full-time yeshiva studies can coexist with family duties, Eliyahu, a student attending a well-known Lithuanian yeshiva, explained:

> Well, our rabbis do not understand this dilemma; they justify every-
> thing in order to keep us in the yeshiva, . . . even if it is not rational at
> all. . . . They use interpretations of the Talmud that contradict the Jewish
> tradition, . . . like the advice to send women to work and support their
> husbands economically . . . or the elevation of yeshiva isolation as an
> ideal model of piety. . . . This is wrong; we cannot feel comfortable with
> this. . . . This is not what the Torah says.

Later, Eliyahu explained what he referred to as the problem of gender
definitions in the community, a subject that received much critical comment in numerous other interviews, in which students maintained that
their detachment from their family's obligations and needs threatened
their masculine identities, their relationship with their wives, and sacredness. The ideal of yeshiva isolation separated men from women and from
the family. Without firm backing at home, students could not concentrate
fully on their studies. They contended that returning to their families as
teachers and emotional therapists redefined their domestic activities and
responsibilities and could improve their position, at home as well as in
the yeshiva.

The new writing style of yeshiva men also has been affected by women's
writings and their voice in the Haredi community today. Shenkar (forthcoming) analyzed novels written by Haredi women, a genre that recently
has flourished despite opposition by traditional male authorities. Shenkar
argues that these female narratives are part of the construction of a new
literary field that offers an alternative to male religious writings. These
novels enable women to ask questions about and find answers to family
and gender issues and are an attempt to change the position of women
in the community. This comparison of men's and women's writing illumi-
nates the differences between the reinterpretations of men's and women's
positions in the family, their self-identity, and their piousness.

The Domestication of Piety and the Holy Family

The fundamentalist model of the yeshiva requires that men study full time
at the study hall as well as fulfill the religious commandment to increase
and multiply (Boyarin 1995, 90). These requirements, however, place an
impossible burden on Haredi women, who are expected to work and also
take care of their families. Moreover, this burden on the women is exacerbated by the worsening economical situation and crowded conditions

in the Haredi community, which have created tensions in the yeshiva world. As reflected in the texts and interviews, feminist egalitarian discourse has influenced the Haredi model of piety. First, the general public discourse on gender and feminism has infiltrated many aspects of Haredi life. Second, the Haredi community has been growing, owing to the various groups of Jewish returnees (*hozrim betshuva*), who joined the Haredi community and who have been strongly affected by the current thought on gender and the family (Caplan 2007). Third, the writing of realist narrative fiction by and for women uses various models of the family within the Haredi world and emphasizes issues such as family chores, work, livelihoods and children's education (Shenkar forthcoming). These trends have influenced younger male writers and have caused the youngest students to challenge the traditional division of labor and the family.

Yeshiva students are called on to become teachers in their families by bringing the spiritual atmosphere of the yeshiva into their homes. The position of teachers in the home is defined as a moral task and, in psychological terms, as a new way to spend time with their children and support their wives. By linking domestication and the family to the debate on crisis in the yeshiva, to the problem of the body, and to the ambiguous meaning of the military as a symbol and as practice, we have arrived at an entirely new perspective on the kinds of questions to be asked. What are the new demands placed on the yeshiva student? What is the nature of the new piety? When analyzing male piety today, we learn that yeshiva students are asked to be vigilant on more fronts than ever before: the evil inclination, an emotional crisis, and now the question of self image vis-à-vis secular society and, particularly, the new emphasis on the family and its many demands, as well as on women's needs and frustrations. These are seen as placing a heavy burden on men, as expressed in interviews and in many popular texts. Because they are perceived as problems of modernity, they require new solutions and form the motivation for men in the yeshiva world to negotiate a different piety, by reinterpreting or replacing the restrictions that the old model imposed on them.

This redefinition of gender roles and of the meaning of gender in the dichotomy between family and yeshiva reflects an important change that is currently taking place in the community and is related to the institutionalization of the yeshiva world. With its growth, the yeshiva world has extended its demands, and many new educational institutions have appeared. Conversely, state policies with regard to Haredi stipends, especially allowances for child care, are being reduced, directly affecting the load that Haredi women with large families must carry. The yeshiva world is affected by the exigencies of state policies, on the one hand, and by women's condition in the community, on the other. The fundamentalist ideal of yeshiva-based religiosity is no longer viable and is being reassessed and recombined with an ideal of the holy family.

In a fundamentalist society, male piety must be protected, and egalitarianism is not a possible model for elite religious men. Nonetheless, the ascetic model is being updated accordingly, and the ideal of the holy family, which must be educated and protected by the pious husband/father, is being emphasized. Pious men are being asked, moreover, to take care of the holy family. While the sacredness of male learning was the dominant task when the Haredi community was established after World War II, nowadays men and women are told to reinforce its continuity through the Haredi family in accordance with the ideals of procreation and women's well-being. The family has become a mutual, sacred enterprise for the younger generation of men and women, posing new challenges to the Haredi community and the Israeli state. Writing influenced by contemporary psychological and feminist thinking now is calling young fundamentalist husbands to involve themselves more in domestic life.

The next chapter explains how this redefined male piety can be achieved through volunteer work. Changes and redirections of piety in the yeshiva world are reflected in the many volunteer tasks Haredi members have been assuming in increasing numbers since the 1990s. By joining many organizations, Haredi members have become involved in civil society, contributing to and participating in civil duties while at the same time aspiring to new models of religiosity. ZAKA is one example of the implementation of a new Haredi piety.

7

A Case Study

Terror, ZAKA, and the "Soldiers of Piety"

And the time drew nigh that Israel must die: and he called his son Joseph, and said unto him, If now I have found grace in thy sight, put, I pray thee, thy hand under my thigh, and deal kindly and truly with me; bury me not, I pray thee, in Egypt.

—Genesis 47:29

On October 4, 2003, twenty-nine-year-old Hanadi Taysir Jaradat, a Palestinian attorney and a new member of Islamic Jihad, entered Maxim, a well-known restaurant in Haifa, and blew herself up. Nineteen people were killed that day, and more than fifty were wounded. Haim, a Haredi paramedic and a ZAKA volunteer who helps evacuate victims described the work after the attack: "When we saw the destruction and the amount of victims and blood, we realized the scope of this dreadful incident. People were in a terrible condition. There was complete silence inside, and unfortunately, some of them were taking their last breath."

ZAKA is the all-male Haredi team that identifies the bodies of victims of disaster after multiple-casualty incidents (MCI), such as terrorist attacks, and if necessary, assembles their remains, making sure that in accordance with Jewish law, not one shred of flesh or drop of blood is left on the scene (Stadler 2006).

The objectives of this Haredi organization is an example of the new ways of achieving piety. Indeed, ZAKA demonstrates that the new construction of piety is a driving force in the Haredi community today and has developed into new practices in Israel. Although yeshiva students generally accept the fundamentalist discourse on sexuality, they do not accept the fundamentalist attitudes toward work and the military. In response, the traditional views of family, gender, and, especially, volunteer work in Israeli society as a whole have changed. It has been mainly through volunteer work that Haredi men have been able to leave the yeshiva and put these new interpretations into practice, serving society while creating their own piety. ZAKA is the best example of this transfiguration of piety.

ZAKA was established by Haredi men during the 1990s, prompted by the significant increase in terrorist attacks and suicide bombings in Israel. This escalation of attacks on Jewish civilians led to a demand for more people with a knowledge of Jewish burial law and death rituals. These experts were found among the Haredi Jews, who quickly agreed to help in these urgent public concerns.

Members of the Haredi community formed several volunteer organizations (after ZAKA, the next largest is Hatzolah Israel),[1] with the aim of providing Halachic solutions to dealing with mutilated and dismembered bodies and offering aid to the larger Israeli public. These new organizations furthermore became a legitimate avenue for male Haredim to practice and experience a new piety, by working outside the community and offering their services to larger segments of Israeli society. Accordingly, Haredim were dispatched to traffic accidents, bombings, and other tragic events, putting to use their expertise in Jewish law and especially in burial rites, as well as in their newly acquired skills in first aid.

ZAKA is currently Israel's largest and best-known voluntary organization dealing with events involving multiple deaths and injuries, and since 1995 it has extended its role and institutionalized its practices. ZAKA volunteers have many tasks: administering first aid to wounded victims of terrorist attacks, locating and reassembling dismembered body parts, washing blood off the dead, overseeing the ritual treatment of victims, and transferring them to the Israeli Institute of Forensic Science. ZAKA offers Haredi men new opportunities to challenge the yeshiva's religiosity and to reconstruct fundamentalist male practices and piety. Through their public position as specialists and death workers in Israel, these volunteers have created alternative religious models that challenge the ascetic vision of the Haredi man and the established models of yeshiva text–based piety.

This chapter shows why ZAKA volunteers see their actions as sacred work, and it explores their views of death as martyrdom. Through their involvement in the death work required by Jewish law, ZAKA volunteers have formed new narratives of identity and heroism unlike the traditional yeshiva piety. These narratives reveal that volunteers' actions following terrorist attacks enable them to monopolize the handling of dead bodies, thereby bringing into the public sphere the Jewish view of corpses and death. Through these practices, the ZAKA volunteers have established a this-worldly orientation of piety and constructed new forms of inclusion and participation in the larger Israeli society.

ZAKA and Haredi Masculine Piety

Since the outbreak in October 2000[2] of the most recent intifada (see Kepel 2002, 150–58), often termed "the second Palestinian Uprising," and characterized by an increase in suicide bombings, ZAKA has intensified its activities.[3] ZAKA texts and my interviews with members made clear that the impetus for establishing the organization was the attack on bus 405 in 1989, near Telz-Stone, a Haredi settlement on the road to Jerusalem. The interviewees told me this story many times, and it can be found on the ZAKA website as well:

> In 1989, while studying in a yeshiva, Yehuda Meshi Zahav, the founder and chairman of ZAKA, and his fellow students were startled into reality by a thunderous boom, two minutes of silence, and then scores of bloodcurdling screams. The number 405 bus had been steered over the mountainside by a terrorist. The bus exploded; seventeen people died, and scores were injured. Yehuda and his colleagues rushed to the scene and began to care for the wounded and dead. The chaos was chilling and horrifying, Yehuda remembered. For six years after this incident, Meshi Zahav and a dedicated group of volunteers continued this work of *chesed shel emet*, the work that "makes God smile"—true kindness, unconditional giving to those who cannot give thanks. The volunteers of ZAKA selflessly overcome horror to recover the human remains—fulfilling the biblical imperative to bury the dead "on the same day" and handle the shattered flesh and bones with respect for the divine spirit that had filled them. (http://www.zaka.org.il/en/about.asp)

According to ZAKA's reports, this dramatic incident prompted Haredi people to join the Israeli police's and army's rescue units, a kind of participation that had been banned previously and, until then, had been regarded as taboo in the Haredi community. In this early attack, the Haredis' participation is described as spontaneous, carried out by a variety of persons. The dissemination of this heroic story, the escalation of terrorist attacks in the mid-1990s, and the actions taken by the organization's founder, Yehuda Meshi Zahav, succeeded in coordinating these individual acts into a large organization of approximately nine hundred volunteers distributed throughout the country (Stadler 2006; Stadler, Ben-Ari, and Mesterman 2005).[4] The organization became fully institutionalized in 1995. ZAKA was founded with the official, more general aim of ensuring that people who die unnatural deaths, in terrorist attacks or other tragic ways, are identified, treated, or buried according to Jewish law (Abramovitch 1991; Heilman 2001).

The mass participation of Haredi men in public death work necessitated by incidents with multiple victims was as unusual and surprising at the time to the secular public as it was to the Haredi community and its leadership, given the Haredis' inclination to withdraw from the general obligations of secular society, especially from the military and the labor market. As we have seen, Haredi withdrawal was known as the "passive" or quiet element of Haredi fundamentalism and was explained as opposition to the violence implicit in a secular, modern society (Heilman 1994; Sprinzak 1993). The establishment of ZAKA, therefore, indicates a shift in yeshiva fundamentalism toward a this-worldly, active piety that involves working in public, collaborating with various state institutions, and participating in the larger collective concerns of terrorism, death, and public mourning.

The organization of ZAKA has also created a new relationship between Haredim and the Israeli state. The increase in terrorist attacks in Israel has forced all state institutions and death professionals to reorganize their activities and expertise. Institutions such as the Israeli military, the police, Magen David Adom (literally, the Red Star of David, i.e., the Israeli Red Cross), and hospitals have had to add to their training programs techniques for handling multiple deaths by explosive devices. But the lack of trained workers became evident, a gap that was filled, rapidly and surprisingly, by ZAKA.

ZAKA thus has brought new respect to the Haredi community and has led to the Israeli public's withdrawing some of their charges of Haredi parasitism (Stadler, Ben-Ari, and Mesterman 2005). ZAKA offers a new conception of social decency, responsibility, and civic accountability that the general public had not expected from members of the Haredi community. Israeli newspapers and television reports describe ZAKA as creating a bridge, giving the Haredi and secular communities a sense of shared destiny and mutual respect. Some observers even see ZAKA as the forerunner of cooperation and unity (Shapiro 2002). Some secular

Israelis consider ZAKA volunteers to be "the 'good Haredim,' the ultra-Orthodox who don't just make demands on Israeli society but actively contribute . . . as opposed to the 'bad Haredim,' who live off of government subsidies, shirking all national service and battling police in protests" (Halevi 1997, 18).

Its various awards have given ZAKA further public recognition. Yehuda Meshi-Zahav, its founder, was invited to light one of the ceremonial torches on Israel's fifty-fifth (2003) Independence Day, which only a few years earlier would have been unthinkable, and even more unimaginable that the invitation would be accepted. This change of orientation, from total exclusion to well-defined inclusion in state and social affairs, is also related to ZAKA's cooperation with state organizations. For example, ZAKA now takes advantage of the training courses offered by different aid organizations in Israel.

In 2006 the organization's website updated its definition of its work using much more inclusive rhetoric:

> ZAKA is a humanitarian voluntary organization, coordinating nearly one thousand volunteers responding to tragic incidents in Israel. ZAKA has expanded and emerged as the principal nongovernmental rescue, life-saving, and recovery organization in Israel, working alongside law enforcement and emergency personnel in responding to incidents of terrorism, accidents, or disasters. (www.zaka.org.il/en/about.asp)

ZAKA's emphasis on humanitarian work places the organization in the same ethical framework as other Israeli and international organizations like the Red Cross or Amnesty International. In addition, ZAKA's rhetoric accords with the politics of altruism, charity and care, which enable it to take advantage of the philanthropy, tax benefits, and local and state funds needed for its day-to-day operations. Because ZAKA also appeals to the Haredi community as a whole and to the rabbinical authorities in particular, it has crossed the Haredi–state and Haredi–secular divide and now is seen as essential by all sides. The presence of identifiable Haredi men wearing rescue-team overalls and latex gloves, picking over the remains of a gruesome bombing, became for a while a regular and, to some extent, a comforting public spectacle.

This trend of cooperating with the secular world is not unique to ZAKA, as at least one other Haredi organization was created with the same purpose. In 1976 the Haredim established Yad Sarah, a charitable association offering health and social welfare assistance, to compensate for the weakening welfare state and specifically to fill the gap in physical aid for the poor and the elderly. Yad Sarah has developed and extended a Jewish theological justification for the wider public, and the newly poor secular middle class has flocked to its doors. Like ZAKA, the organization has extended the boundaries of the Haredi community by giving aid to all comers.

Changes in Haredi Leadership

As an organization emerging from a fundamentalist Jewish context, ZA-KA's challenge to the traditional forms of Haredi piety and masculinity has also produced a leadership that supports its participation and new assignments. ZAKA now operates under the spiritual guidance of various community rabbis, who assist by answering religious questions concerning the volunteers' work and practical training and by offering religious affirmation of the various demands of ZAKA's rescue work.[5] These rabbis rule on religious practices such as the correct treatment of corpses and address questions of Jewish ritual purification and regulations that arise during terrorist events.[6] The volunteers' questions and the rabbis' answers were recently printed and distributed in the Haredi community.

With the support of this leadership, ZAKA has broadened its practices and qualifications to include the rescue, treatment, and support of terrorist victims and their families. According to its website, ZAKA's work includes MCI emergencies, disasters, and unnatural deaths, whether caused by terrorist attack, car accident, suicide, murder, drowning, earthquake, building collapse, and so forth. Its website also describes the training needed for these missions:

> ZAKA volunteers are trained in emergency health services in conjunction with the police in forensics and with the Justice Department and the Ministry of Religious Affairs in Halacha. ZAKA volunteers are extremely professional and trained in the latest technology in the identification and recovery of bodies and body parts. Moreover, because of ZAKA's vast experience and knowledge, it has been asked to help in the identification and recovery of disaster victims around the world. (www.zaka.org.il/en/units_zaka.asp)

ZAKA's website notes that the organization can offer religious services in time of death that no other institution can offer, and it stresses the importance of cooperating with state institutions such as the police, the army, and emergency services.

ZAKA presents new options to yeshiva students, combining a universalistic vision with the particularistic symbols, practices, and values of Jewish death rituals as an alternative to yeshiva asceticism and as a bridge between mainstream Israeli society and the Haredi enclave. For young yeshiva students, ZAKA enables a new piety that is this-worldly and legitimizes their position in Israeli society through their participation in state institutions and contribution to civil society.

Jewish Death Customs and the Burial Society

Participation in ZAKA demands training in new practices that are not familiar to Haredi men and are different from those acquired at the yeshiva. To work in ZAKA necessitates not dedicating oneself exclusively to Torah studies, as ideally all Haredi men must. Instead, volunteers are trained in anatomy, first aid, the use of medical equipment, scientific forms of identification, the techniques of driving ambulances and motorcycles, and more. But according to my interviewees, they learn all these skills only after they have studied and understood the ultra-Orthodox theology of death, handling of the dead, and burial. The meaning of death in Jewish culture, and in Haredi culture in particular, is a large issue (cf. Geertz 1973; see Goldberg 1995, 75–98; Heilman 2001), but just a brief description of the long-established Haredi burial society, Hevra kaddisha, and its status in Israel is enough to show the uniqueness of ZAKA's new death work (Stadler 2006).

The Hevra kaddisha (Holy Society), or Communal Fraternal Burial Society in Israel, is in charge of disposing of the dead in accordance with Jewish law for all Jewish citizens, religious as well as secular (Abramovitch 1986, 127; Heilman 2001; Hillers 1971, 442–44). Following Jewish ritual practices, the dead must be buried as soon as possible, as much out of respect for the dead as out of concern that they might ritually pollute their environment and make it unfit to live in. Texts commenting on the impurity of human remains are abundant, and the laws relating to this subject are very strict: people and utensils that have been in contact with a cadaver become impure, as does the place where they have lain (Goldberg 1995, 82). Accordingly, the Haredi burial society takes bodies away from the homes or hospitals where they have died and performs the ritual of purifying them, wrapping them in shrouds, and making all the formal and practical funeral arrangements. The society also acts as a ritual expert, guiding inexperienced mourners through the funeral (Abramovitch 1991, 80).

Originally, the Haredi burial society was a collection of prestigious volunteer organizations in the various Jewish communities in the Jewish diaspora. In Israel, however, the society's position is much different, as most of the burial work is handled by the Ministry of Religion, and most funerals, with few exceptions,[7] are handled by Hevra kaddisha. Although this control has given Hevra kaddisha authority and proficiency in everything pertaining to death rituals, it also has caused tension and sometimes resentment in the surrounding society.

ZAKA can be seen as an extension of the traditional burial society. Similar to the society, members of ZAKA see themselves as having comparable religious expertise regarding death and the handling of bodies as well as the ability and religious motivation to provide death-related services for all Jewish Israelis, whether or not observant. In contrast, however, to Hevra kaddisha, which is responsible mostly for Jewish burial rituals, ZAKA manages the moments after unnatural death and sees to the correct handling of the remains before burial: locating and reassembling dismembered body parts and washing them—all according to ritual—and transferring them to the relevant authorities (see Weiss 2002). ZAKA is one of the few organizations that responds to the carnage left in the wake of bombing attacks, which distinguishes it from Hevra kaddisha and all other secular institutions that deal with routine deaths, such as police, hospitals, and emergency services. Consequently, the meaning of ZAKA's various practices at the scenes of accidents or multiple-casualty incidents (MCI) has not yet been institutionalized or ritualized in Israel.

Terror and New Haredi Piety

The fieldwork presented in this chapter began in the summer of 2002, a particularly intensive period of suicide bombings when intifada events reached their peak.[8] I conducted interviews with twenty-two ZAKA volunteers (most of them lasting between one and three hours) in Jerusalem at the organization's center, as well as in other cities, including Rehovot, Tel Aviv, and Holon.[9] The interviews took place in a variety of locations, such as hotel lobbies, shopping malls, volunteers' homes, and Haredi restaurants. In the initial stage of my project, most of the informants were recruited by the founder and head of ZAKA. Although some volunteers might have agreed to be interviewed without the founder's encouragement, his willingness to cooperate clearly helped me find my first contacts and helped make them comfortable answering questions they might not have answered without his approval. Through these initial contacts, I found others to interview. Contact by phone was usually the first step, during which I described my research project, explained the technical aspects of the interview, and gathered some information about the interviewee's background.[10] To understand the context in which ZAKA was established and supplement the interview data,[11] I read newspaper articles and the organization's website and watched films[12] and television reports describing ZAKA.

Like other Haredi institutions, ZAKA keeps men and women separated. Although I regularly asked about the absence of women in the organization, the answer usually was brief but stressed the possibility of admitting them in the future (mainly to do secretarial work). When asked about the possibility of women helping after terrorist attacks, the interviewees expressed reluctance, citing the religious difficulties of these tasks and their inherent physical danger.

The ZAKA volunteers that I interviewed insisted that after a terrorist attack, they alone were responsible for the gathering and preliminary identification of organs and corpses. The volunteers see this duty as a sacred task and work for hours recovering every piece of every body and, if possible, matching them with the body. In the interviews, the volunteers used various religious symbols and justifications to underscore the great importance and complexity of this task. Consequently, the volunteers interpret their work as both a sacred duty and an act of piety. The organization's leaders also told me that many young Haredim wish to join because, as one of my interviewees confirmed, "They can do sacred work while at the same time make use of the energies young people have." Thus, this sacred work also offers the benefit of vigorous exercise.

To reinforce this new Haredi piety, volunteers use such religious concepts as true kindness (*hesed shel emet*),[13] the ultimate act of charity toward someone who can never repay it, that is, a dead person; the commandment of respect for the dead (*kvod hamet*);[14] and the comparison of dead bodies to burning bible scrolls as an expression of sacrifice and martyrdom. Volunteers blend these religious symbols with masculine images of risk taking, courage, a military-like toughness and group cohesion, and professionalism. The mixture of such images highlights the volunteers' special position as the exclusive mediators among death, religion, and life in the critical moments after a terrorist attack.[15] By reinforcing these symbols, volunteers reconstruct ideals of piety in the community that are not studious, intellectual, or ascetic but instead involve action, danger, and physicality.

Terror Rescue and the Torah Scroll

When ZAKA volunteers began taking over the task of recovering body parts after bombings, they introduced a variety of pious expressions into their performance. During the interviews, the volunteers spoke at length about the condition of bodies after an explosion, the complexity of the treatments and techniques that they used to "clean" an area after an incident (leaving the responsibility of dealing with concerns of the afterlife and resurrection to Hevra kaddisha).

Many volunteers emphasized the importance of these missions and the changes that ZAKA introduced in dealing with dead bodies. Daniel, a ZAKA volunteer, explained:

> Before ZAKA was established, when there was a death—like after a car accident, for example—they used to wash the road, and that was it; we lost all the pieces of the bodies and the blood. Other organizations, like Hevra kaddisha or the army, had no responsibility for these deaths. [Consequently,] when massive terror attacks began all over Israel, people did not know how to deal properly with dead bodies. We realized that we needed to do this job, to handle the dead after attacks, and to take care of them according to Jewish law and with religious enthusiasm and respect.

To dramatize the sacredness and value of their work, the volunteers compared a dismembered corpse to a burning Bible scroll, which contains holy scripture and must be saved at all costs, and at the same time represented themselves as martyrs performing sacred tasks of body disposal and respect. Abraham, a ZAKA volunteer, used this metaphor to justify ZAKA's work and its need to work appropriately and rapidly to remove the bodies from the street after an attack:

> The scroll of the Torah is something physical, corporeal . . . the parchment, taken from a pure animal, the writing in ink obtained from trees . . . these are physical and corporeal materials. But when they are joined together: the animal leather is used for holy acts. . . . A piece of

leather or parchment that is used to write the sacred words of the Torah is not sacred until we begin writing the sacred words. . . . If a book of Torah is, God forbid, burned, a Jew will definitely hurry to save it, with all his soul.

Like many other volunteers, Abraham used this image to justify his tasks and connect the pious Haredi man and the handling of dead bodies, thus emphasizing and accepting full responsibility for the swift religious treatment of the corporeal body at disaster scenes. The equation of the dead and wounded after an explosion with burning Bible scrolls that must be saved emphasizes the importance of arriving at the scene of disaster as quickly as possible and thus being exposed to additional explosions. The willingness to work voluntarily at a death scene while constantly being exposed to danger and constantly being aware of impending martyrdom, is the central act and experience of religious sacrifice in ZAKA.

Honoring the Dead

ZAKA's concept of sanctity is connected to the Jewish concept of respect toward the dead (*kvod hamet*). Safeguarding the dignity of the dead is central to the work of Hevra kaddisha and is fulfilled mainly through strict adherence to funerary rites (Abramovitch 1991, 80). ZAKA volunteers have turned this religious duty into an obligatory and sacred public practice. Body parts, like the burned scroll with the word of God inscribed on it, must be rapidly and systematically gathered and recomposed and, only then, covered and removed. In fulfilling this task, organs must be meticulously collected, scattered blood soaked up with cloths, and body parts collected and identified. This is a new form of a public, technologically advanced fulfillment of the traditional commandment of respect for the dead, which the volunteers explained as the most honorable performance possible for people whose manner of death is a travesty of divine creation.[16]

The volunteers showed pride at being the exclusive agents to carry out this task correctly and to perform the important sacred rituals after such an event.

Respecting the dead is related to honoring the corpse, just as a burned Bible would be. The ashes and all that is left are not thrown away but must be retrieved and buried. . . . A dead body is exactly the same, and we must protect its dignity. . . . It was created in God's image and in his likeness, and therefore man's image must be kept . . . and not tortured, humiliated, or harmed.

Both body and Torah scroll contain the same holy spirit and are owed the same respect (Stadler 2006). Shlomo, a volunteer from Jerusalem, explained the behavioral aspect of respecting and maintaining the dignity of the dead:

In principle we refer to the lack of respect for the human body shown by terrorism. If the body is discarded, just like that, on the street, this is disrespectful. Moreover, if it is visible, and everybody can see it, this is a lack of respect, shameful, and is why the first thing we do is to cover the body. It is the first thing I do when they call me after an attack. I drive an ambulance, so I'm often called to a terror scene, so I go around and cover the dead bodies to show my respect for the dead, to fulfill my religious obligation. The second thing I do is if I realize that the body is not in one piece, I collect the pieces of the corpse, and I act according to Jewish law. When parts of the body are scattered about, I follow the rule about scattered bones. We are talking about a person who has just died, so the law is even stricter, so I collect pieces of human flesh. This is an act of respect, and I fulfill this religious duty.

Respect for the dead is shown in two ways, as expressed in many interviews: covering the body and reassembling flesh and blood. Many interviewees see these practices as both the most important and the most religiously rewarding. Shlomo mentioned the Jewish law regarding scattered bones and how, based on the same law, he treats bodies after bombing incidents. Like many other volunteers, he sees himself as the exclusive agent fulfilling these sacred Jewish duties for the rest of society.

Another interviewee from ZAKA, Daniel, offered his view:

Because we believe in the immortality of the soul, death is not the end of the road; it is only a movement from one world to the next. This is why we respect the body, because of the spirit that it still contains, and we cannot disrespect it. This is why we treat the dead body as if it were alive. We know scientifically that after retrieving and identifying the pieces, the body parts can be buried separately. But according to our belief and law, this is a lack of respect for the dead, so we recompose the body and try to bury the dead whole. . . . This is how we keep sacredness and how we do this holy work.

Many volunteers emphasized these ideas about the body and the spirit of the dead after terrorist attacks. Furthermore, many of them raised the idea that people who have just died a violent death still possess their spirits and thus must be treated accordingly. ZAKA volunteers are responsible for maintaining religious order even, or especially, during the most chaotic moments and for performing their tasks properly.

Another volunteer, Rafael, described dealing with corpses and violent death as both an imitation of God and a fulfillment of God's commandments:

In Jewish law it is known that God himself dealt with burial. He took care of Moses; therefore each one of us hopes to be worthy of performing this act of God. This is a very big thing in Jewish law. We treat the victim as sacred, even after death, because we believe that even if he is without soul, it does not mean that he is without honor. The corpse deserves respect because it was created in God's image. This is why the Torah refers to it with respect even after death.

Of Moses it is said that "he [God?] buried him in a valley in the land of Moab," but "no man knows" his place of burial (Deuteronomy 34:6), thus elevating ZAKA's treatment of the dead to the highest levels of religious performance, imitating God. Rafael emphasized the sacredness of the body and the sacredness of respect for it after death. The body, a creation of God, is considered holy, and therefore disposing of it is returning God's creation to its maker.

By telling these stories about re-membering and handling bodies, volunteers stress the uniqueness of their mission to honor any death, especially in those cases in which the established institutions fail to do so, thus making their work the greatest and most courageous act of religious devotion and piety.

The Theology of Death and Compassion

"True kindness," as the website http://www.zaka.org.il translates *hesed shel emet*, refers to the genuine compassion that the living must show to the dead. It is an act that has a religious reward for performing public acts related to death. Volunteers explained their preoccupation with covering, gathering, and matching body parts with this Jewish concept of "true kindness." Devotees regard this as the ultimate act of generosity, pure religious charity conceived as a voluntary and disinterested act, performed with no expectation of a this-worldly reward. As the ZAKA website observes:

> The biblical commandment to honor the dead is a sacred duty acknowledging that man was created in the image of God. Collecting the bodies and body parts of all disaster victims and giving them a proper burial is the highest form of charity of which a human being is capable—unconditional, thankless giving—true kindness [*hesed shel emet*].

According to the volunteers, in order to fulfill these duties, members must join the organization; volunteer in public; be ready to work at any time, day or night; and frequently renounce their primary religious obligations to the yeshiva. Hillel, a nineteen-year-old ZAKA volunteer, explained his reasons for joining ZAKA and the meaning of this work for him:

> I was at the Sarei Israel Street incident; it was bus number 18. I stopped and saw the work of the volunteers—how they behaved. It was the first time I had seen this kind of event. I was thrilled. For me, the work that they were doing was actually *kiddush shem shamaim*,[17] so I decided to join. . . . This is really sacred work, straight and simple . . . the feeling that you can contribute, help somebody, and that it is *hesed shel emet*, the "true kindness"— meaning that this person cannot pay you back— . . . is to know that the person who died at this event with his body scattered all around will at least gain respect and will reach burial as any of us would want.

Using ZAKA's interpretation of the ideology of fulfilling the final kindness and rites, ZAKA volunteers perceive the treatment of the body and the proximity to death as extremely rewarding acts of religious devotion. In the film *Zaka: Living with Death*, the head of a major ZAKA unit also refers to this:

> You get an announcement about an explosion. . . . Then from the moment I arrive at the scene—I feel awful saying it—but there is no emotion. . . . It's like going to work; it seems natural, just like doing your own everyday job. . . . From the moment you arrive, you begin to work, you

forget everything. . . . You take a brain, you take a liver, you take other parts, and you don't feel anything, any emotion; . . . it is a mission.

Recomposing the body after an explosion becomes the most generous act of devotion. Elijah, a twenty-nine-year-old volunteer from Jerusalem, describes the saving of one soul's life in Israel as the most otherworldly rewarding act:

> It is much harder to be in ZAKA than in any other organization. That is why I would say that it is much more sacred to be in ZAKA. Your place in heaven is much higher. If you have saved someone else's life, you de- serve the world—as we say, he who saves one soul in Israel saves a whole world—but in heaven they say that for things that are much more difficult, we gain more. . . . Honoring the dead [*kvod hamet*] is hard to do. You can go to Abu kabir [the Institute of Forensic Science] and see how we honor the dead . . . how every piece of flesh is collected, how we scratch a wall with pieces of flesh and blood, how we match parts of flesh so that the birds won't eat them. Indeed, these are difficult tasks to carry out.

The act of reassembling the bodies was often explained using the logic of the biblical sacrificial system, specifically, the biblical spreading of the sacrificial body's organs on the altar (cf. Douglas 1999, 76–77). This is de- scribed as an act of regeneration that has pious meanings to those involved in death tasks (Bloch and Parry 1982). The new identity constructed by ZAKA volunteers while working at death sites, cleaning blood, treating people, and handling corpses allows them claim a unique social status and identity in their society.

"Search, Rescue, and Save": The New Heroic Masculinity

Joining ZAKA leads to a necessary decline in Torah study as a way of life and a breach of community boundaries between the disorder of death and the public sphere. Men who participate in ZAKA thus are challenging traditional piety, the yeshiva institutions, and the community leadership. But they regard this violation of the sacredness of yeshiva-based life as an alternative religious path to a true and pious masculinity.

"Search, Rescue, and Save" is the slogan used by ZAKA members to summarize their religious tasks. The new religious aspects of ZAKA are mixed with a new look and dress for Haredi men, appropriate to scenes of

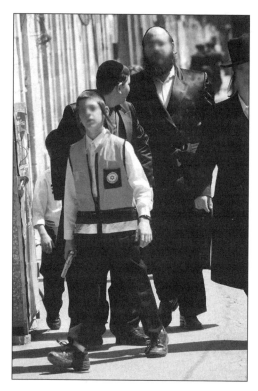

Figure 7.1. A boy dressed up as ZAKA volunteer. Mea She'arim, Purim, 2006.

bombings, emergencies, and rapid deployment. One indication of the pop-ularity of ZAKA in the Haredi world is the great number of people wear-ing ZAKA and Hatzolah Israel costumes in the streets of Mea She'arim in Jerusalem during the Purim celebrations. As mentioned earlier in relation to military imagery, during the Jewish holiday of Purim, adults and youth dress up in costumes, offering a glimpse into the fantasy world of Haredim (Heilman 1992; Jacobs 1971, 1390–95). On the Purim celebrations in 2005, 2006, and 2007, together with soldiers' and police officers' costumes, the fa-vorite costume worn by Haredi children was the yellow or orange outfits of Hatzolah Israel and ZAKA (see figure 7.1). The popularity of these costumes reflects the growing status of death workers in the Haredi community and their becoming a new model of imitation for Haredi children, particularly boys. I rarely saw a girl in a ZAKA outfit, although there were some.

When asked about the popularity of the ZAKA costume, Meshi Za-hav, the founder of ZAKA, explained in an interview to NRG (the *Ma'ariv* daily newspaper's online website, March 4, 2004):

Haredi children identify with our missions. We do not have our own elite army units, but after terror attacks, the children see us and realize that our force is important; it is just like the costume of the paratrooper during the 1980s. Of course this makes us all very proud: although we would rather be unemployed, we take great pride in being so popular in our community. However, I must say that all of us are very concerned about what is happening in the volunteers' homes. We know that the children are pretending that they are doing the work of ZAKA and Magen David Adom, that they are working on a terror scene evacuating corpses.

On the Purim celebrations of 2006 and 2007, in almost every family I observed on the streets, at least one boy was dressed in an orange or yellow outfit. Most children dressed in ZAKA or Hatzolah Israel outfits were holding toy guns as well, and some wore knives or swords, although these are not part of the volunteers' outfits, thereby further mixing categories of manliness (see figure 7.2). They all had identity cards with photographs, a peaked cap with a sheriff's tag or a star, sunglasses, a first aid kit, and a set of keys for an ambulance or motorcycle. These are some of the items that the members of ZAKA carry with them, creating a new manly look utterly unlike the traditional black-and-white Haredi suit of the yeshiva.

Figure 7.2. Children dressed up as ZAKA volunteers. Mea She'arim, Purim 2006.

Three attributes of ZAKA's new piety are courage, professionalism, and militarism. The courage and toughness of ZAKA's missions are exemplified by its motorcycle unit, which its website describes as follows:

> The rapid-rescue motorcycle unit, founded in 2001, enables ZAKA to provide a rapid response to medical emergencies. The goal of the rapid-rescue unit is to arrive to the scene of a disaster within four minutes, . . . the four golden minutes that can mean the difference between life and death. Because the agility and speed of the motorcycles allow them to maneuver through the narrow streets and traffic jams, precious minutes are saved and the ZAKA volunteers arrive within minutes in order to save as many lives as possible. The unit, with its mobility, advanced technology, and professional treatment, has saved hundreds of lives to date. ZAKA has one hundred motorcycles deployed throughout the country. ZAKA's rapid-rescue motorcycle unit arrives first to the scene of a disaster and spearheads the Israel Emergency Medical Services. (http://www.zaka.org.il/en/about.asp)

The mission of the motorcycle unit is explained in professional, medical, and rescue terms as the only way of arriving at a scene within minutes in order to save lives. The interviewees, as well, discussed the motorcycle unit at length, enthusiastically describing its importance to the organization. When interviewed for newspaper articles, ZAKA volunteers are photographed on their motorcycles. The image of Haredi men riding motorcycles equipped with first aid equipment rushing to help in an event with mass casualties represents a new type of Haredi masculinity: tough, courageous, risk-taking individualists, who also are angels fighting against death, agile, fast, mobile, advanced, and technologically savvy, a united force of dedicated leaders: everything that traditional yeshiva models taught them not to be.

Yitzhak is a member of the motorcycle unit and explained the significance of his missions:

> ZAKA is no longer only a "true kindness" organization doing holy work for the dead; it is also devoted to prompt rescue. We realized the need to arrive very fast, and motorcycles are much faster and can enter a scene much better than an ambulance. At the beginning, we had only five Sym 125 cc [motorcycles], but now we have more than fifty heavy and medium-size motorcycles, because light motorcycles did not survive the overwhelming requirements. . . . They call us "the commando unit." . . .

We were the first on the scene of the bombing attack at the Hebrew University because we had motorcycles, and we were the first to give aid to people there. . . . This is why at first, I had doubts about joining this unit, . . . because in the Haredi street, driving a motorcycle is unthinkable; it is considered "exaggerated masculinity," too much machismo behavior.

Yitzhak argued that ZAKA provides religious rewards other than those from death work and that the job required using a motorcycle, despite the disapproval in Haredi circles. He used military terms to define the motorcycle unit, which hinted at their adventurous aspects.

The pioneering aspect of the use of motorcycles was pointed out in an interview with *Ma'ariv* (Kotesberg 2002) by one of the members of the motorcycle unit: "In our neighborhoods, we were not even allowed to ride bicycles. We had no background in these things, and suddenly we found ourselves on motorcycles. . . . You drive around with your coat and helmet in a Haredi neighborhood, and at first it was not natural."

The heroic nature of ZAKA's work was brought up in many interviews, even though the use of motorcycles and other technologies is not acceptable to Haredim, for fear of being accused of immodesty. In an interview in the ZAKA center in Jerusalem, David, a member of the motorcycle unit, told me:

On a personal level, people admire me. The children see me as an idol. Every time they see me on the street, people are alarmed and ask, "What happened?" It's as though I am on my way to an incident. I can't even go the grocery anymore. I just touch the motorcycle, and the children come running and asking, "What happened? Who died?" I am the source of information for them. . . . In this neighborhood I am admired, and nobody has anything against [ZAKA]. Many members of the public want to join ZAKA and contribute to society. There are not many places to which the Haredi public can contribute. They can't join the military . . . so at least they can contribute through ZAKA, through rescue and other organizations. They want to help, but not everyone is accepted.

Besides the features promoted through the use of motorcycles, the volunteers pointed to ZAKA's increasing professionalism. The interviewees described in detail the many training courses they attended and the various steps in being accepted by the organization. According to ZAKA's website,

ZAKA's Search and Rescue Unit was launched in conjunction with Israel's Home Front Command. Hundreds of ZAKA volunteers are qualified as certified rescuers after successfully completing the Homeland Security Command's carefully designed courses. These courses include special training in mountain climbing and glider rescue. This unit forms the volunteer civil rescue unit for emergency situations and works together with the Home Front Command's rescue unit. The Search and Rescue Unit deals with disasters such as collapsing buildings, earthquakes, or missing persons.

This definition of ZAKA's tasks goes beyond the usual religious aspects of help, rescue, and kindness, as claimed when ZAKA was first established. The preceding description of professional training also cites ZAKA's partnership with state security organizations—their members attending their courses and training units—and its emphasis on the heroic, masculine, adventurous, risky nature of its missions, including mountain climbing, handling earthquake disasters, and the like. These missions obviously require different kinds of training that are far from the standard yeshiva socialization.

Haredim who wish to serve in ZAKA must learn law enforcement, become familiar with Israeli police units, talk with rabbis about special religious issues, and meet a few times with psychologists. In order to join, volunteers must pass an initiation centered on the purification ceremony of washing the dead before the burial (a ritual performed for all deaths). At this stage, according to the interviewees, many quit. This acceptance ritual is regarded—in ways similar to the military—as demonstrating one's ability to remain composed under stress, so those who do not pass must be considered unsuitable for ZAKA's missions.

After this ceremony, prospective volunteers must take further extensive training in several fields such as first aid, basic firefighting, rappelling, and psychological therapy, practices that obviously are not part of regular education in the yeshiva world. All ZAKA volunteers are given technological equipment. They are connected to cell phones and beepers and are called to their missions based on their residence and qualifications. In an event of a multiple-casualty incident, a special team is alerted and rushed to the area. Each volunteer is equipped with a special ZAKA ID and a police certificate specifying his skills.

The meanings and symbols discussed earlier in relation to the image of the Israeli combat soldier appear here in a directly valorized form. Added to the ZAKA members' courage and professionalism is their use of military terms and images.

Volunteers likewise describe bombing scenes in short phrases and military terms. For example, Amos, a young volunteer, talked about his work after a bomb attack:

> I arrive and start treating a few of the wounded. . . . I begin resuscitating someone, finish treating the wounded. [Finally there are] no more wounded. I look at my beeper to find out where the ZAKA meeting point is located. I drink something after the work I did. I and all the guys who are also in ZAKA don't go back to the Magen David Adom (Israeli Red Cross) station or home. We stay out in the field. We gather next to the bus station. Everyone is signed up for his crew. We get ready. Put on vests. There was a lot of work there. It was actually a big explosion, and a lot was scattered over the whole street. We divide into crews and do our work. It takes several hours. Magen David's work is over very quickly. Within twenty minutes, none of their teams are around. ZAKA's work takes many hours. . . . There are various sites: on the rooftops, on balconies; there is the floor, the sidewalk, there is the bus or the car. You can't put everyone in one place. Each crew does its own work. There are always five guys at the area, and they are always the bosses. . . . The squad leaders are those who know the work, who have been at it for years.

The references to the military extend to the internal hierarchy where the volunteers receive training as part of their specialization: "Really like the army—each team has its commander, platoon commander. . . . To gather a body into a bag, it is not enough to have one person or two, especially if the body is so smashed up that you need . . . teamwork."

Amos stressed the importance of teamwork to fulfill ZAKA's personal requirements and achieve its collective aims by comparing it with that of an army unit. These similarities to the military are evident as well in ZAKA's divisions into territorial commands, its uniforms, its use of advanced equipment, and its coining of acronyms (Stadler, Ben-Ari, and Mesterman 2005).

Besides the use of military symbolism and imagery to describe ZAKA's actions, it also points to young yeshiva members' yearning for a new concept of masculinity. To fulfill this desire, ZAKA enables its members not only to gain status through their holy work but also to gain recognition and support from Israeli society at large, who see ZAKA and, through them, the Haredi community in general as allies and active participants in the response to terrorism and suicide bombings.

Conclusion

The members of ZAKA use the new meanings of its work—its occupational features, heroic masculinity, and alternative Haredi piety—to form their own identity. Previous chapters discussed how religious models and notions are being challenged by the youngest yeshiva students, by criticizing the yeshiva's work ethics and withdrawal from the labor market, by changing the relations between the genders within the family, and by questioning the ascetic model of yeshiva piety and the exclusion from state affairs, especially the military. These criticisms are now being replaced by a more egalitarian model of thinking and a new proposal for gender relations and fatherhood in the Haredi family. ZAKA is another, albeit more extreme, example of the current shifts in Haredi religiosity and the yeshiva lifestyle.

ZAKA reflects the transformation of piety and patterns of behavior that the Haredi community is undergoing. It offers a this-worldly piety oriented to the inclusion of Haredi members in state and civil society. Because its task is religious, ZAKA's volunteers are principally involved in reviving various religious symbols, such as pious suffering, noble death, martyrdom, self-sacrifice, as well as the reuse of these symbols by different cultural and political agents (Van Henten and Avemarie 2002). Moreover, while reinforcing this piety, ZAKA volunteers are challenging the ideals of the yeshiva and its traditional form of socialization.

By joining ZAKA, Haredi men are allowed access to worlds of knowledge and practice banned by the fundamentalist authorities when the community was established. Participation in these worlds is legitimized by the sacredness of their work: rescuing the wounded and handling the dead after multiple-casualty incidents, a mission exclusive to Haredi men. Indeed, they regard ZAKA's immediate response and presence at such incidents as an act of sacrifice and devotion by these men for both the Haredi community and the Jewish people and the state. Just as the suicide bomber is perceived by his or her faction as a martyr, a "soldier" representing true religious passion (Zulaika and Douglass 1996, 152), ZAKA volunteers are perceived as holy servants, offering to sacrifice their lives for their religious beliefs. This new model of Haredi devotion and participation is a blend of different features of piety: the reinterpretation and publication of Haredi death work and the invention of a public theology of death expressed through militaristic qualities like courage, heroism, and professionalism.

In contrast to other areas we have considered, such as the military, the family, and the labor market, ZAKA has actually transformed otherworldly orientations of the yeshiva culture into this-worldly, semimilitaristic, inclusive, and professional norms and conduct. Moreover, the collective Haredi ideals of the fundamentalist leadership are being replaced by more individualistic modes of thinking and behavior. In Israel, the constant threat of war and threat to security, along with the weakening of the welfare state, have led to the emergence of different social groups performing or taking over functions that the state is no longer able to perform wholly or in part. Haredi volunteers have responded to the changes in their society and in the world around them by centering on practices that make them good citizens and pious men at the same time. In so doing, they have widened the boundaries of the yeshiva world by anchoring it in a theologically justified discourse on death and sacrifice.

8

Conclusion

A Reconstruction of Fundamentalism and Piety

Piety, as I have argued throughout this book, is not a permanent pattern of belief; it is always shifting, being revised, reinterpreted, and contested. As we have seen, in the Jewish fundamentalist world, male piety is being reconsidered and reconstructed as a result of, and in response to, the challenges of modernity. The changing economy, politics, feminism, and new ideas about the family all have penetrated the fundamentalist enclave, reconsidering its basic models and religious experiences. This encounter between fundamentalism and the various trends and issues of modernity has created new religious phenomena and raised questions about the unique nature of piety and its current implementations by young fundamentalist devotees.

At the beginning of this book, I asked how male piety was reconstructed in the fundamentalist context and in what way this redefinition has led to social and cultural changes. In contrast to the views of scholars of the Haredi culture (M. Friedman 1991, 1993), who describe yeshiva piety in Israel as a text-based elite fundamentalist culture, I maintain that Haredi piety is shifting and, with it, the nature of Jewish fundamentalism in general.

After World War II and the Holocaust, the yeshiva culture in Israel was formed as part of what Almond, Appleby, and Sivan (2003) call the reinforcement of "strong religion," the intensification of morality that helped mobilize people to establish and protect the fundamentalist enclave, even while living in a secular liberal state. As defined by Menachem Friedman (1991), this intensification of the society of learners and its yeshiva-based institutions was the key to a world that would renew the spirit of the Jewish social ethic in the decadent modern era. But after examining students' attitudes, reading yeshiva writings, and watching films and DVDs on the military, family, work, and gender, I have concluded that this religiosity is shifting to what Max Weber termed *this-worldly piety* (Weber 1904/5), a new set of pious ideals reflecting the institutionalization and popularization of current fundamentalism. That is, yeshiva students are now demanding a piety that is more inclusive, heroic, profane, and militaristic, as well as experiencing religion as individualistic, domestic, and popular. This shift in the nature of piety, the core of the fundamentalist mind, also has resulted in changes in the fundamentalist group, including the yeshiva's relations with the state and civil society and its conceptions of citizenship.

As we have seen, the transformation of male piety is not only the result of inner pressures and shifts but has also been influenced by the state and Israeli society as a whole. Since the mid-1980s, Israel's society and polity have undergone several interrelated transformations that have influenced the Haredi community and its modes of religiosity. First, the threats to Israel's survival and the conflicts in which the country is involved have affected conceptions of membership, citizenship, and the links between individuals and the nation-state. The first Palestinian intifada (1987–92), the first Gulf War (1990/1), the Iraq War (2003–), the second intifada (beginning in 2000), and the Second Lebanon War (summer 2006) all have altered basic conceptions about relations between the civil and military worlds and the links between the state and civil society. Because the attacks by the Palestinians and Hezbollah have targeted civilians as well as soldiers, and Jewish as well as Arab citizens of Israel, the differentiation between the military front and the civilian rear and the boundaries of the Israeli collective, albeit always fluid, are changing as well.

The second broad sweep of changes was the result of a new emphasis on Israel's neoliberalist policies. In brief, neoliberal policies have weakened the Israeli state, undermined state-mandated arrangements for supplying social and health services, and led to new forms of citizen participation and have significantly undermined social privileges associated with citizenship (Shafir and Peled 2002).

Beginning in the 1980s, neoliberalism—the privileged status of Jewish law and, particularly, the status of the Orthodox rabbinate—has given the Haredim many advantages in politics, education, and more. For example, because the Haredi political parties wield great power in Israel, the increase in the state's support of education has allowed an unprecedented growth of such Haredi institutions as yeshivas. Furthermore, the Haredi community itself has grown since the 1980s, with the addition of new populations. Accordingly, the traditional separation of Lithuanians and Hasidic sects has been blurred with the arrival of the Sephardic Haredim and an influx of returnees (the Teshuvah movement). Over the last two decades, various mysticists and spiritual and New Age and study-based groups also have influenced the Haredi community and are part of the forces urging it to rethink its identity, community, and religious boundaries. These changes, I have tried to show, have both necessitated and arisen from a new fundamentalist model of male piety.

This book has tried to capture these transformations, the challenge by one set of rules of another, through the lens of piety, when certain major practices and models are replaced or modified by devotees. As my interviews revealed, yeshiva students are questioning their rabbis' ideas and are suggesting alternative definitions of the group's fundamentalism.

Yeshiva students, the core of Haredi fundamentalism, are acting as the agents of reformation. Their project is not monolithic, however, as they are demanding different levels of change in the different spheres of their own piety. That is, the students are not trying to change attitudes toward sexuality, but they do find unacceptable the prohibition on working and want to break down the strict separation of genders.

Through their writing and narratives, they have expressed their wish to be more involved in family life. Students tell of their desire, and frustration, to earn extra income for the family, to serve in the military, and to join the public debate on current state and security issues. Haredi devotees begin by fantasizing and progress to demanding and, in some cases, constructing acceptable alternatives to the traditional model of yeshiva withdrawal. These alternatives include participation in and responsibility for affairs that were not possible before. The creation of and volunteer participation in ZAKA is one example of the new thinking about piety in the yeshiva world. Another is the adoption of Israeli models of masculinity, especially that of the heroic combat soldier, and a new interpretation of piety to match them.

Previous analyses, the yeshiva students' narratives, and popular verbal and visual texts all make clear that piety is not monolithic. Although traditional idea of piety is learned, used, protected, and reinforced by fundamentalists, it does not prevent devotees from reevaluating male power and status or from criticizing and reshaping old interpretations and creating new ones. Indeed, it is those yeshiva students who embody the highest level of piety in the group—whose actual and potential dominance would seem to make them want to protect their privilege and reproduce the sacred tradition—who are constantly refining and critiquing their own religious paradigms.

In the larger yeshiva world, some are even challenging the very nature and validity of what is considered sacred in their culture. Besides belonging to a system whose adherents are striving to protect and defend its boundaries and identities, piety and devotion have also formed a paradigm of resistance, in which revisions and incorporations have been forced on the holders of traditional authority. Young yeshiva men worship and accept the sacred in its traditional form but at the same time are revamping its meanings and structures to suit nontraditional ideologies and value systems (Levi-Strauss 1976). This move questions both the hegemonic view of male fundamentalist piety based on yeshiva learning and the ideology behind the creation of alternatives to the model of pious masculinity. This evolution of piety in turn causes us to rethink how Haredi fundamentalism in Israel has shifted and how the ideas of the sacred and of transcendental experience are being contested by a new generation of devotees. We have learned that members of the fundamentalist group are in constant negotiation with the different agents of modernity, such as the state, the military, the labor market, and civil society, and also how they are reacting to these widespread social transformations.

The Fundamentalist Elite, the Holy Family, and the Text

The students' challenge to yeshiva piety must be situated in a more general framework of worldwide fundamentalism. I have emphasized three central religious foundations that are being challenged today: the religious elite, the fundamentalist family, and the ways of approaching the sacred (see Ammerman 1987; Antoun 2001; Aran 1991; Heilman 1994; Riesebrodt 1993). The distinctiveness of fundamentalism is based on the interpretation of each of these aspects and their reinterpretation in everyday life.

The religious elite are supposed to defend the boundaries of the group, reinforce scripturalism, determine prohibitions, and supervise the mechanism of exclusion and inclusion. The family, the basic unit of reproduction and economic support, provides the social, emotional, and cultural legitimation of the elite. Finally, the sacred texts are kept and interpreted exclusively by male members of the elite as codes governing normative moral behavior. In accordance with the rabbinical tradition and Jewish morality, this approach to the texts is presumed to be direct and explained as an authentic reading. Although these textual interpretations should regulate all situations and spheres of life and validate the true path, I do not believe that they do.

As the interviewees often explained, each of these assumptions reflects new tensions in the fundamentalist group, which have led to the current changes. In the yeshiva world these three—elite, family, and approach to the sacred—permeate almost every aspect of the students' everyday life and experiences. For example, students are expected to excel at study as a sign of their pious learnedness. Yet the growth in numbers at the yeshivas has led to a popularization of the Talmudic culture and the yeshiva spirit, so paradoxically, despite—or, rather, because of—the exponential growth in numbers of *bnei Torah* and the drop in their academic level, it now is much harder to achieve academic excellence or piety. Because men must study for the benefit of all men, the notion of elite in the yeshiva world has lost its meaning.

As study has become less attractive, the domestic realm, next in importance, offers new ways for yeshiva students to achieve piety and to transfer place and function to their own families and homes. Students are expected to dedicate their life to the study hall as well as to get married and have large families. How they can support their families is one of the principal issues that, I believe, will change. According to the traditional model, pious masculinity cannot accommodate men as breadwinners, active fathers, and supportive husbands. Therefore, everyday life is left to individual interpretations. In these cases, the achievement of piety and the burden of domestic and existential tasks clash, producing frustration and tension. One of the likely consequences will be a change in the fundamentalist structure of gender, especially the role of women and the conceptions of womanhood in Haredi public and private display.

The yeshiva's approach to texts, which parallels the approach to authority in general and rabbinic authority in particular, poses another problem for the students. Yeshiva scripturalism assumes that all the moral codes of everyday life can be found in the sacred Jewish canon. Behavior should thus be the product of careful interpretation of scriptures and exercise of God's true morality. But the constant changes in the modern world, technology, politics, demographics, and social pressures demand a careful examination of fundamentalism as an intellectual, textual-based elite culture. The popularization of the yeshiva world and, with it, the need to reexamine morals and behaviors contradict authenticity, selectivity, and other elite features, which are the main issues of the fundamentalist view of scriptures. Tensions between the fundamentalist text-based culture and the religious revival have created new demands for popular religious ideas and practices. It is not surprising, therefore, that in all aspects of religion in everyday life, such frustrations and occasional aggressiveness or even violence have resulted. The question is how these tensions will be interpreted or resolved in the future. Comparing fundamentalist groups can give us a more comprehensive view of religious changes, as well as indicate the future of fundamentalism.

Fundamentalism and the Question of Freedom

The study of transformations in the concept of piety in fundamentalism raises questions about freedom and power. In the introduction I asked why those who hold power—male fundamentalists, the elite—would want to struggle for a different kind of piety. Following Martin Riesebrodt (1993, 198–99), we can see that the students are reconsidering the quietistic nature of fundamentalism and are politicizing theodicy, and that the elite is offering a radical challenge to power and morality as well as to the authorities.

In addition, we would assume that these liberal and secular ideologies would have produced more liberated and unbounded approaches to the body, even in religious milieus. But religious revivals have instead produced a variety of strict behaviors, like meditation, which are gaining popularity in Israeli society. These behaviors require specific training programs, dietary rules, athletic programs, and medical knowledge, all of which demonstrate that the traditional fundamentalist models of piety are only one option available to men and women who wish to adopt a religious way of life.

Once again, the question of freedom and power in religious life is crucial. Why do people who are free to choose from a variety of modern body techniques and images prefer pious models of self-control? We need to investigate fundamentalist conceptions of body and freedom in relation to politics, because they not only influence fundamentalism but also have enormous implications for its future.

Yeshiva students are trying to deconstruct their power in order to realize the sacred in their everyday life. In the yeshiva world, studious acts are no longer the only way of gaining power and position. Rather, as agents of change, yeshiva students use popular knowledge and modern images to rethink and reconstruct their piety. They read popular texts about finding true Judaism and manuals on yeshiva morality, masculinity, femininity, and marriage; they watch films and use computers, translating text codes into visual and performative knowledge.

The experience of yeshiva sacredness that used to be scriptural and elitist thus has been popularized. By criticizing text-based piety—the exclusive training in Talmudic exegesis—and asceticism, students are seeking a this-worldly piety that includes citizenship, sociopolitical participation, and contributions. In contrast to feminist examinations of women in fundamentalist groups, in which the resistance and challenges of the socially and politically deprived are the obvious starting point, the struggle of the powerful and how they effect change must be investigated further. I hope that the model of analysis that I have suggested has added to our understanding of fundamentalism as it is today.

Notes

1. My analysis of women's access to fieldwork dominated by men is influenced by Edna Lomsky-Feder's work (1996).

2. Key informants are considered central to ethnographic endeavors, as they perform a variety of roles, chief among them helping the researcher obtain access to the field.

3. Make yourself into groups [*kittot*] to study the Torah, since the knowledge of Torah can be acquired only in association with others" (Benedictions, 63b).

4. The fellowship, *hevruta*, is a unique form of studying in a male peer group, with the aim of improving the understanding, memory, and debating skills of sacred texts (Heilman 1983, 203). This *hevruta* form of studying is very popular in the Haredi community and also has important meanings at the community level. Many members of the community told me how proud they were that their son was in the *hevruta* of a certain individual, especially if he was the son of a famous rabbi. Thus, the *hevruta* also is a reflection of the student's social hierarchy, networks, and future position. Many yeshiva students talked about their *hevruta* partners as a way of clarifying their level and status at the yeshiva.

5. I bought most of the audiocassettes from three Haredi organizations: Kol-Hadaf, Ner-Lamea, and Hasdey-Neomi.

1. Today the Musar tradition continues in the yeshiva world at, for example, the Mir, Hebron, and Ponevezh yeshivas in Israel and U.S. yeshivas like Chofetz Chaim in Forest Hills, New York, and the Lakewood yeshiva in New Jersey.

1. The book was first published in 1740 by R. Moshe Chaim Luzzatto, known as the Ramchal. It is a classical work on Jewish piety and a manual for devotion and piety, and it is studied in all Haredi yeshivas.

2. The protection of the body from the temptation of the evil inclination.

3. Abramovitch (1991, 78) noted that at the end of the ritual of purification in the Jerusalem burial ceremony, it is customary for the eldest son to place soil over the eyes of his parent. Abramovitch's informants told him that because the eye is the organ of desire and envy, it needs to be specially treated in order for it to accept its demise.

4. Men are known to be prone to the evil sexual inclination, a disease of the heart, whereas women have, in addition, a disease of the mouth, or "tongue gossiping," *leshon hara* (evil tongue). Furthermore, women are taught that their bodies are arousing to men, so they should dress modestly, and that they can also be dangerously polluting during and after menstruation. They thus are subject to the particular rule and ideology of *tzniut* (modesty) (Baskin 1985, 5; Douglas 1966; Neusner 1979, 99; Yanay and Rapoport 1997). In official Haredi writings, women are driven by wild, uncontrollable instincts, even madness (Oryan 1994; Satlow 1996, 27; Yanay and Rapoport 1997). Both men and women are threatened by depraved internal desires, but women lack the sexual self-control that men are expected to have, and by nature, women are almost incapable of achieving such control. In this they are unlike men, who are usually portrayed as rational and able to control their desires and urges. Women are a constant threat to men, which is a great challenge to overcome. Accordingly, even relations between the sexes before and after marriage must be strictly governed and monitored.

5. The title of this book is taken from the Rambam's Mishneh Torah, the book of Adoration, Prayers, 9. Morning Benediction: "Enlighten our eyes in Thy law, and make our hearts cleave to Thy commandments."

CHAPTER 4

1. The term *Torato omnuto* is from the Talmud (Sabbath 11, 1).

2. In contrast to texts produced by community organs for the secular camp (such as newspapers and cassettes), for other religious camps, or as proselytizing literature (see Caplan 1997, 2007).

3. The use of a miracle in Haredi Lithuanian literature to explain economic existence is surprising, since the Lithuanian tradition is characterized (by both scholars and community members) as rejecting miraculous beliefs and practices and highlighting rational religious practices (according to the teachings of the Vilna *gaon* (1720–97) (Nadler 1997), and preferring the use of rational theories to explain world events (see Ben-Sasson 1984). The Lithuanian tradition, in turn, refers to the tradition of the Mitnagdim, who emphasized rational study and methodology while vehemently rejecting the mysticism and messianic experiences of the Hassidim. The Haredi community in Israel sees in the resurgence of the miracle a device for the maintenance and construction of its boundaries and a way of reinforcing faith. When the miracle emerges as the sole explanation for economic

success or a course of action, it then presents a novel mystical interpretation of everyday behavior. Rather than expand models of participation and achievement to mundane activities, devotees emphasize miraculous events and contemplative practices as a bonding exercise.

4. This miraculous appearance can be compared with the revelation of the numinous (in Rudolf Otto's words, 1917) as an epiphany or a gift of grace (see also Wuthnow 1994, 1).

CHAPTER 5

1. Despite this decision, during the 1948 war and the first few years after the nation of Israel was established, Haredim did join the military. Frankel (1994) argues that it was thought that the Jewish population of Jerusalem could not mobilize enough people to defend itself and had particular difficulties mustering representatives of the Old Yishuv, Neturei Karta and Bnei Yeshivot. In addition, the Haredim were believed to be willing to surrender Jerusalem to a foreign occupier. Basing his contentions on the actual numbers of people mobilized, Frankel states that most male members of the Haredi community actually were recruited and that they included many yeshiva students who joined the battles, despite the rabbis' objections. Frankel also notes that even though a full company of yeshiva students was recruited at the time, those denouncing the Haredi community continued to spread these accusations. Clearly, the declared ideology of many rabbis at that time was very different from that of today.

2. R. Avraham Yeshayahu Karlitz (1878–1953), the leading rabbinic figure of ultra-Orthodox Jewry in prestate Palestine.

3. In the Haredi book *Splendor of Our Generation: The Life of the Hazon Ish* (*Pe'er hador hayei haHazon Ish*), dedicated to the Hazon Ish, the authors quote him arguing against the army: "And even if they put off their studies for one moment, this is a terrible thing . . . and this is a dangerous thing to all of Israel" (see Cohen 1973, 4:259).

4. It is important to note that individual Haredim like teachers or *kashruth* supervisors have always served in the army (Stadler and Ben Ari 2003).

5. The Haredi NACHAL (an acronym for "fighting pioneer youth") was established as a Haredi combat unit. In addition to its homogeneous makeup, this unit enjoys special conditions designed to serve, and even advance, its religious needs. For example, special times are set aside in the unit's crowded schedule for prayer and Talmud study. Moreover, not only is the command in religious hands, but teachers and religious "supervisors" also are brought in to oversee the soldiers' observance and studies (Drori 2005; Stadler and Ben Ari 2003).

6. Ehud Barak set up the Tal Committee while he was prime minister in the late 1990s. The committee was mandated to seek a legal basis for issues related to recruiting yeshiva students (August 22, 1999; see Ilan 2000, 114, 122).

7. In 2007, the committee's conclusions and recommendations were still being contested by many of the major political factions.

8. This booklet was published in many versions, for example, *Tal's Law* (2001).

9. This poster is a play on words. *NACHAL* means "stream" and also is an acronym for an army unit. Also see note 5.

10. Aside from reading the Book of Esther, the main features of Purim are "carnivalesque" (Bakhtin 1984), and even the public reading of the book is punctuated by the sound of rattles and horns every time the name Haman, "the evil one," is mentioned. Gifts, mainly sweets and pastries, are exchanged; gifts are given to the poor; and inebriation among men on this day is customary, even mandatory, as is the wearing of costumes, mainly by children (see Jacobs 1971, 1390–95).

11. I discuss this organization in chapter 7. ZAKA is the Jewish ultra-Orthodox rapid-response team that identifies victims of disaster in Israel and reassembles their dismembered body parts.

12. Hatzolah Israel (Save Lives), formerly known as Hatzolah Jerusalem, is a volunteer, nonprofit, emergency medical service that assists victims of disaster and other medical emergencies throughout Israel. See http://www.hatzolah.org.il/e-about.htm.

13. For example, R. Moshe Einhoren, "The Land of Israel and the State of Israel"; R. Eliezer Ben-David, "Religion and the State"; R. Yehuda Yosefi and R. Arie Shehter, "What Is Our Duty in the War?"; R. Zvi Karlistein, "Religious Lessons from the War"; R. Mordehai Neugerschal, "Yeshiva Students' Enlistment"; and R. Emanuel Tehila, "Yeshiva Students and the Army."

14. Also translated in the original video as *The Real Soldiers*.

15. One example of this is a petition by Haredi soldiers, published on May 4, 2001, in *Iton Yerushalaim*, the weekend supplement of *Ma'ariv*, a daily Israeli newspaper. The soldiers' complaint was that the army was not honoring its promise to allow them to train as paratroopers, which was the reason that they joined the army in the first place. In the petition, the soldiers specifically mention their desire to reach a certain proficiency rating that would confirm their status as "elite" combat soldiers (as opposed to "regular" combat soldiers). The petition illustrates not only the students' desire to serve in the military but also their admiration of combat units and training. Here the fantasy of the studious ascetic becomes a reality, as the young Haredi boy becomes a soldier in the IDF.

CHAPTER 6

1. The title is from Job 5:24: "And thou shalt know that thy tent is in peace; and thou shalt visit thy, habitation, and shalt miss nothing."

CHAPTER 7

1. Hatzolah Israel; see http://www.hatzolah.org.il/e-about.htm.

2. In September 2000, a bomb was detonated at a bus stop in the town of Netanya, wounding more than twenty people. Hamas, an Islamic resistance movement, claimed responsibility for the attack. Stork claims that from this moment on, this method was embraced by a large proportion of the Palestinian public, making suicide bomb attacks the principal form of Palestinian resistance in the region (Stork 2002, 12). So far, four main groups have launched suicide bomb attacks: Hamas, Islamic Jihad, the secular Popular Front for the Liberation of Palestine, and the Al-Aqsa Martyrs' Brigade. Stork (2002) sees the actions of these groups as an inevitable consequence of the suffering of the Palestinian people and the Israeli state's violation of their rights.

3. Hizbollah, in Lebanon, was the first group to use suicide bomb attacks. In November 1982, a suicide bomber destroyed a building in Tyre, killing seventy-six Israeli security personnel. In October 1983, two more suicide explosions—one killing 241 American servicemen, mostly marines, and the other killing fifty-eight French paratroopers—forced the United States and France to leave Lebanon (see Margalit 2003).

4. The charismatic leader and founder of ZAKA, Yehuda Meshi Zahav, was a former anti-Zionist who participated in many demonstrations and acts of violence against the state.

5. The committee of ZAKA rabbis is an association dealing with the religious aspects of ZAKA's work and providing answers to many issues and dilemmas in accordance with the Halakha. Recently the committee decided that every volunteer had to take classes on Halakha learning (i.e., the study of Jewish laws and practices).

6. Some of the Haredi publications regarding death that ZAKA volunteers use in their work are Adler (n.d.); Avidan 1978; Rabinowicz 1989; Roje 2004a, 2004b; and Vaad Rabanei ZAKA (n.d.).

7. Menucha nehona (Rest in Peace), is a secular burial society located in Beer Sheva. The organization's website explains that Menucha nehona "operates the country's first cemetery for either a Jewish or alternative civil burial ceremony." See http://www.menucha-nehona.co.il.

8. March 2002 is considered the bloodiest month for Israeli casualties, in which Palestinian suicide bombers killed at least eighty civilians and wounded or maimed around 420.

9. I thank my three research assistants, Einat Mesterman, Sagi Genosar, and Jonathan Ventura, for their help with my fieldwork for this chapter.

10. I assume that the volunteers' reasons for being interviewed were a combination of the difficulties of their many tasks, the danger of their work and its

proximity to death, their cultural marginality in Israeli society, and the social criticism of the Haredi lifestyle, all matters that were not easy to discuss (Stadler 2004). Indeed, these factors may have prompted their desire to talk about their actions and ways of life. The volunteers provided many examples of their work, stressing and describing in some detail the horror of numerous events. The interviewees spoke at length about ZAKA, the reasons for their involvement, their religious justification and motivation, and their own experiences in such attacks and in other assignments. Most of the time, I interviewed them shortly after the incidents, when their memories and impressions were still fresh.

11. For this chapter, I analyzed only those reports in which ZAKA members were interviewed or those texts that were produced by the volunteers themselves. I did not investigate the images of ZAKA in the Israeli media, a subject that deserves a separate analysis.

12. Especially the documentary film by Noam Shalev, *ZAKA: Living with Death* (2004).

13. When asked about the specific source and interpretation of the expression "true kindness," volunteers gave me a booklet entitled "Passages from and Interpretations of True Kindness" (Psukim vebi'urim legabei hesed shel emet), according to which *hesed shel emet* was taken from Genesis 47:29: When Jacob is dying, he makes Joseph swear to bury him not in Egypt but with his forefathers in the cave of Machpelah in Hebron. He asks him to "deal kindly and truly with" him. The booklet then offers several interpretations of this passage, including how it should be understood in the present. True kindness is a central virtue of Hevra kaddisha, that is, "speeding the dead to their new abode and returning the living to the web of community connections" (Heilman 2001, 31). The meaning of "true loving-kindness" is connected to the idea also stressed by ZAKA volunteers, a kindness for which the givers cannot expect any direct compensation. ZAKA volunteers emphasize this virtue, practicing it in both letter and spirit.

14. *Kvod hamet*, the obligation to respect the dead, is a fundamental Jewish principle. Many books on Jewish laws and customs of mourning cite 2 Chronicles 32:33: "And Hezekiah slept with his fathers . . . and the inhabitants of Jerusalem . . . did him honor [*kavod*] at his death." An important feature of *kvod hamet* is that the dead should never be left alone but be watched until the funeral. Accordingly, while these watchers are standing watch over the dead, they are not to carry out any commandments except reading psalms. Jewish law requires immediate burial, both to avoid corruption and to keep *kvod hamet*. Autopsies are strictly forbidden, as they damage the body for resurrection (Rabinowicz 1989, 10–18). These obligations and customs are well known and were formerly the almost exclusive preserve of the Hevra kaddisha, the Haredi burial society. But as I show later, they were reinterpreted by ZAKA members after the mass bombings (see also Toktzinsky 1960).

15. I borrowed the term *death specialists* from, and base my analysis on, Jonathan Parry's various works (1980, 1982, 1994), especially his analysis of the Benares funeral priests (1980, 88–111; also see Lambek 1993).

16. This interpretation can be connected to the idea that attacks against Jews in present-day Israel (especially by suicide bombers) are reconfigurations of the collective Jewish past, references to and repetitions of previous events. These date back to biblical times (Arabs are compared with Amalek, a vicious mythical tribe, which all Jews are sworn to remember and never forgive), to the Crusades and blood libels of the Middle Ages, the pogroms of nineteenth century, and the exterminations of the Holocaust. Through this "iterative reality," which replaces "historical" reality, the past is viewed in a messianic manner, and historical thought is sacralized, so that contemporary terrorist acts against Jews are related to other violent acts against Jews in the past. As active and vital agents, ZAKA members see themselves as bravely fulfilling ritual duties under fire, in contrast to the accepted image of Jews as weaklings, particularly in the diaspora and during the Holocaust, when Haredi Jews were presumed to have been led passively to their death. The respectful handling of corpses and burials is related to the collective memories of the corrupted and disregarded corpses of the holy Jewish communities in ghettos and villages, left unattended in the streets, and remembered as a major violation of Jewish moral principles. For a comparison of the term *hessed shel emet* during the Holocaust (see Ferbstien 2002, 251–52).

17. Usually ZAKA volunteers use the term *kiddush hashem*, "sanctification of the divine name," to describe their work (see Ben-Sasson 1971). Accordingly, the collocation *kiddush shem shamaim* is uncommon, a difference that needs to be investigated further.

References

Abramovitch, Henry. 1986. The Clash of Values in the Jewish Funeral, a Participant Observer Study of "Hevra Kaddisha." In *Proceedings of the Ninth World Congress of Jewish Studies* 9:86–79. Jerusalem: World Union of Jewish Studies.

Abramovitch, Henry. 1991. The Jerusalem Funeral as a Microcosm of the "Mismeeting" between Religious and Secular Israelis. In *Tradition, Innovation, Conflict, Jewishness and Judaism in Contemporary Israel*, edited by Zvi Sobel and Benjamin Beit-Hallahmi, 71–99. Albany: State University of New York Press.

Abu-Lughod, Lila. 1986. *Veiled Sentiments, Honor and Poetry in a Bedouin Society*. Berkeley: University of California Press.

Adler, I. n.d. *In Time of Trouble: The Laws for Burial and Death*. Jerusalem (in Hebrew).

Almog, Ozz. 2000. *Sabra: The Creation of the New Jew*. Berkeley: University of California Press.

Almond, Gabriel, Scott Appleby, and Emmanuel Sivan. 2003. *Strong Religion, the Rise of Fundamentalism around the World*. Chicago: University of Chicago Press.

Ammerman, Nancy T. 1987. *Bible Believers, Fundamentalism in the Modern World*. New Brunswick, NJ: Rutgers University Press.

Ammerman, Nancy T. 2005. *Pillars of Faith, American Congregations and Their Partners*. Berkeley: University of California Press.

Antoun, Richard T. 1989. *Muslim Preacher in the Modern World: A Jordanian Case Study in Comparative Perspective*. Princeton, NJ: Princeton University Press.

Antoun, Richard T. 2001. *Understanding Fundamentalism: Christian, Islamic and Jewish Movements*. Oxford: Altamira Press.

Aran, Gideon. 1991. Jewish Zionist Fundamentalism: The Bloc of the Faithful in Israel (Gush Emunim). In *Fundamentalisms Observed*, edited by Martin E. Marty and R. Scott Appleby, 265–344. Chicago: University of Chicago Press.

Aran, Gideon. 1993. Return to the Scriptures in Modern Israel. *Bibliothèque de l'École des hautes études sciences religieuses* 99:101–31.

Aran, Gideon. 2003. The Haredi Body. In *Israeli Haredim*, edited by Emanuel Sivan and Kimmy Caplan, 99–133. Jerusalem: Van Leer Institute (in Hebrew).

Aran, Gideon, Nurit Stadler, and Eyal Ben-Ari. 2008. Fundamentalism and the Masculine Body: The Case of Jewish Ultra-Orthodox Men in Israel. *Religion* 38 (1):25–53.

Asad, Talal. 1986. The Idea of an Anthropology of Islam. Washington, DC: Center for Contemporary Arab Studies, Georgetown University.

Asad, Talal. 2003. *Formation of the Secular: Christianity, Islam, Modernity.* Stanford, CA: Stanford University Press.

Avidan, M. A. 1978. *Ways of Kindness: A Theology of the True Kindness.* Jerusalem (in Hebrew).

Ba Gad-Elimelech, Vered. Forthcoming. From Ancient Past to Present Days: Rabbinical Images in Haredi Films. In *Authority and Power in the Haredi Community in Israel,* edited by Kimmy Caplan and Nurit Stadler. Tel-Aviv: Hakibutz Hameuhad and the Van Leer Institute (in Hebrew).

Bakhtin, Mikhail. 1984. *Rabelais and His World.* Translated by Helene Iswolsky. Bloomington: Indiana University Press.

Bartkowski, John P. 2000. Breaking Walls, Raising Fences: Masculinity, Intimacy and Accountability among the Promise Keepers. *Sociology of Religion* 61 (1):33–53.

Bartkowski, John P. 2004. *The Promise Keepers: Servants, Soldiers, and Godly Men.* New Brunswick, NJ: Rutgers University Press.

Bashevis Singer, Isaac. 1962. *Yentl the Yeshiva Boy.* New York: Farrar, Straus & Giroux.

Baskin, R. Judith. 1985. The Separation of Women in Rabbinical Judaism. In *Woman, Religion and Social Change,* edited by Yvonne Yazbeck Haddad and Ellison Banks Findly, 3–18. Albany: State University of New York Press.

Beeman, O. William. 2001. Fighting the Good Fight: Fundamentalism and Religious Revival. In *Exotic No More: Anthropology on the Front Lines*, edited by Jeremy MacClancy, 129–44. Chicago: University of Chicago Press.

Belcove-Shalin, Janet S. 1988. Becoming More of an Eskimo: Fieldwork among the Hassidim of Boro Park. In *Between Two Worlds: Ethnographic Essays on American Jewry*, edited by Jack Kugelmass, 77–102. Ithaca, NY: Cornell University Press.

Ben-Ari, Eyal. 1998. *Mastering Soldiers: Conflict, Emotions and the Enemy in an Israeli Military Unit.* Oxford: Bergham Books.

Ben-Ari, Eyal, and Edna Lomsky-Feder. 2000. Introductory Essay: Cultural Constructions of War and the Military in Israel. In *The Military and Militarism in Israeli Society*, edited by Edna Lomsky-Feder and Eyal Ben-Ari, 1–36. Albany: State University of New York Press.

Ben-Ari, Eyal, and Edna Lomsky-Feder, eds. 2000. *The Military and Militarism in Israeli Society.* Albany: State University of New York Press.

Ben-Sasson, Haim Hillel. 1971. Sanctification of the Divine Name and Defamation of the Divine Name. In *Encyclopedia Judaica,* edited by Roth Cecil, 978–86. Jerusalem: Keter.

Ben-Sasson, Haim Hillel. 1984. *Continuity and Change.* Tel Aviv: Am Oved (in Hebrew).

Bendroth, Margaret L. 1993. *Fundamentalism and Gender, 1875 to the Present.* New Haven, CT: Yale University Press.

Berman, Eli. 1998. *Sect, Subsidy and Sacrifice: An Economist's View of Ultra-Orthodox Jews.* Jerusalem: Jerusalem Institute for Israel Studies.

Berman, Eli. 2000. Sect, Subsidy and Sacrifice: An Economist's View of Ultra-Orthodox Jews. *Quarterly Journal of Economics* 115 (3):905–53.

Biale, David. 1988. The Lust for Asceticism in Hassidim. In *Sexuality and the Family in History,* edited by Israel Bartal and Isaiah Gafni, 213–24. Jerusalem: Zalman Shazar Center for Jewish History (in Hebrew).

Biale, David. 1992a. *Eros and the Jews.* New York: Basic Books.

Biale, David. 1992b. Zionism as an Erotic Revolution. In *The People of the Body, Jews and Judaism from an Embodied Perspective,* edited by Howard Eilberg-Schwartz, 283–308. Albany: State University of New York Press.

Bilu, Yoram. 2000. Circumcision, the First Haircut and the Torah: Ritual and Male Identity among the Ultraorthodox Community of Contemporary Israel. In *Imagined Masculinities, Male Identity and Culture in the Modern Middle East, edited by* Mai Ghoussoub and Emma Sinclair-Webb, 33–64. London: Saqi Books.

Bleich, J. David. 1983. Preemptive War in Jewish Law. *Tradition* 21 (1):1–39.

Bloch, Maurice, and Jonathan Parry, eds. 1982. *Death and the Regeneration of Life.* Cambridge: Cambridge University Press.

Bourdieu, Pierre. 1977. *Outline of a Theory of Practice.* Cambridge: Cambridge University Press.

Boyarin, Daniel. 1993. *Carnal Israel: Reading Sex in Talmudic Culture.* Berkeley: University of California Press.

Boyarin, Daniel. 1995. Body Politics among the Brides of Christ: Paul and the Origins of Christian Sexual Renunciation. In *Asceticism,* edited by Vincent L. Wimbush and Richard Valantasis, 459–78. Oxford: Oxford University Press.

Boyarin, Daniel. 1997. *Unheroic Conduct.* Berkeley: University of California Press.

Brasher, Brenda. 1998. *Godly Women: Fundamentalism and Female Power.* New Brunswick, NJ: Rutgers University Press.

Breuer, Mordechai. 2003. *Oholei Torah (The Tents of Torah): The Yeshiva, Its Structure and History.* Jerusalem: Zalman Shazar Center for Jewish History (in Hebrew).

Brown, Peter. 1988. *The Body and Society.* London: Faber & Faber.

Bruce, Steve. 2000. *Fundamentalism.* Malden, MA: Blackwell.

Building the World (*Sefer binyan olam*). 1996. Jerusalem (in Hebrew).

Bynum, Caroline Walker. 1987. *Holy Feast and Holy Fast: The Religious Significance of Food to Medieval Women.* Berkeley: University of California Press.

Caplan, Kimmy. 1997. God's Voice: Audiotaped Sermons in Israeli Haredi Society. *Modern Judaism* 17:253–79.

Caplan, Kimmy. 2001. Israeli Haredi Society and the Repentance (Hazarah Biteshuvah) Movement. *Jewish Studies Quarterly* 8 (4):369–99.

Caplan, Kimmy. 2003a. The Internal Popular Discourse of Israeli Haredi Women. *Archives de sciences sociales des religions* 123:77–101.

Caplan, Kimmy. 2003b. On the Haredi Community in Israel: Characteristics, Achievements and Challenges. In *Israeli Haredim: Integration without Assimilation?* edited by Kimmy Caplan and Emmanuel Sivan, 224–78. Tel Aviv: Hakkibutz Hameuchad and the Van Leer Institute (in Hebrew).

Caplan, Kimmy. 2007. *Internal Popular Discourse in Israeli Haredi Society.* Jerusalem: Zalman Shazar Center for Jewish History (in Hebrew).

Cohen, Shlomo. 1973. *Splendor of Our Generation: The Life of the Chazon Ish, Part 4.* Bnei Brak: Netzach.

Cohen, Stuart. 1997. *The Scroll or the Sword? Dilemmas of Religion and Military Service in Israel.* Amsterdam: Harwood Academic.

Cohen, Stuart. 1999. From Integration to Segregation: The Role of Religion in the IDF. *Armed Forces and Society* 35(3):387–405.

Cohen, Yekhezkel. 1993. Giyus Kahalakha: On the Exemption of Yeshiva Students from the Army. Tel-Aviv: H'akibutz H'adati (in Hebrew).

Comaroff, Jean. 1985. *Body of Power, Spirits of Resistance: The Culture and History of a South African People.* Chicago: University of Chicago Press.

Crapanzano, Vincent. 1980. *Tuhami: Portrait of a Moroccan.* Chicago: University of Chicago Press.

Cromer, Gerald. 1993. Withdrawal and Conquest: Two Aspects of the Haredi Response to Modernity. In *Jewish Fundamentalism in Comparative Perspective: Religion, Ideology and Crisis of Modernity,* edited by Laurence J. Silberstein, 164–80. Albany: State University of New York Press.

Dahan, Momi. 1998. *The Haredi Population and the Local Authority.* Jerusalem: Jerusalem Institute for Israel Studies (in Hebrew).

Davidman, Lynn. 1991. *Tradition in a Rootless World: Women Turn to Orthodox Judaism.* Berkeley: University of California Press.

Davidman, Lynn, and L. Arthur Greil. 2007. Characters in Search of a Script: The Exit Narratives of Formerly Ultra-Orthodox Jews. *Journal for the Scientific Study of Religion* 46 (2):201–16.

Deeb, Lara. 2006. *An Enchanted Modern: Gender and Public Piety in Shii Lebanon.* Princeton, NJ: Princeton University Press.

de-Lange, Nicholas. 2000. *An Introduction to Judaism.* Cambridge: Cambridge University Press.

Demerath, N. Jay. 1999. Varieties of Sacred Experiences. *Journal of the Scientific Study of Religion* 39 (1):1–11.

Don-Yehiya, Eliezer. 1994. The Book and the Sword: The Nationalist Yeshivot and Political Radicalism in Israel. In *Accounting for Fundamentalism: The Dynamic Character of Movements*, edited by Martin E. Marty and R. Scott Appleby, 264–302. Chicago: University of Chicago Press.

Doron, Gideon, and Udi Lebel. 2003. *Politics of Bereavement*. Tel Aviv: Hakibbutz Hameuchad.

Douglas, Mary. 1966. *Purity and Danger*. London: Routledge & Kegan Paul.

Douglas, Mary. 1993. *In the Wilderness: The Doctrine of Defilement in the Book of Numbers*. Sheffield: JSOT Press.

Douglas, Mary. 1999. *Leviticus as Literature*. Oxford: Oxford University Press.

Drori, Ze'ev. 2005. *Between Faith and Military Service: The Haredi Nahal Battalion*. Jerusalem: Floersheimer Institute for Policy Studies. (in Hebrew)

Ehrenreich, Barbara. 1983. *The Hearts of Men: American Dreams and the Flight from Commitment*. New York: Doubleday Dell.

Eilberg-Schwartz, Howard. 1992. The Problem of the Body for the People of the Book. In *The People of the Body, Jews and Judaism from an Embodied Perspective*, edited by Howard Eilberg-Schwartz, 17–46. Albany: State University of New York Press.

Eilberg-Schwartz, Howard. 1994. *God's Phallus and Other Problems for Men and Monotheism*. Boston: Beacon Press.

Eisenblat, S. Hacohen. 1983. Observations for *Avrechim* [married yeshiva students]. Jerusalem (in Hebrew).

Eisenstadt, Shmuel Noah. 1995. Fundamentalism, Phenomenology, and Comparative Dimensions. In *Fundamentalism Comprehended*, edited by Martin E. Marty and R. Scott Appleby, 259–76. Chicago: University of Chicago Press.

Eisenstadt, Shmuel Noah. 2000. *Fundamentalism, Sectarianism and Revolution: The Jacobin Dimension of Modernity*. Cambridge: Cambridge University Press.

El-Or, Tamar. 1993a. Are They Like Their Grandmothers? A Paradox of Literacy in the Life of Ultraorthodox Jewish Women. *Anthropology and Education Quarterly* 24:61–81.

El-Or, Tamar. 1993b. The Length of the Slits and the Spread of Luxury: Reconstructing the Subordination of Ultra-Orthodox Jewish Women through the Patriarchy of Men Scholars. *Sex Roles* 29:585–98.

El-Or, Tamar. 1994. *Educated and Ignorant: On Ultra-Orthodox Jewish Women and Their World*. Translated by Haim Watzman. Boulder, CO: Lynne Rienner.

El-Or, Tamar. 2002. *Next Year I Will Know More: Literacy and Identity among Young Orthodox Women in Israel*. Translated by Haim Waitzman. Detroit: Wayne State University Press.

El-Or, Tamar. 2006. *Reserved Seats: Religion, Gender and Ethnicity in Contemporary Israel*. Tel Aviv: Am Oved (in Hebrew).

Emerson, Michael O., and David Hartman. 2006. The Rise of Religious Fundamentalism. *Annual Review of Sociology* 32:127–44.

Eyali, Meir. 1987. *Workers and Artisans.* Givataim: Mesada (in Hebrew).

Ferbstien, Esther. 2002. *Hidden in Thunder: Perspectives on Faith, Theology and Leadership during the Holocaust.* Jerusalem: Mossad Harav Kook (in Hebrew).

Foucault. Michel. 1997. Technologies of the Self. In *Ethics: Subjectivity and Truth,* edited by Paul Rabinow, 223–51. New York: New Press.

Frankel, Yuval. 1994. The Haredi and Religious Jewish Communities during the Siege on Jerusalem. *Hazionut* 18:249–80 (in Hebrew).

Friedl, Erika. 1996. Ideal Womanhood in Postrevolutionary Iran. In *Mixed Blessings, Gender and Religious Fundamentalism Cross Culturally,* edited by Judy Brink and Joan Mencher, 143–58. New York: Routledge.

Friedlander, Haim. 1986. *And Thou Shalt Know That Thy Tent Is in Peace.* Bnei Brak (in Hebrew).

Friedman, Menachem. 1987. Life Tradition and Book Tradition in the Development of Ultra-Orthodox Judaism. In *Judaism Viewed from Within and from Without,* edited by Harvey E. Goldberg, 235–55. Albany: State University of New York Press.

Friedman, Menachem. 1988. Back to the Grandmother: The New Ultra-Orthodox Woman. *Israel Studies* 1:21–26.

Friedman, Menachem. 1991. *The Haredi [Ultra-Orthodox] Society.* Jerusalem: Jerusalem Institute for Israel Studies (in Hebrew).

Friedman, Menachem. 1993. The Haredim and the Israeli Society. In *Whither Israel: The Domestic Challenges,* edited by Joel Peters and Keith Kyle, 177–201. London: Chatham House and I. B. Tauris.

Friedman, Menachem. 1994. Habad as Messianic Fundamentalism: From Local Particularism to Universal Jewish Mission. In *Accounting for Fundamentalisms: The Dynamic Character of Movements,* edited by Martin E. Marty and R. Scott Appleby, 328–57. Chicago: University of Chicago Press.

Friedman, Menachem. 1995a. The Structural Foundation for Religio-Political Accommodation in Israel: Fallacy and Reality. In *Israel: The First Decade of Independence,* edited by S. Ilan Troen and Noah Lucas, 51–82. Albany: State University of New York Press.

Friedman, Menachem. 1995b. The Ultra-Orthodox women. In *A View into the Lives of Women in Jewish Societies,* edited by Yael Azmon, 273–91. Jerusalem: Zalman Shazar Center (in Hebrew).

Friedman, Theodore. 1996. Study. In vol. 15 of *Encyclopedia Judaica,* edited by Roth Cecil, 458. Jerusalem: Keter.

Friedman, Yaakov. 1997. *The Soul of the Yeshiva.* Jerusalem: Torhat Haim (in Hebrew).

Friend, Moshe Ariel. 1995. *The Kindness of Your Youth.* Jerusalem: Frank (in Hebrew).

Gallagher, K. Sally. 2003. *Evangelical Identity and Gendered Family Life.* New Brunswick, NJ: Rutgers University Press.

Geertz, Clifford. 1973. *The Interpretation of Cultures.* New York: Basic Books.

Gellner, Ernest André. 1981. *Muslim Society.* Cambridge: Cambridge University Press.

Goldberg, Harvey. 1987. Text in Jewish Society and the Challenge of Comparison. In *Judaism Viewed from Within and from Without*, edited by Harvey Goldberg, 315–29. Albany: State University of New York Press.

Goldberg, Sylvie-Anne. 1995. *Crossing the Jabbok, Illness and Death in Ashkenazi Judaism in Sixteenth- through Nineteenth-Century Prague.* Berkeley: University of California Press.

Goldsmith, S. 2004. *Enlighten Our Eyes.* Kiryat Sefer (in Hebrew).

Gonen, Amiram. 2000. *From Yeshiva to Work: The American Experience and Lessons for Israel.* Jerusalem: Floersheimer Institute for Policy Studies (in Hebrew).

Goodman, Yehuda. 1997. The Exile of the Broken Vessel, Reality Construction and Therapeutic Discourse at Jewish Ultraorthodox Settings for the Mentally Disturbed. PhD diss., Hebrew University of Jerusalem (in Hebrew).

Griffith, R. Marie. 1997. *God's Daughters: Evangelical Women and the Power of Submission.* Berkeley: University of California Press.

Gurovich, Norma, and Eilat Cohen-Kastro. 2004. *Ultra-Orthodox Jews, Geographic Distribution and Demographic, Social and Economic Characteristics of the Ultra-Orthodox Jewish Population in Israel 1996–2001.* Jerusalem: Central Bureau of Statistics, Demography Sector (in Hebrew).

Hakak, Yohai. 2003. *Yeshiva Learning and Military Training: An Encounter between Two Cultural Models.* Jerusalem: Floersheimer Institute for Policy Studies (in Hebrew).

Hakak, Yohai. 2006. *The Haredi Body Returns from Exile, Moving among the Yeshiva Army, Work and Politics.* PhD diss., Hebrew University of Jerusalem (in Hebrew).

Halbertal, Moshe, and Tova Hartman-Halbertal. 1998. The Yeshiva. In *Philosophers on Education: New Historical Perspectives*, edited by Amelie Oksenberg Rorty, 458–69. New York: Routledge.

Halevi, Yehuda. 1997. Militant Mercy. *Jerusalem Report* 18:18–19.

Halliday, A. K. Michael. 1976. Anti-Language. *American Anthropologist* 78 (3):572–84.

Harding, Susan. 2000. *The Book of Jerry Falwell.* Princeton, NJ: Princeton University Press.

Heilman, Samuel C. 1983. *The People of the Book: Drama, Fellowship and Religion.* Chicago: University of Chicago Press.

Heilman, Samuel C. 1992. *Defenders of the Faith: Inside Ultra-Orthodox Jewry.* New York: Schocken Books.

Heilman, Samuel. C. 1994. Quiescent and Active Fundamentalisms: The Jewish Cases. In *Accounting for Fundamentalism: The Dynamic Character of Movements*, edited by Martin E. Marty and R. Scott Appleby, 96–173. Chicago: University of Chicago Press.

Heilman, Samuel C. 1995. The Vision from the Madrasa and Bes Medrash: Some Parallels between Islam and Judaism. In *Fundamentalism Comprehended*, edited by Martin E. Marty and R. Scott Appleby, 71–95. Chicago: University of Chicago Press.

Heilman, Samuel. C. 2001. *When a Jew Dies*. Berkeley: University of California Press.

Heilman, Samuel, and Menachem Friedman. 1991a. *The Haredim in Israel*. New York: American Jewish Committee.

Heilman, Samuel, and Menachem Friedman. 1991b. Religious Fundamentalism and Religious Jews: The Case of the Haredim. In *Fundamentalisms Observed*, edited by Martin E. Marty and R. Scott Appleby, 197–264. Chicago: University of Chicago Press.

Helmreich, William B. 2000. *The World of the Yeshiva: An Intimate Portrait of Orthodox Jewry*. Hoboken, NJ: Ktav.

Hertzman, Elhanan Yossef. 1982. *A Faithful Home*. Jerusalem: Mashabim (in Hebrew).

Hervieu-Léger, Danièle. 2000. *Religion as a Chain of Memory*. Cambridge: Polity Press.

Hillers, Delbert Roy. 1971. *Hevra Kaddisha* [Holy Brotherhood]. In vol. 8 of *Encyclopedia Judaica*, edited by Roth Cecil, 442–46. Jerusalem: Keter.

Horowitz, Neri. 2002. *Our Town Is Burning, Ultra-Orthodox Politics between the Elections of 1999 and 2001*. Jerusalem: Floersheimer Institute for Policy Studies (in Hebrew).

Iannaccone, Laurence. R. 1998. Introduction to the Economics of Religion. *Journal of Economic Literature* 36 (3):1465–96.

Ilan, Shahar. 1999. *Deferment of Recruitment of Yeshiva Students: A Proposal for Policy*. Jerusalem: Floersheimer Institute for Policy Studies (in Hebrew).

Ilan, Shahar. 2000. *Haredim Ba'am*. Jerusalem: Keter (in Hebrew).

Jacobs, Louis. 1971. Purim. In vol. 13 of *Encyclopedia Judaica*, edited by Roth Cecil, 1390–95. Jerusalem: Keter.

Jenkins, E. Kathleen. 2005. *Awesome Families: The Promise of Healing Relationships in the International Churches of Christ*. New Brunswick, NJ: Rutgers University Press.

The Jew from Beit Jalla. n.d. Directed by Ohad Amzaleg. Jerusalem: Galraz Chemed Production (in Hebrew).

Juergensmeyer, Mark. 2000. *Terror in the Mind of God: The Global Rise of Religious Violence*. Berkeley: University of California Press.

Kahane, Reuven. 1988. Multicode Organizations: A Conceptual Framework for the Analysis of Boarding Schools. *Sociology of Education* 61 (4):211–26.

Kahane, Reuven. 1997. *The Origins of Post Modern Youth*. Berlin: De Gruyter.

Kaplan, Lawrence. 1992. Hazon Ish: Critic of Traditional Orthodoxy. In *the Uses of Tradition: Jewish Continuity in the Modern Era*, edited by Jack Wertheimer, 145–74. New York: Jewish Theological Seminary of America.

Kaul-Seidman, Lisa R. 2002. Fieldwork among the Ultra-Orthodox: the "Insider"–"Outsider" Paradigm Revisited. *Jewish Journal of Sociology* 44 (1–2):30–55.

Kepel, Gilles. 2002. *Jihad: The Trail of Political Islam*. Translated by Anthony F. Roberts. London: Tauris.

Kimmel, Michael. 1996. *Manhood in America: A Cultural History*. New York: Free Press.

Kimmerling, Baruch. 1979. Determination of Boundaries and Frameworks of Conscription: Two Dimensions of Military Relations. *Studies in Comparative International Developments* 14:22–41.

Kotesberg, Chen. 2002. He Is a Zakai on a Motorcycle [Hu Zakai Al Ofnoa]. *Ma'ariv*, November 29 (in Hebrew).

Krannich, S. Richard, and Craig. R. Humphrey. 1986. Using Key Informant Data in Comparative Community Research. *Sociological Methods & Research* 14 (4):473–93.

Kuran, Timur. 1993. Fundamentalism and the Economy. In *Fundamentalisms and the State: Remaking Polities, Economies, and Militance*, edited by Martin E. Marty and R. Scott Appleby, 289–301. Chicago: University of Chicago Press.

Kuran, Timur. 2004. *Islam and Mammon: The Economic Predicaments of Islamism*. Princeton, NJ: Princeton University Press.

Lambek, Michael. 1993. *Knowledge and Practice in Mayotte, Local Discourse of Islam, Sorcery, and Spirit Possession*. Toronto: University of Toronto Press.

Lawrence, Bruce B. 1989. *Defenders of God: The Fundamentalists Revolt against the Modern Age*. San Francisco: Harper & Row.

Lehmann, David. 1998. Fundamentalism and Globalism. *World Quarterly* 19 (4):607–34.

Lehmann, David, and Batia Siebzehner. 2006. *Remaking Israeli Judaism: The Challenge of Shas*. New York: Oxford University Press.

Levi-Strauss, Claude. 1976. *The Savage Mind*. Translated by Rodney Needham. London: Weidenfeld and Nicolson.

Liebman, Charles S. 1993. Jewish Fundamentalism and the Israeli Polity. In *Fundamentalism and the State: Remaking Polities, Economies and Militance*, edited by Martin E. Marty and R. Scott Appleby, 68–87. Chicago: University of Chicago Press.

Liraz, M. 2000. *For Thou Shalt Eat the Labour of Thine Hands: Happy Shalt Thou Be, and It Shall Be Well with Thee.* Hamodia 51, 8 (in Hebrew).

Lomsky-Feder, Edna. 1996. A Woman Studies War: Stranger in a Man's World. In *Ethics and Process in the Narrative Study of Life,* edited by Ruthellen Josselson, 232–42. London: Sage.

Lomsky-Feder, Edna, and Tamar Rapoport. 2003. Juggling Models of Masculinity: Russian–Jewish Immigrants in the Israeli Army. *Sociological Inquiry* 73 (1):114–37.

Lupo, Jacob. 2003. *A Shift in Haredi Society: Vocational Training and Academic Studies.* Jerusalem: Floersheimer Institute for Policy Studies (in Hebrew).

Mahmood, Saba, 2005. *Politics of Piety, the Islamic Revival and the Feminist Subject.* Princeton, NJ: Princeton University Press.

Maor, M. Z. 1984. *The Believer versus the Actor.* Jerusalem: Hamahon Le'mehkar Torani (in Hebrew).

Margalit, Avishai. 2003. The Suicide Bombers. Available at http://www.nybooks.com/articles/15979.

Marty, Martin E., and R. Scott Appleby. 1991. The Fundamentalism Project: A User's Guide. In *Fundamentalisms Observed,* edited by Martin E. Marty and R. Scott Appleby, vii–xiii. Chicago: University of Chicago Press.

Melovitzky, Aharon. 1994. *Guide Book for Yeshiva Students.* Bnei Brak: Greentec Media (in Hebrew).

Messner, A. Michael. 1997. *Politics of Masculinity, Men in Movements.* London: Sage.

Morgan, David. 1994. Theater of War: Combat, the Military and Masculinities. In *Theorizing Masculinities,* edited by Harry Brod and Michael Kaufman, 165–81. London: Sage.

Muesse, Mark W. 1996. Masculinity and Fundamentalism. In *Redeeming Men: Religion and Masculinity,* edited by Stephen B. Boyd, W. Merle Longwood, and Mark W. Muesse, 89–102. Louisville: Westminster John Knox Press.

Nadler, Allan. 1997. *The Faith of the Mithnagdim.* Baltimore: John Hopkins University Press.

Narkiss, Bezalel. 1969. *Hebrew Illuminated Manuscripts.* Jerusalem: Keter (in Hebrew).

Nason-Clark, Nancy, and Mary Jo Neitz, eds. 2001. *Feminist Perspectives and Narrative in the Sociology of Religion.* Walnut Creek, CA: Altamira Press.

Neitz, Mary Jo. 1987. *Charisma and Community: A Study of Religious Commitment within the Charismatic Renewal.* New Brunswick, NJ: Transaction Books.

Neusner, Jacob. 1979. *Method and Meaning in Ancient Judaism.* Brown University Judaica Series 10. Missoula, MT: Scholars Press.

Obeyesekere, Gananath. 1995. Buddhism, Nationhood, and Cultural Identity: A Question of Fundamentals. In *The Fundamentalism Project.* Vol. 5 of

Fundamentalisms Comprehended, edited by Martin E. Marty and R. Scott Appleby, 231–55. Chicago: University of Chicago Press.

Oryan, Shulamit. 1994. None Is More Beautiful Than the Virtue of Modesty: Communication Patterns in the Socialization of Orthodox Girls. Master's thesis, Haifa University (in Hebrew).

Otto, Rudolph. 1917. *The Idea of the Holy*. Reprint, London: Penguin Books, 1959.

Parry, Jonathan. 1980. Ghosts, Greed and Sin: The Occupational Identity of the Banares Funeral Priests. *Man* 15 (1):88–111.

Parry, Jonathan. 1982. Sacrificial Death and the Nacrophagous Ascetic. In *Death and the Regeneration of Life*, edited by Maurice Bloch and Jonathan Parry, 171–83. Cambridge: Cambridge University Press.

Parry, Jonathan. 1994. *Death in Banaras*. Cambridge: Cambridge University Press.

"Passages from and Interpretations of True Kindness." Available at http://www.zaka.org.il/.

Peshkin, Alan. 1986. *God's Choice: The Total World of a Fundamentalist Christian School*. Chicago: University of Chicago Press.

Putney, Clifford. 2001. *Muscular Christianity: Manhood and Sports in Protestant America, 1880-1920*. Cambridge, MA: Harvard University Press.

Rabinowicz, Tzvi. 1989. *A Guide to Life: Jewish Laws and Customs of Mourning*. London: Jason Aronson (in Hebrew).

Rapoport, Tamar. 1999. The Pedagogical Construction of Traditional Woman: An Ethnographic Study of "Holiness Class." *Megamot* 39 (4):492–517 (in Hebrew).

Rapoport, Tamar, Anat Penso, and Yoni Garb. 1994. Contribution to the Collective by Religious-Zionist Adolescent Girls. *British Journal of Sociology of Education* 15 (3):375–88.

Rapoport, Tamar, Anat Penso, and Yoni Garb. 1995. Religious Socialization and Female Subjectivity: Religious-Zionist Girls in Israel. *Sociology of Education* 68 (1):18–61.

Rapoport, Tamar, Anat Penso, and Tova Halbertal. 1996. Girl's Experiences of Artistic Ambition: The Voices of a Religious-Zionist and a Kibbutznik. *Journal of Contemporary Ethnography* 24 (4):438–61.

Ravitzky, Aviezer. 1994. The Contemporary Lubavitch Hasidic Movement: Between Conservatism and Messianism. In *Accounting for Fundamentalisms: The Dynamic Character of Movements*, edited by Martin E. Marty and R. Scott Appleby, 303–27. Chicago: University of Chicago Press.

Riesebrodt, Martin. 1993. *Pious Passion: The Emergence of Modern Fundamentalism in the United States and Iran*. Translated from German by Don Reneau. Berkeley: University of California Press.

Roje, Jacob. 2004a. "And the Living Will Lay It to His Heart," Death Customs for Those Who Deal with the Holy Work, ZAKA and Hevra Kadisha. Jerusalem (in Hebrew).

Roje, Jacob. 2004b. *ZAKA's Rabbinical Committee: A Collection on Human's Nature*. Rehovot (in Hebrew).

Rotundo, Anthony, E. 1993. *American Manhood: Transformations in Masculinity from the Revolution to the Modern Era*. New York: Basic Books.

Sasson-Levy, Orna. 2002. Constructing Identities at the Margins: Masculinity and Citizenship in the Israeli Army. *Sociological Quarterly* 43 (3):357–83.

Sasson-Levy, Orna. 2006. *Identities in Uniform: Masculinities and Femininities in the Israeli Military*. Jerusalem: Hebrew University Magnes Press (in Hebrew).

Satlow, Michael, L. 1996. Try to Be a Man: The Rabbinic Construction of Masculinity. *Harvard Theological Review* 89 (1):19–40.

Schiffer, Varda. 1998. *The Haredi Education System: Allocation, Regulation and Control*. Jerusalem: Floersheimer Institute for Policy Studies (in Hebrew).

Schwartz, Yoel. 1978. *Young Yeshiva Scholar: Instructions and Recommendations*. Jerusalem: D'var Yerushalaim Yeshiva (in Hebrew).

Schwartz, Yoel. 2000. *Son of the Torah and Yeshiva*. Bnei Brak (in Hebrew).

Secret Mission in Damascus. Directed by Alon Alsech. Ateret Production and Tehilot (in Hebrew).

Selengut, Charles. 1994. By Torah Alone: Yeshiva Fundamentalism in Jewish Life. In *Accounting for Fundamentalisms: The Dynamic Character of Movements*, edited by Martin E. Marty and R. Scott Appleby, 236–63. Chicago: University of Chicago Press.

Shalif, Yishai. 1995. The Motives for Learning Torah by Yeshiva and Kollel Students and Their Development. PhD diss., Hebrew University of Jerusalem (in Hebrew).

Shafir, Gershon, and Yoav Peled. 2002. *Being Israeli: The Dynamic of Multiple Citizenship*. Cambridge: Cambridge University Press.

Shapiro, Marchall. 2002. Eventually You Can Go Crazy. *Jewish Tribune*, July 25.

Shenkar, Yael. Forthcoming. Haredi Female Writers. In *Authority and Power in the Haredi Community in Israel*, edited by Kimmy Caplan and Nurit Stadler. Tel Aviv: Hakibutz Hameuhad and the Van Leer institute (in Hebrew).

Shilhav, Yosseph. 1991. *A Town in the City: Geography of Separation and Integration*. Jerusalem: Jerusalem Institute for Israel Studies (in Hebrew).

Shilhav, Yosseph. 1998. *Ultra-Orthodoxy in Urban Governance*. Jerusalem: Floersheimer Institute for Policy Studies (in Hebrew).

Sivan, Emmanuel, 1995. The Enclave Culture. In *Fundamentalisms Comprehended*, edited by Martin E. Marty and R. Scott Appleby, 11–68. Chicago: University of Chicago Press.

Sivan, Emanuel, and Kimmy Caplan, eds. 2003. *Israeli Haredim: Integration without Assimilation?* Tel-Aviv: Van Leer Institute and Hakibutz Hameuhad (in Hebrew).

Soldiers without Uniforms. Directed by Ofir Shteinbaum. Bnei Brak: Greentec Media (in Hebrew).

Soloveitchik, Haym. 1994a. Migration, Acculturation, and the New Role of Texts in the Haredi World. In *Accounting for Fundamentalisms: The Dynamic Character of Movements*, edited by Martin E. Marty and R. Scott Appleby, 197–235. Chicago: University of Chicago Press.

Soloveitchik, Haym. 1994b. Rupture and Reconstruction: The Transformation of Contemporary Orthodoxy. *Tradition* 28)4):64–130.

Sprinzak, Ehud. 1993. Three Models of Religious Violence: The Case of Jewish Fundamentalism in Israel. In *Fundamentalism and the State: Remaking Polities, Economies and Militance*, edited by Martin E. Marty and R. Scott Appleby, 462–90. Chicago: University of Chicago Press.

Stacey, Judith. 1990. *Brave New Families: Stories of Domestic Upheaval in Late Twentieth Century America.* New York: Basic Books.

Stadler, Nurit. 2002. Is Profane Work an Obstacle to Salvation? The Case of Ultra-Orthodox (Haredi) Jews in Contemporary Israel. *Sociology of Religion* 63 (4):455–74.

Stadler, Nurit. 2004. Taboos, Dreams and Desires: Haredi Fantasies on Militarism and the Military. *Sociologia Israelit* 6 (1):69–90 (in Hebrew).

Stadler, Nurit. 2005. Fundamentalism. In *Modern Judaism: An Oxford Guide*, edited by Nicholas de-Lange and Miri Freud-Kandel, 216–27. Oxford: Oxford University Press.

Stadler, Nurit. 2006. Terror, Corpse Symbolism and Taboo Violation: The "Haredi Disaster Victim Identification Team in Israel" (ZAKA). *Journal of the Royal Anthropological Institute* 12 (4):837–58.

Stadler, Nurit. 2007. Playing with Sacred/Corporeal Identities: Yeshiva Students' Fantasies of the Military Participation. *Jewish Social Studies* 13(2):155–78.

Stadler, Nurit, and Eyal Ben-Ari. 2003. Other-Worldly Soldiers? Ultra-Orthodox Views of Military Service in Contemporary Israel. *Israel Affairs* 9)4):17–48.

Stadler, Nurit, Eyal Ben Ari, and Einat Mesterman. 2005. Terror, Aid and Organization: The Haredi Disaster Victim Identification Teams (ZAKA) in Israel. *Anthropological Quarterly* 78 (3):619–51.

Stallybrass, Peter, and Allon White. 1986. *The Politics and Poetics of Transgression.* Ithaca, NY: Cornell University Press.

Stampfer, Shaul. 2005. *The Lithuanian Yeshiva.* Rev. and expanded ed. Jerusalem: Zalman Shazar Center for Jewish History (in Hebrew).

Stark, Rodney. 1999. Secularization, R.I.P. *Sociology of Religion* 60 (3):249–73.

Stolow, Jeremy. 2004. Transnationalism and the New Religio-Politics: Reflections on a Jewish Orthodox Case. *Theory, Culture and Society* 21 (2):109–37.

Stork, Joe. 2002. *Erased in a Moment: Suicide Bombing Attacks against Israeli Civilians.* London: Human Rights Watch.

Tal's Law: A Trap to the People of the Torah. 2001. Jerusalem: Association of Students and Rabbis.

Taussig, Majid. 1998. Transgression. In *Critical Terms for Religious Studies,* edited by Mark C. Taylor, 349–64. Chicago: University of Chicago Press.

Tishby, Isaiah. 1989. *The Wisdom of the Zohar: An Anthology of Texts.* Vol. 2. Oxford: Oxford University Press.

Toktzinsky, Yechiel Michael. 1960. *The Bridge of Life* (Part 1). Jerusalem: Solomon Press (in Hebrew).

Vaanunu, Shimon. 1998. *The Joy of the Torah.* Jerusalem: Shimon Chen–Mordechai Chen (in Hebrew).

Valantasis, Richard. 1995. A Theory of the Social Function of Asceticism. In *Asceticism,* edited by Vincent Wimbush and Richard Valantasis, 544–52. Oxford: Oxford University Press.

Van Henten, Jan Willem, and Friedrich Avemarie. 2002. *Martyrdom and Noble Death.* London: Routledge.

Vazner, Haim Meir Halevi. 1986. *Spend Your Life with the Woman You Love.* Jerusalem (in Hebrew).

Wagner, Richard J. 1998. The Image and Status of Women in Classical Rabbinical Judaism. In *Jewish Women in Historical Perspective,* edited by Judith R. Baskin, 73–100. Detroit: Wayne State University Press.

Walzer, Michael. 1996. War and Peace in the Jewish Tradition. In *The Ethics of War and Peace: Religious and Secular Perspective,* edited by Terry Nardin, 95–114. Princeton, NJ: Princeton University Press.

Weber, Max. 1904/5. *The Protestant Ethic and the Spirit of Capitalism.* Translated by T. Parsons. Reprint, New York: Scribner, 1958.

Wegshel, Shaul. 1998. *The Happiness of the Wife of a Yeshiva Scholar.* Jerusalem (in Hebrew).

Wegshel, Shaul. 2000. *The Ways of the Just: A Moral Handbook for the Yeshiva Student.* Jerusalem (in Hebrew).

Weiss, Meira. 2002. *The Chosen Body: The Politics of the Body in Israeli Society.* Stanford, CA: Stanford University Press.

Williams, H. Rhys. 2001. Promise Keepers: A Comment on Religion and Social Movements. In *Promise Keepers and New Masculinity: Private Lives and Public Morality,* edited by Williams, H. Rhys, 1–10. Lanham, MD: Lexington Books.

Wolbe, Shmuel. 1989. *A Note of Guidance to Yeshiva Students.* Jerusalem: Bet Musar (in Hebrew).

Wuthnow, Robert. 1994. *Producing the Sacred: An Essay on Public Religion.* Urbana: University of Illinois Press.

Yamane, David. 2000. Narrative and Religious Experience, *Sociology of Religion* 61 (2):171–89.

Yanay, Nitza, and Tamar Rapoport. 1997. Ritual Impurity and Religious Discourse on Women and Nationality. *Women's Studies International Forum* 20 (5):651–63.

ZAKA: Living with Death. Documentary Film. 2004. Directed by Noam Shalev. Tel Aviv: High Light Films (in Hebrew).

Zalkin, Mordechay. 2006. City of Torah—Torah Studies in the Lithuanian Urban Spaces during the 19th Century. In *Yeshivot and Battei Midrash*, edited by Immanuel Etkes, 131–62. Jerusalem: Zalman Shazar Center for Jewish History (in Hebrew).

Zohar, Zion. 2004. Oriental Jewry Confronts Modernity: The Case of Rabbi Ovadiah Yosef, *Modern Judaism* 24 (2):120–50.

Zulaika, Joseba, and William Douglass. 1996. *Terror and Taboo: The Follies Fables and Faces of Terrorism*. New York: Routledge.

Index

About the Author

NURIT STADLER is Assistant Professor in the Department of Sociology and Anthropology at the Hebrew University of Jerusalem.